SHADOWS
IN THE
VALLEY

SHADOWS
IN THE
VALLEY

A Cultural History of
Illness, Death, and Loss
in New England,
1840–1916

ALAN C. SWEDLUND

University of Massachusetts Press
Amherst & Boston

LC 2009054454
ISBN 978-1-55849-720-7 (paper); 719-1 (library cloth)

Designed by Jack Harrison
Set in Monotype Dante and Adobe Jenson Pro
Printed and bound by Thomson-Shore, Inc.

Library of Congress Cataloging-in-Publication Data
Swedlund, Alan C.
Shadows in the valley : a cultural history of illness, death, and loss
in New England, 1840–1916 / Alan C. Swedlund.
p. cm.
Includes bibliographical references and index.
ISBN 978-1-55849-720-7 (paper : alk. paper) —
ISBN 978-1-55849-719-1 (library cloth : alk. paper)
1. Diseases—Social aspects—New England—History—19th century.
2. Diseases—Social aspects—New England—History—20th century.
3. Death—Social aspects—New England—History.
4. Mortality—Social aspects—New England—History.
5. Loss (Psychology)—Social aspects—New England—History.
6. New England—Social conditions—19th century.
7. New England—Social conditions—20th century.
8. New England—Statistics, Medical.   I. Title.
RA418.3.N427S94 2010
614.4'273—dc22
2009054454

British Library Cataloguing in Publication data are available.

To my daughters Sara and Jennie,
and to my daughters' daughters

CONTENTS

ILLUSTRATIONS

ACKNOWLEGMENTS

This book became a gleam in my eye, plus several pages of notes, during the spring of 1996, while working on a study of infant mortality in nineteenth-century Massachusetts. In 1995–96 I was fortunate to receive a Weatherhead Resident Scholarship to the School for American (now Advanced) Research in Santa Fe, New Mexico. This beautiful and inspiring place, and the bright colleagues with whom I shared that time, gave me the opportunity and insight to see this as a future project. Two subsequent summer scholarships at SAR over the intervening years provided additional time and space for this book to rise and take shape. I would like to thank Douglas Schwartz, George Gumerman, and James Brooks of SAR for all their encouragement and support.

For the spring of 2001, I was invited to be a scholar-in-residence at St. John's College, Oxford University, which provided another haven for research and writing. For this exceptional experience I am indebted to my longtime friend and colleague Dr. Anthony Boyce of St. John's College. Travel and other support were provided by the European Program, Department of Anthropology, University of Massachusetts. Having access to the Radcliffe Science Library resulted in much of the content for Chapter 8. This leave also afforded the opportunity for me to explore my ideas with Anne Hardy, director of the Wellcome Trust Center for the History of Medicine, whose own work has been very influential on me.

In the spring of 2004, I received support for data analysis as an external faculty member-in-residence at the Santa Fe Institute. Additional financial support has included grants from the National Science Foundation and the National Institutes of Health for initial data collection and analysis. These form the basis for estimating the magnitude and structure of cause of death discussed in the chapters, and for the appendixes at the end of the book. The Wenner-Gren Foundation provided support for student research assistants, as did faculty research grants from the University of Massachusetts. The writing of this book would not have been possible without a long history of data collection, completed primarily by graduate student assistants including Richard Meindl, Helena-Temkin-Greener, Alan McArdle, Margaret Gradie, Caren

Ginsberg, Nancy Folbre, Judith Nydon, Deborah Rotman, Susan Hautaniemi Leonard, Alison Donta, Helen Ball, and Nicole Falk Smith. Alan McArdle merits special mention for his tenacious archiving of the data over many years; Nicole Falk Smith for help with figures in the appendixes and managing the bibliography; and Susan Hautaniemi Leonard for her long-standing interest in the project and careful reading of the book manuscript. Thanks to former Hampshire College undergraduate Laurie MacLeod for first introducing me to Dr. Stephen West Williams and "the dyspepsia generation."

I have been fortunate to live in western Massachusetts, close to the site of my research, and in contact with many gifted scholars who generously talked ideas, shared their knowledge, and read and commented on chapters. The so-called Five College area is rich in talent and those willing to share their expertise. I especially want to thank Robert Paynter and Brooke Thomas from my own department, and Randall Knoper from English (University of Massachusetts Amherst), also Karen Sanchez-Eppler, Kevin Sweeney, and Marni Sandweiss (Amherst College). Medical anthropologist Lynn Morgan (Mt. Holyoke College) has been an always-willing sounding board, reader, sage, critic, and supportive friend.

I approached this project as an anthropologist, wanting to focus on specific communities and individuals and working up to larger observations and comparisons, rather than starting with a broad, geographically diffuse study of illness, death, and loss. What made this approach possible is the extraordinary collections of the Memorial Libraries of Historic Deerfield, Inc., and the Pocumtuck Valley Memorial Association. I am grateful for all the help I received from David Bosse, director of the Memorial Libraries, and his staff, particularly Martha Noblick. I owe a special debt of gratitude to Shirley Majewski, PVMA librarian. It was Shirley who, time after time, found the document I was looking for and often found the document that I did not know existed but which supported an argument or provided the perfect example for a premise. Thank you, Shirley, for becoming interested and excited in what I was trying to do. Thanks to Memorial Hall Museum (PVMA) curator Suzanne Flynt for all her help with the images and making what I envisioned possible.

Because this book crosses many disciplines and yet required in-depth knowledge of local history, I invited several individuals to read and comment on various chapters and, at times, the whole manuscript. No one turned me down, each generously gave me valued feedback, and usually the validation I sought. New England historians Donald Friary, Susan McGowan Titus, and Kevin Sweeney each kept an eagle eye on my accuracy in representing the history of Deerfield and the other towns of Franklin County. Cultural historians Katherine Ott and Karen Halttunen, medical historian Michael Sappol, demographic anthropologist Susan Greenhalgh, and historical archaeologist Sarah Tarlow each sharpened my theoretical gaze in various chapters. Epidemiologist-anthropologist Anne Buchanan and medical anthropologist D. Ann Herring each read the entire manuscript and offered their valued insights. The usual disclaimer applies—I listened, I heeded, but I own any errors.

I am compelled to acknowledge a few individuals who were not directly involved with this book, but who, as professional friends, have shaped my work and my thinking so much that I feel their presence here. Thank you Marjorie Abel, Shirley Lindenbaum, Elinor Ochs, Mary Orgel, Larry Sawchuk, and Jacqueline Urla.

When I stared at the first draft of this book and it stared back menacingly, I consulted with my good friend and professional editor Jane Kepp, in search of reconciliation. Thank you, Jane, for your gifts at mediation. I thank Clark Dougan of the University of Massachusetts Press for wanting this book and for his enthusiastic and unwavering support. Thanks to Deborah Smith for a great eye and a thorough and professional job of copyediting, to Jim O'Brien for preparing my index, and to Jack Harrison for his care in design. Thank you, Carol Betsch, for so ably seeing this book to completion, for sharing your interest and expertise on the cemetery as landscape, and for your lovely photographs when my own compositions failed.

And finally, I think it is customary at this juncture to thank one's spouse for all his/her help on a book project. I can honestly say that my wife, M.A., did not help on this book. In fact, it might have been done two years earlier without her influence, but, oh, the joys I would have missed. Thank you, M.A., for constantly reminding me—while I wrote about death—to savor life, family, and friends.

SHADOWS
IN THE
VALLEY

INTRODUCTION

THIS BOOK IS ABOUT the circumstances that occur when illness leads to death, and death to loss and mourning. Anthropologists sometimes remark that birth and death are the only true universals for humankind. But though death is universal, the way it is experienced is not. This book also is about death in a specific place and time: Massachusetts from the mid-nineteenth to the early twentieth century. It is about those who attended the dying, from a parent or spouse to the doctor, undertaker, and officiating civil authority. Most of all, it is about how death informed life for the people of New England during the long nineteenth century.

As an anthropologist who "does" history, I frequently feel that I do some things and see some things differently from scholars who are trained in the discipline of history. I think of my work as doing "fieldwork" in the archives. The differences blur when I compare my perspective and intentions with those of cultural historians and some medical historians, and then, on occasion, differences appear in sharp relief when I compare myself with still others. I mention this here because one thing that anthropologists and cultural historians often do is identify ourselves as such and situate ourselves at the outset of the task at hand. So, what follows is a brief overview of the way I approach illness and death in this book.

Illness, death, and mourning form a cycle of closely related events bound together by subjects, objects, performances, and time. Between 1840 and 1916 we can expect to find cycles and transitions in the cultural practices and therapies surrounding health and sickness—and even in the named causes of death. Historians, anthropologists, and others often try to navigate between the particularities and uniqueness of everyday experience and the generalizations that can be drawn by assembling these particularities into a larger whole. Each side has contributions to make to our broader understanding of illness, death, and loss.

On the side of generality, I work with some basic premises. The first is that practices surrounding illness, death, and loss are socially constructed and culturally embodied. Death may be a natural, biological process, but the way it is manifested in a community is laden with social, cultural, and psychological

1

dimensions. In the contemporary West our experiences of illness and the loss of family members and friends differ from the experiences of people in the nineteenth century. To take a simple example, in 1840 there were no mortuaries or funeral directors in the United States; these came much later.

Today, it is possible for many of us, if we were born as healthy, middle- or upper-class citizens of Europe or North America, to live into or beyond our eighties and have all our children survive us. Unlike in 1840, it is even possible for a few of us never or rarely to witness a death by accident, heart attack, virulent infection, or cancer.[1] Death has become more private, and we more successfully screen it from public view than people did in nineteenth-century New England.[2] Life expectancy at birth in the United States is now about eighty years for women and seventy-five for men.[3] In the 1870s the comparable values were about half that—approximately forty years. The difference is explained mostly by the extraordinary reduction in infant and early childhood mortality that was accomplished between about 1880 and 1930, but the risk of dying at all ages has also changed dramatically.[4]

In this book I aim to capture some of the differences between past and present in the relationships individuals and communities have had with death and to describe people's more uncertain "expectations" of life in the past. I also trace changes in cultural notions and classifications of illness and death. As Katherine Ott observes, "The meaning of a disease evolves from the interrelationship of people, technology, medical doctrines, and state affairs."[5] Biomedical anthropologists, like epidemiologists, tend to view disease as an interaction among pathogens, hosts, and the environment—that is, in terms of the biology of micro-organisms and the people they infect. They look at issues of risk, at the incidence and prevalence of disease, and at the ecological factors predisposing populations to disease. Medical anthropologists and sociologists in the past tended to look at health practices as reflections of cultural systems. A more recent medical anthropology has emerged, however, that recognizes the value of combining biological and cultural views of health and disease into a biocultural perspective—one that acknowledges the biological realities of infectious, chronic, and degenerative diseases but also foregrounds the fact that these "realities" and our understandings of them take place in a social realm of beliefs, values, customs, and human relationships.[6]

A second premise has to do with the more organic and biological side of illness and death. Today, when we consult a physician about an illness, we expect a diagnosis and treatment based on scientific medicine. This was not always so; medical practices were once commonly referred to as the healing arts. In the 1840s, Europeans and Americans suspected a vague entity called contagion but had no solid grasp of germs. Thirty years later they had identified germs (bacteria) and could even observe them under a microscope. But a germ is never "just" a germ. It has multiple, layered meanings that change with time and place and purpose, whether to a mid-nineteenth-century housewife, a physician in the 1880s, or a twenty-first-century molecular biologist. Even well into the early twentieth century, the association between a germ and an illness was often tenuous and somewhat ambiguous. People could "carry" a germ but be asymptomatic. Until the discovery of the *Helicobacter pylori* bacterium in the 1980s, ulcers were thought to be unrelated to germs.

Science and medicine have built an ever-growing base of knowledge about what a particular germ is, under what conditions it becomes infectious, and how it "penetrates" the human body, activates its virulent effects, and manifests its presence in symptoms of illness. Yet, embedded in that progressive story are many shadings, disputed interpretations, and professional disagreements. Ineffective therapies and harmful side effects color medical practice in all times and places. Anthropologists and other social scientists often find it easier to recognize and describe these effects and contested meanings in the medical practices of non-Western cultures, but as several medical anthropologists have pointed out, these same issues are always present in our own medicine and medical culture as well, and they deserve our attention.[7]

In Massachusetts—and the United States—in the 1840s, a person could consult a wide array of health practitioners. The options might include trusted members of one's own family, a knowledgeable midwife, a regular physician, an herbalist, a homeopath or hydropath, an eclectic physician, and even a spiritual healer. By the 1870s the range had grown even greater, and one might see an osteopath or a Christian Science practitioner. Ott calls this period a medical free-for-all.[8] It was unlikely that the regular physician, to his chagrin (and it was always *he* in New England in the 1840s), was the first person consulted. Today in many parts of the United States we find a similar range of biomedical and alternative therapies. Thus, the progressive narrative suggesting that today's medical practices are all objective and science-based or that superstition and quackery characterized only the past ignores the historical diversity of medical practices in the United States.

Western anthropologists studying non-Western cultures are likely to view healing practices and burial customs in their symbolic and ritualized context. They may understand people's treatment of illness in Western terms—that is, possibly by believing the treatment to be more psychologically comforting than physiologically efficacious—although they are cautious about passing judgment. Western medical anthropologists are likely to apply this same methodology and questioning to practices in Western medicine.[9] By contrast, some medical historians, particularly if they are trained in Western medicine, look at the practices of their predecessors not so much as matters of ideology and ritual but as the naive practices of as-yet-uninformed doctors or the futile performances of quacks.[10]

Yet in an age when studies document the power of the "placebo effect" and the efficacy of acupuncture, we can no longer draw simple oppositions between Western scientific and alternative practices, or make a simple dichotomy of effective and ineffective treatments. The Cartesian divide between mind and body, too, has become more tenuous and permeable. Medical anthropologists are unlikely to contrast Western medicine with non-Western, or allopathic medicine with homeopathic. They are unlikely to tell a linear story reaching from the ignorance of the past to the enlightenment of the present. It is interesting to think of our Western medical practices, past or present, as embedded not just in facts or the absence thereof but also in ideas and beliefs. In looking at the past I continually struggle with my own scientific background and positivist leanings as I try to look at nineteenth-century mortality and medicine in more holistic ways.

Conventional narratives in the history of medicine or health often elide the way illness, death, loss, mourning, and remembrance are intertwined for those who knew the deceased and for the community that must react and adjust to the loss of one of its members.[11] A third premise underlying this book is that there is a place in medical history for integrating events of illness and death with the emotional and social responses to loss. For people in many communities in the nineteenth century mortality was a common fact of everyday life. How might this experience have been reflected in expressions of grief and in mourning practices? If death was a more frequent and visible event in the past than it is now, does that hold implications for the way relatives and friends experienced loss? For the way they grieved or mourned?

Bringing together the events of illness, death, and loss enables me to address some questions that persist in the literature and that in many respects transcend nineteenth-century New England. One of these has to do with the emotional experience of losing a loved one, particularly a child. Some scholars have proposed that in past times, when mortality was much higher in the Western world, as well as in the contemporary third world or other settings where mortality is high, people adapt—or cope—by maintaining some level of acceptance and emotional detachment at the death of a child. The intensity of their grief is tempered by the knowledge that childhood is a period of risk for survival, and an infant lost might be replaced by a future birth.

Montaigne is alleged to have said, "I have lost two or three children in their infancy, not without regret, but without great sorrow."[12] Lawrence Stone argues that parents in England in the 1600s withheld emotional investment in their children because of high mortality, and Sheila Johansson suggests that a certain amount of mortality in early modern Europe can even be attributed to the willing neglect of young children because of high fertility and the constant threat of death.[13]

One of the most compelling cases for Stone's argument is made by Nancy Scheper-Hughes in her 1992 book *Death without Weeping*.[14] She tells a gripping story of poor women in twentieth-century Brazil who daily confronted extreme poverty, inadequate hygiene, and shortages of food and clean water. Her argument is that, under such persistent deprivation, mothers accepted the losses of infants and young children stoically, trusting that God had called them away. Johansson takes up a similar theme with reference to European peasants.

In contrast, Linda Pollock and Pat Jalland have each argued that even at times of high mortality in North America and Britain, parents made a strong emotional investment in their children.[15] Diaries from nineteenth-century New England tend to support Jalland's and Pollock's opinions that children were highly valued and deeply mourned. Yet interviewing and witnessing one's subjects, as Scheper-Hughes did during her fieldwork, are quite different from reading historical records. Might the sort of psychological adaptation discernible in contemporary economically depressed, resource-depleted, and war-torn regions also have existed in places like the nineteenth-century United States, where knowledge of effective therapies and health prevention measures was poor and where economic inequalities could be great? Does frequency of loss diminish its effect on people, so that the mother of a deceased child in 1890 might have felt less pain than her great-great-granddaughter would have under the same circumstances in 1990? We can assume that as a culture we do experience death differently in the twenty-first century, but how and in what ways?

Religious preferences and cultural differences in perceiving the value of children can play a part in responses to death, too. Even in a small New England town, differences existed among families with regard to religion, class, occupation, and what we might call social and material well-being. We should not necessarily expect, therefore, to find a simple, homogeneous pattern in the chances of child survival or in people's mourning observances after death.

I believe that families in all circumstances in nineteenth-century New England were likely to grieve for their lost children, but the debate lingers, and variation should be expected. It does not follow that all families in all circumstances mourned in the same way or to the same degree. To capture some sense of the broader range of expressions of emotion at death requires sensitivity to the unwritten as well as the written—to records that were destroyed as well as those that survive. As Jalland found in researching family records in England, the families in New England who were most likely to leave testimonials were middle or upper class, and the writers were usually spouses, parents, or friends who were describing what Jalland calls the "good death" of a child or an adult. The household facing a suicide or the downward spiral of an alcoholic family member might have been less inclined to memorialize the loss. Furthermore, one would assume that descendant generations were more likely to preserve the positive, poignant, and sentimental than the angry, painful, or sordid. Impoverished, working-class families seldom left any records at all. Illiteracy, the lack of writing materials, the grinding pace of life, and the absence of a tradition of expressive writing all came into play. In conducting archival research, one must take care not to overgeneralize from documents that originated in one social class, institution, or group.[16]

Grief over the loss of a loved one is a genuine human emotion, but it finds different ritualized expressions in the mourning practices of different cultures. In Victorian and Progressive Era North America, mourning took on specific protocols that varied with the religious and secular context. In New England, Congregationalists and Roman Catholics, for example, had roles to play and different expectations associated with funerals. Throughout this book, I want to draw readers' attention to individual expressions of grief and to the culture of mourning, showing the ways in which mourning changed with the age of the deceased and the decade under consideration.

Ann Douglas, in her classic essay on the American way of death in the nineteenth century, argues that women then were caught up in a culture of death that found its expression in what she calls "consolation literature."[17] Through such writing, women, whose sexual and social status was marginalized, could achieve recognition outside the home and kitchen. By offering advice on the etiquette of mourning, describing life after death, and helping to define the rituality and religiosity surrounding death, they were able to achieve status in one important domain. Consolation literature had a large following, but it also had its detractors, among them Mark Twain. The outward manifestation of genuine emotion takes place in a cultural context. Expressions of sincere and heartfelt grief can be codified, ritualized, and romanticized well beyond what the innermost feelings of family members might otherwise dictate. Douglas's work reminds us that recognition, reputation, and monetary reward are also a part of ministering to the sick and dying.

With the rise of photography beginning in the mid-nineteenth century, many family members memorialized their dead loved ones by posing them in their caskets or by creating "live" poses. Mementos, including locks of hair, were collected from the dead and sometimes placed in a locket or transformed into elaborate, decorative pieces. Etiquette manuals narrowed the options for many families by describing what a proper funeral was, what to wear, and how long to mourn. As Jessica Mitford documents in *The American Way of*

Death, the rise of the funeral industry created new arenas and expectations for what constitutes proper recognition of death.[18] Examples of these cultural practices show us the extent to which formal modes of mourning can find cultural acceptance or can change in a relatively short time.

The messy reality of historical archives is that different sources capture different snapshots of the "reality" of an event. As one overlays the various sources (or different people's interpretations of them), certain events emerge clearly and incontrovertibly, but others remain slightly out of focus. Diagnoses, attributions, and accounts of events are always in question and contested. For me, acknowledging this fact was an important step as I developed my approach to historical epidemiology. It means that one must relinquish certain standards of precision and embrace all reliable sources and all the dimensions of inference that are available to the inquirer.

In the end I drew on historical and statistical documents about medicine, mortality, and institutions that promoted health. But I also relied heavily on diaries, letters, and other sources that people wrote at times when they or their family members were sick or dying. These accounts represent the voices of those outside the medical establishment. Newspaper reports, advice manuals, and treatises on etiquette at times of mourning provide a cultural context for interpreting the actions of patients, doctors, loved ones, and those in authority over sickness and death. Combining these resources enabled me to capture something of the way people felt about medical treatment, the way doctors regarded patients (and their sick bodies), and the way the community responded to the "problem" of sickness and death.

"To record," from the Latin root *recordari*, means, literally, to remember.[19] Thus, the historical record, so often interpreted as a compilation of literal facts, is more accurately facts as remembered or even remembrances. Historians normally consider the statistics gathered by the state to fit more closely with their notion of historical records as facts. But what about diaries? Account books? Newspaper stories? The minutes of a meeting of the Franklin District Medical Society? Are these records or remembrances also facts? Anyone who works with documents derived from both official record-keeping and the "subjective" accounting of events knows that they can agree, can both be in error, or can simply differ in their interpretations. In the pages that follow I recount many recorded facts, but a death certificate might tell one story, an obituary another, and a letter to a grieving widow still another, even though all refer to the same person and event. The diagnosis of a disease in 1850 might be very different from the diagnosis of the same disease in 1880, even if made by the same doctor. I want to bring these disparate records together and capture, but not necessarily always resolve, their inconsistencies, differences, and shadings of meaning. The many-layered and multivoiced interpretations of those who lived and died in the past merit our attention, even when they disagree.[20]

The period between 1840 and 1916 is one of profound social and economic change in the United States. Rather than a neat, linear progression from one decade to the next, I see dynamic changes in the social order. Michael Sappol describes them as "remarkable" and even "dizzying."[21] Because I believe that transitions and innovations are at times asynchronous, or more punctuated than at others, like some anthropologists, I pay less heed to the strict delineations of the historians' eras and epochs.

Some of the subjects that appear in this book are the diseases themselves and even the pathogens—the microbes—that promoted a sometimes fatal infectious disease. Others are prominent members of the community, such as Dr. Stephen West Williams and George Sheldon, whom we meet in Chapter 1. We also meet a child who died too young to be given a name and a working-class immigrant who left barely an imprint of his presence in the town when he died in service to his employer, striving to provide for his family. In each chapter, my intent is to characterize the actions, beliefs, attitudes, decisions, and feelings of people engaged in trying to save lives, administer appropriately to the deceased, or comfort the surviving family and friends. It is a given that the topic of death is sad. When an epidemic strikes a community and claims some of its young, the loss is profoundly painful. But in death there can also be honor, celebration, and humor. The death of a long-lived and respected member of the community might be celebrated as much as mourned while friends and family honor the deceased's life and accomplishments. Along with sad stories come interesting and even humorous ones. Humor often accompanies human frailty and offers a means of coping with sadness or tragedy. The spirit of this book is not to be unrelenting in telling of the loss of life, though neither is it to sterilize the realities of death in a community by removing everything but the cold, hard statistics.

Sarah Tarlow and others have written wryly about how death can hardly be considered an understudied topic considering the hundreds, if not thousands, of books and articles in print.[22] I agree that there is no lack of research on death. Yet, I also agree with Tarlow that there is still much to learn through cultural histories that engage the record in the broadest sense. This approach includes attention to, and critical analysis of, the complex, varying, emotion-laden, and universal cycle of illness, death, and loss.

1

HISTORIES OF
ILLNESS AND DEATH

IN THE EARLY SPRING OF 1842 a country doctor sits at his writing desk. As he writes, he ponders a recent epidemic of dysentery in his town, unaware that another is soon to follow. The doctor's name is Stephen West Williams, and he lives in the small agricultural town of Deerfield, County of Franklin, Commonwealth of Massachusetts. A third-generation medical man, he began his career in the Deerfield practice of his father, William Stoddard Williams, whose own father, Thomas Williams, served as a surgeon in the French and Indian War.

A visitor to Deerfield in the spring of 1842 would have observed a rich flood plain laid out in well-tended fields to the north and south of the village. The main street, on higher ground, was wide and tree-lined. Large houses with erect barns and tidy farmyards faced it. The appearance was one of successful harvests and good fortune, not one of disease and death. Dr. Williams's house, still standing to this day, was located south of Pratt's Store, the Brick Church, and the town common.

The epidemic that held Dr. Williams's attention came in the late summer and early fall of 1841. The symptoms of acute diarrhea affected many, but it was lethal to infants and young children. The first week of September was devastating for the community. Among those who died were little Mary Hoyt and Francis Hawks's son, and the Reverend Rodolphus Dickinson bore the heavy task of recording his own grand-daughter's death in the church's records. Dr. Williams and his associate, Dr. Sumner Haskell, made house calls and treated the sick. Williams believed the adults responded to treatment, but there was little to do for the children.[1]

Like many others physicians at the time, Stephen West Williams received little formal training. He apprenticed in medicine under his father and then trained at Columbia College in New York in 1812–13; physicians commonly had less than a full year's medical training then, and many had much less or none at all.[2] Williams was elected to the Massachusetts Medical Society in 1817, and in 1818 he married Harriet Goodhue, the daughter of a doctor from Portsmouth, New Hampshire.

Stephen West Williams. Courtesy of Historic Deerfield, Inc. (HD).

The home of Dr. Stephen West Williams, c. 1900, photographed by the Allen Sisters. Courtesy of PVMA.

View looking south from the north end of Deerfield's main street. Bradford stereograph. Courtesy of Memorial Hall Museum, Pocumtuck Valley Memorial Association, Deerfield, Mass. (PVMA).

By 1840 Williams had gained considerable prominence in the Commonwealth. Besides being active in the Massachusetts Medical Society, he was a founder and the first president of the Franklin District Medical Society, and he frequently published articles in the *Boston Medical and Surgical Journal*, which later became the *New England Journal of Medicine*. Williams was in the prime of his professional life in the second quarter of the nineteenth century—an invigorating moment in the history of American medicine.

During this period local medical societies began recruiting more actively and practitioners envisioned a national organization. Eager to improve their professional standing, physicians took pains to distinguish themselves from other varieties of medical and health practitioners, with whom they competed for patients. Commonwealth officials began trying to improve the registration of births, deaths, and marriages—so-called vital statistics. They especially wanted more accurate statistics on mortality, for the number of deaths every year had become alarming, especially in the coastal and industrializing parts of the Commonwealth.[3]

A small but growing class of bureaucrats and interested citizens urged the state to better monitor the health of its citizens and collect data on the risk of illness and death. Improving transportation brought the towns and smaller cities of interior Massachusetts—and New England in general—closer to their urban counterparts. Political and economic affairs of state drifted more readily from capitals to outlying towns. The extent of health disparities between rural areas and urbanizing centers was largely unknown, but a sense of unease was stirring that some districts were much less healthy places in which to live than others.

By the 1840s, the individual in illness, the community and its health practitioners, the county, the Commonwealth of Massachusetts, the nation, and the world, for that matter, were at least loosely interconnected through various means of communication. Someone in a rural New England town, sick with gastroenteritis, might open his weekly newspaper and read with alarm about a cholera epidemic in England. A physician in Boston could consult with his counterpart in London and, at roughly the same time, with his country colleague in a small New England town.

The 1840s—and indeed the entire nineteenth century—witnessed repeated epidemics of dysentery in New England. Infants, young children, and the elderly were the most likely to succumb. Deerfield was hit hard in 1841 and 1842, and Dr. Williams worried about the cause and proper treatment of the disease. As we picture him at his writing desk, we can imagine he is preparing the address he will make to the Massachusetts Medical Society in Boston in a few weeks' time, where he describes his scientific observations about dysentery in Franklin County.

He undoubtedly knew that although western Massachusetts experienced epidemics and other medical crises, there were other parts of the eastern United States where the conditions of life were worse and the probability of death higher. Boston, about ninety miles east of Deerfield, could make a legitimate claim to be a center of medical knowledge at mid-nineteenth century but that hardly assured good health to all its citizens. Along the streets running off Boston's harbor and in the dwellings of its poorest neighborhoods, conditions were in fact much worse than along the tree-lined streets of a small town in the Connecticut River valley.

Steven West Williams shows us just how well informed and respected that country colleague might have been. He would become a representative from his region to the first national medical convention in Philadelphia in 1847 and a charter member of the American Medical Association. In May 1842 Williams made the arduous two-day trip to Boston by horse-drawn carriage to deliver the keynote address at the annual meeting of the Massachusetts Medical Society.[4] No doubt he wondered whether the distinguished Dr. Oliver Wendell Holmes, with whom he had corresponded, would be in the audience.

In the address, Williams apologizes to his colleagues for not having attended the society's meetings before. "[I feel] peculiarly honored," he explains, "in the choice you have made for me for your speaker," adding, "[I trust I have] not been wanting in activity and zeal, in the promotion of the grand and philanthropic objects of this highly useful and respectable Society." Then he recounts the recent history of epidemics in Deerfield and surrounding towns and describes the events in 1841.

> It seemed to follow the courses of streams, and was most severe in the towns of Deerfield and Greenfield. There were nearly one hundred cases in each of these towns, and these were confined almost exclusively to the town streets, so called, in both these places. There were but few deaths, and it is supposed by the physicians who attended the complaint, that the astringent method of treating it had much efficacy in arresting the ravages of death from it. After the first evacuations, it was not uncommon to administer from 20 to 60 grains of the sugar of lead in a day, and from 5 to 10 grains of opium, with decidedly beneficial effect.

Williams is interested also in proportionality—he is a collector of data. He moves on to compare mortality rates in rural Franklin County with those in other regions.

> In this way I make the average mortality for all the towns which I have heard from in the county to be about one in 80 inhabitants. The lowest mortality in any town, as shown by the tables, was about one in ninety-two, and the highest about one in sixty. Had it been extended to four or five such periods, there can be no doubt that the result would have been more favorable. That is considered to

be a healthy country [*sic*] where the average mortality is one in sixty. According to this, Franklin county much more than averages the healthy standard.[5]

How did he reach the conclusion that one death in sixty signified a healthy county? The statement hints at his knowledge of a question then being addressed in England and taken up by health reformers in Boston. It suggests that he was attuned to the most recent research.

Williams was no bumbling country doctor; he was a distinguished peer to his urban counterparts. Though we might cringe at the thought of taking "60 grains of the sugar of lead" for loose bowels, we can assume that his prescription was their prescription. He was an experienced, well-read physician keeping track of the latest medical findings, speaking to a group of "respectable" medical men in what might be considered the medical capital of the United States in the 1840s.[6] We learn, from this moment and these passages, that at least this country doctor was not sheltered from the larger world of medicine.

Stephen West Williams practiced medicine in Deerfield until 1853, when, at age sixty-three, he retired with his wife, Harriet, to Illinois to live with their son. Williams repeatedly enters and exits the pages of this book, but he is not its prime subject, nor is the town of Deerfield or even the history of medicine for that matter, though each has a prominent role. Instead, I want to look more broadly at the way people in western Massachusetts and the United States as a whole experienced and dealt with illness, death, and loss between 1840 and 1916.[7] Williams in Deerfield provides a useful entry point—very different from, say, Oliver Wendell Holmes in Cambridge and the nearby offices of the Massachusetts Medical Society, the Harvard Medical School, or the Boston Sanitary Commission. In the United States in the 1840s, issues of health and mortality were still largely local matters, not state or federal ones. No surgeon general yet existed, nor did a U.S. department of health and welfare. Massachusetts had no department of health.

Histories of American medicine most often concentrate on power centers such as New York, Philadelphia, Boston-Cambridge, and Baltimore.[8] My intention, however, is to work up rather than down, from the hinterlands to the centers, and to place individuals and families rather than institutions in the foreground. From that perspective, Dr. Williams, Deerfield, and the Connecticut River valley make excellent places to start. I want to shift the emphasis away from the epic and the famous and visit places that, although close to the great medical center of Boston, were far enough away to have their own distinguishing experiences and local encounters with the diseases of a growing nation. Deerfield and Franklin County lie west and a little north of Boston. Farther to the west and north of Deerfield are the town of Shelburne (and the village of Shelburne Falls), the small city of Greenfield, and to the east

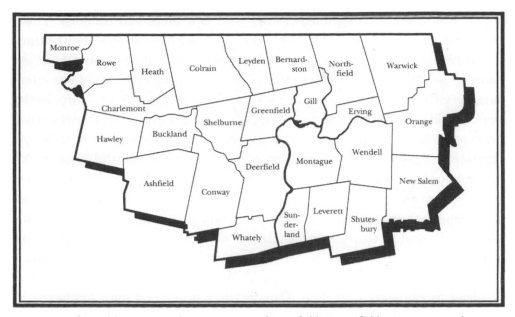

Map of Franklin County, showing towns of Deerfield, Greenfield, Montague, and Shelburne. Courtesy of J. Ritchie Garrison.

the town of Montague with its industrial village, Turners Falls. These four communities offer a window into the world of health, sickness, and death in nineteenth-century America.

In this book I use a biocultural approach to investigate the interconnections among illness, death, and loss. I do this by tracking the movement of ideas about disease, causes, treatments, and the management of death from the mid-nineteenth to the early twentieth century. I focus attention on a set of critical points in the life cycle from birth to death and view transitions through the cultural institutions of family and friends, doctors, churches, funeral directors, and government bureaucracies. As noted in the introduction, I consider myself more an anthropologist doing "fieldwork" in the archives than a conventional historian. The intense study of smaller communities at the margins of the mainstream is at the core of the anthropological tradition. My attention is on illness, death, and loss among ordinary people in their everyday lives, and how these connect to larger processes and events.

As infants we are susceptible to many infections, though our immature immune systems may receive some help from antibodies passed from our mothers through breast milk. In childhood our still developing immune systems put us at some risk of other infectious diseases, and as we explore the

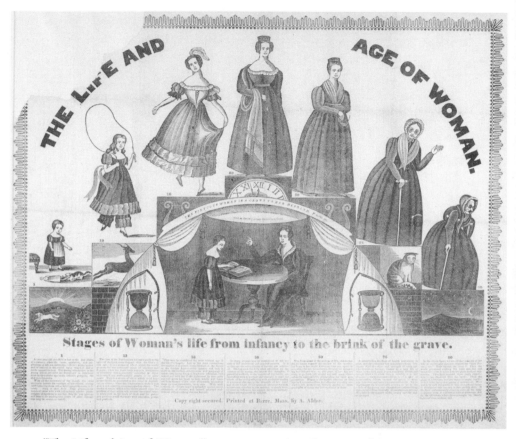

"The Life and Age of Woman," c. 1840, engraving. Courtesy of PVMA.

world we suffer our share of accidents. Once our immune systems become fully developed, diet, habits, and the daily "insults" of life bring on another set of risks—in addition to infections and accidents, wear and tear and the infirmities of age, which produce degenerative and chronic diseases. The relationship between disease and the life course, by no means well understood in the 1840s, was becoming more clearly delineated by 1916. The two offer a useful organizational framework for this book. My chapters are focused on the major stages of life: infancy, childhood, adolescence, adulthood, and old age—what might be called "life-course time."

I start in the 1840s and, moving from Deerfield into ever-larger spheres of geographical and political influence, end just before the United States entered World War I in 1917. On this timetable, an infant born in 1840 who lived into old age would have been seventy-six in 1916. He or she had managed to avoid or survive the epidemics, accidents, medical treatments, and other causes of death that I describe in Chapters 3 through 6. Several children born in Franklin

County in the 1840s indeed lived into their seventies, eighties, and even nineties, but many more died before their "three score and ten."[9] Then as now, more women than men survived into old age.

What we might call "disease time" has no such direct relationship with chronological or calendar time. Diseases, particularly infectious ones, come and go, wax and wane, and sometimes become endemic, or ever-present. Infectious diseases such as tuberculosis and genetic diseases such as cystic fibrosis may persist generation after generation. Hence we speak of epidemics, endemic diseases, and diseases that are either episodic or chronic. To enhance synchrony in subsequent chapters, I identify an infant epidemic in the 1840s, a childhood epidemic in the 1850s, and an endemic disease affecting adolescents in the 1860s and 1870s, though an epidemic of dysentery or scarlet fever always has the potential to come back and affect infants or children born decades later. Tuberculosis respects no single point on the calendar and no particular age; indeed, it remains a significant health problem in the twenty-first century. In this way disease time illustrates how opportunistic, changing, and resilient disease pathogens can be and allows us to discover how communities responded in different ways to the same disease throughout calendar time.

There was even a point when many people believed that disease time—at least with respect to infectious diseases—had ended. In the mid-twentieth century some claimed that it was difficult to recruit doctors into research and practice centered on infectious diseases because, with vaccines and antibiotics—the "miracle" drugs—diseases were soon to become a problem of the past.[10] Progressive medical narratives talked about "conquering" infectious disease. Soon after the appearance of antibiotics, however, came signs of antibiotic resistance. The recognition of rapidly mutating pathogens and newly emerging diseases quickly followed.[11] The dawn of the understanding of microbial infection came in 1870, and by 1970 we Westerners smugly thought we were on the eve of conquering it. Yet today infectious disease is an ongoing menace and a growing and extremely important field of medical specialization. We are warned of new strains of influenza viruses that could cause pandemics, killing millions. HIV/AIDS persists as an international health crisis. With our current awareness of potential disease crises, perhaps it is easier for us to relate to the subjects of this book—people living in the second half of the nineteenth century—than it would have been for readers at mid-twentieth century.

One question that often arises, implicitly if not explicitly, about the history of medicine between 1840 and 1916 is why doctors persisted for so long in prescribing treatments that seldom helped the patient and that today seem counterintuitive. This question lies at the heart of a medical anthropological inquiry into healing practices. What scientific, cultural, and religious beliefs were in play that gave men (and a very few women) the confidence that their therapies and nostrums were working despite evidence to the contrary? Approaches taken in the historical literature on this subject tend to careen from criticism of doctors for being so slow to recognize the error of their ways to apologias in which honorable men were doing the "best they could" to conquer disease at a time when little was known about it.[12]

Neither position is particularly wrong, but I believe they both miss an important aspect of the way cultures of health form and the way the members of such a culture support and reinforce one another. I look at nineteenth-century medical practice as both a system of beliefs and a fraternity in which membership was regulated and restricted. This knowledge-making practice was not static or unbending, but certain forces or factors sustained its conservatism and made it resistant to change. Among these forces was the initial belief in the possession of true knowledge and a resistance to the scientific testing of that knowledge. A second was the collective ambition to achieve and maintain an elevated status of respect and unchallenged authority as doctors. A third was the frequent resilience of the patient's own body to recover some level of health despite the ministrations of regular physicians. With such instances doctors could lay claim to the power of their knowledge.

A closely related issue I explore in this book is that of medical practitioners' understandings of the categories and characteristics of diseases and causes of death. In the Western tradition, theories of the diseased body go back at least to Hippocrates. In nineteenth-century Europe and North America, theories of bodily states in illness were again both conservative and changing. Nosology—the classification of diseases—in the nineteenth century, although informed by the recognition of pathologies during the development of anatomy and physiology in the seventeenth and eighteenth centuries, was still extremely unsystematic. Physicians and health reformers, to correct what they saw as a problem, created logical, "natural" nosologies. The one widely adopted in North America was developed by William Farr and others in Britain. Its basic form persisted until the turn of the twentieth century, when the United States adopted the International Classification of Diseases system.

All classifications, including nosology, depend on a theory of relationships between categories and on extant knowledge about the phenomena—in this case, diseases—being studied. All classifications embed cultural concepts that are continuously negotiated and reinterpreted. At medical society meetings in the nineteenth century, attendees often devoted attention to describing or showing examples of diseases and then discussing them to share knowledge and try to achieve consensus. This process continues today; the International Classification of Diseases system is now in its tenth revision.

Finally, I want to look at the institutional management of illness and death. At its most primal level, a death is a matter for immediate family members and close friends, and in the early nineteenth century these people, perhaps along with the local minister, represented the extent of society's involvement in death. Gradually, however, other people and institutions became involved, including the patient's doctor, the church, the funeral director, the town clerk, the state boards of vital statistics and health, and possibly an insurance agent. Treatment of the dying in a hospital comes relatively late. Now several layers of institutions interpenetrate what was previously a very private and intimate course of events.

In the following chapters I offer ways in which to read the past for insights into the behaviors of different agents—parents, doctors, clergy, civil officials—that tell us something about how nineteenth- and early twentieth-century New Englanders reacted to illness and death and performed the roles expected of them. Some events are readily quantified, and for these I include appendixes at the end of the book. But most topics concerning illness, death, and loss resist easy quantification. They require disentangling, interpretation, and judgment on the part of both writer and reader.

In the nineteenth century the great majority of the U.S. population did not live in the big cities on which most medical history is centered. In 1850, 85 percent lived in small towns and rural areas, places in many ways comparable to Deerfield, Massachusetts.[13] People farmed, managed stores, worked for the railroad, in the lumber mill, or in small manufacturing shops, or otherwise "made do," just like the residents of Deerfield. These were not the port cities where yellow fever and Asiatic cholera wrought their havoc—although epidemics on occasion prevailed. Many of these country towns and rural areas—again like Deerfield and its surrounding towns—were relatively healthy places in which to live. Unlike in the third world today, where rural mortality usually exceeds urban mortality, in rural America of the nineteenth and early twentieth centuries the reverse appears to have been true: mortality was lower and life expectancy higher than in big cities. In this sense, to investigate nineteenth-century mortality in rural America is to view not the backwater but the mainstream.[14]

George Sheldon was born in Deerfield in 1818 and lived to the age of ninety-eight. He was a farmer, a town official, a historian, a state senator, and a representative to the General Court. Like his friend and cousin Stephen West Williams, George Sheldon is an important person, and someone we meet repeatedly in succeeding chapters. His life spanned the period with which this book is concerned. His death in 1916 marks the end of my period of inquiry. In 1870 Sheldon founded the Pocumtuck Valley Memorial Association, one of the oldest historical societies in the United States, and in 1896 he published the two-volume *History of Deerfield, Massachusetts*. Sheldon's historical interests lay primarily in the colonial past, but I am interested in Sheldon as a chronicler of his own time. What did he see in 1841, the time of the dysentery epidemic that Williams described in his speech to the Massachusetts Medical Society? What did he observe in 1859? 1880? 1900? One thing he saw was the deaths of many close friends and family members.

Sheldon was part of a popular movement in late nineteenth- and early twentieth-century America to collect and record local history.[15] Many volumes of local history were published throughout the United States during this period, and though they varied greatly in quality, their authors all sought to preserve the past by commemorating colonial wars and conflicts, the American Revolution, and the nation's early years of independence. That interest coupled with anxiety over growing industrialization and increasing foreign immigration produced a sentimentality about the agrarian past, the founding fathers of towns and counties, and the earliest recollections of the old-timers. Sheldon appears more often to have looked backward than at the present or toward the future. But thanks to his efforts and those of people like him who felt a responsibility to keep a record for the future, we have been granted the gift of a vast resource of documents in the archives of libraries and historical societies throughout New England and elsewhere. Although the collectors tended to focus on the colonial and revolutionary periods, they did accumulate records of nineteenth-century events, especially the Civil War.

At the state level another kind of recording was proceeding apace. Even before American independence, the General Court of Massachusetts ordered an annual count of births, deaths, and marriages among the colony's citizens. These earliest records, going back to an edict in 1639, vary in quality according to the conscientiousness of town clerks and parish ministers.[16] In 1842—the year in which Dr. Williams presented his lecture to the Massachusetts Medical Society—the Commonwealth of Massachusetts passed new laws requiring more systematic recording of births, deaths, and marriages, later adding further requirements for the collection of vital statistics, as well as fines for town clerks who failed to maintain good records and make timely reports to the state offices in Boston.[17] The second half of the nineteenth century also witnessed the creation of the state Board of Health, local boards of health, and many other data-collecting and record-keeping bodies, each mandated to monitor the citizens of the Commonwealth.

To the state, an individual is a statistic, a datum point of interest for bureaucratic purposes. The person's name, sex, cause of death, and other pertinent information might be included with the date of death, but the state's primary interest is in aggregating these data points in order to summarize all the persons

George Sheldon, late 1870s, from Louis H. Everts, *History of the Connecticut River Valley in Massachusetts*, 2 vols. (1879), vol. 2. Courtesy of Historic Deerfield Library (HDL)

surveyed. The individual is intentionally obscured in favor of the aggregate. In a local history, by contrast, a person's death is a socially embedded piece of information, deeply connected to family and community. It is not a single event but a point on a continuum of illness, death, burial, mourning, and remembrance.

In my work here, I bring the statistics and the historical observations and anecdotes together, looking for patterns and ways of characterizing mortality. I identify closely with Pat Jalland when she writes, "Death is one of the most important facts in human life, and experiences of dying and responses to death take us to the heart of human history." Jalland adds that studying the history of human experiences of death and grief can lead to insights into the meaning of life, but that meaning is embedded in a world of private experience that has to be reconstructed from family histories and "contextualized within the profound cultural transformations of the nineteenth and early twentieth centuries."[18]

Medical history deals with sick bodies, but in many instances it tends to stay at least one step removed from the body after death. The doctor's work is done. The reverse can often be true for scholars who study death and dying—they may skim over or neglect prior events. Margaret Lock reminds us that "the study of health, illness, and medicine provides us with one of the most revealing mirrors for understanding the relationship between individuals, society, and culture."[19] To anthropologists, all times and places, notions of health, disease ("dis-ease"), and death are not simply compilations of objective facts but are mediated through cultural values, beliefs, and models of causality. Each ripples outward through the community in many ways and affects or engages other people, if only in the tangible apprehensions others feel in the presence of a diseased or deceased person. Each event is represented and interpreted through a set of cultural practices, treatments, and rituals that allow the community to reintegrate the sick individual or fill the void left by a death. My ambitious task in the chapters that follow is to give readers access to a complex set of interrelated ideas about culture, health, and science in the presence of illness and death.

2

LIFE AND DEATH IN MASSACHUSETTS, DEERFIELD, AND THE CONNECTICUT RIVER VALLEY, 1620–1840

New England is the healthiest country in the United States; and probably inferior in this respect to few in the world.
—Timothy Dwight, *Travels in New-England and New York* (1821)

WHEN TIMOTHY DWIGHT traveled throughout New England in 1796–97, soon after assuming the presidency of Yale University, he saw a landscape dotted with small farming communities and mill sites that reflected prosperity and abundance. New Englanders had been cultivating the land for about 175 years, ever since Plymouth Plantation was settled in 1620. Dwight wrote of Deerfield's center village and the adjacent Deerfield River:

> Few scenes are more delightful than this river and its borders. The intervals, which accompany the whole of its northern and considerable part of its Eastern course, are unusually elegant, and productive. The town itself is situated on a handsome elevation, in the midst of luxuriant meadows and orchards. In union with these objects, the neighbouring mountain on the East, the more distant hills on the West, covered with farms and forests, and the river winding at the bottom, form a landscape, which more than most others, engages the eye of a traveler.[1]

Observers of New England in the late eighteenth and early nineteenth centuries seem to have been struck by the general good health of the people and salubriousness of the rural places they visited, especially in comparison with the bustling port cities in which many of them resided. Life in the countryside was probably better for the average citizen than it was in the cities, though one can become distracted by this image of pastoral plenty and easily forget that at this time, in the rural United States, epidemics came and went, and other diseases, ever present, took a daily toll.[2]

Relating climate, environment, and healthfulness was a tradition of local writers as well. Rodolphus Dickinson, in his 1815 statistical overview of the town of Deerfield, wrote, "It has been stated, and the observation is believed to be correct, that the diseases in this place are generally less inflammatory, than in the neighbouring elevated towns."[3] In 1836, Stephen West Williams claimed in his "Medical and Physical Topography of the Town of Deerfield," "This town may be considered as healthy as any upon [the] Connecticut river, and perhaps as any in the United States." Williams went on to give an account of the topographic and meteorological data for the town going back to the late 1700s. He also demonstrated his early interest in statistics by summarizing the record of deaths that he, Dickinson, local ministers, and others had been compiling for many years.[4]

At roughly the same time Williams was writing his article on medical topography, Thomas Cole was painting his now famous landscape portrait of the Connecticut River valley, *The Oxbow*. The view faces southwest from Mount Holyoke, near the town of Northampton. Deerfield and Franklin County lie a few miles to the north. William Cronon sees in this painting the vestiges of a wilderness that was being transformed through human agency.[5] On the left side of the painting stands a dense forest. To the right, forests have been cut, fields have been cultivated, and shepherds tend sheep. Smokestacks rise in the distance, hinting of industry. The right side of the painting represents wilderness tamed. There are no Indians in the scene. A later, more vernacular and derivative piece by P. F. Goist illustrates a view of the Oxbow looking north from nearby Mount Nonotuck.[6] In the foreground are symbols of progress: the train, the railroad bridge, a steamboat navigating the river, heading toward Deerfield and Greenfield unseen in the distance.

These two artists took liberties with time and space to represent a romantic past and a future marked by technology, industrialization, and white human settlement. In both works, wilderness, always linked to the past, is juxtaposed against progress and the American future. From the time of one painting to the next, the effects of human agency become increasingly apparent. The pictures thus offer a way to contextualize the time of Stephen West Williams as a moment when rural life and country medicine were gradually giving way to technology and science. From his small corner of the world, Williams witnessed the American industrial revolution and the coming of the railroad. He traveled by horse and coach in 1842, by train in 1852. Similarly, he understood health and medicine through both the practices of his father and grandfather and the emerging "sciences" of disease classification and public health. Before turning to Williams and his patients, it is valuable to gain some insight into the period preceding his arrival in Deerfield as a practicing physician. Who occupied this rapidly changing "wilderness"? What constituted medical knowledge?

When colonial settlers first arrived in the late 1600s, the area that became Franklin County was neither vacant land nor virgin wilderness, as artists

Thomas Cole, *The Oxbow*, 1836. The Metropolitan Museum of Art, Gift of Mrs. Russell Sage, 1908 (08.228). Image © The Metropolitan Museum of Art.

P. F. Goist, "View of Connecticut Valley from Mt. Nonotuck," frontispiece to Everts, *History*, vol. 1. Courtesy of HDL.

might have wished to represent it. It had been a center of Native settlement for thousands of years and part of the homeland of the Pocumtuck and Squakheag Indians, who fished the rivers and streams, cultivated and planted the floodplains, and hunted in the surrounding forested hills.[7]

But Europeans brought new pathogens to their New World—plague, smallpox, measles, diphtheria, and influenza—and the American Indians were "virgin soil" for those diseases.[8] They died of them by the hundreds and thousands. Smallpox was undoubtedly the most virulent, but even the less deadly infections could debilitate families or whole villages to the point that many died simply because too few people were healthy enough to get food, water, and firewood.

Long-standing accusations claim that British soldiers and some early English settlers spread diseases to Indians intentionally, through direct contact or infected blankets, to encourage the rapid demise of Natives in advance of British colonizing. Historians have charged, for example, that Lord Jeffrey Amherst, an officer in the British army during the French and Indian War of 1754–63 and the man for whom the town of Amherst, Massachusetts, was named, discussed and sanctioned the issue of smallpox-infected blankets to Natives during Pontiac's Rebellion in 1763. This story has often been cited as an early example of biological warfare, and recent research tends to support these claims. Intentional infection possibly added to the thousands of deaths caused by the unintentional spread of smallpox in New England, New York, Pennsylvania, and Canada. During the American Revolution colonists feared that the British were again using this tactic against soldiers and civilians. Whereas most of the British soldiers had been inoculated, most American soldiers had not.[9]

Even before the French and Indian War, epidemics of smallpox and other infectious diseases had reduced the Native population of New England to a fraction of its precontact number. Some scholars estimate that as few as 5 to 10 percent survived by the late 1600s.[10] Many Indians of the Connecticut Valley of Massachusetts had migrated north and west and joined other tribes as the English advanced. But the valley was not devoid of a Native presence at the time European settlers arrived. Indians were always present to some degree, and traveled through the region,

The popular misconception about contact between Native Americans and Euro-Americans in the Connecticut Valley is that it consisted primarily of violent conflict. And, when violent encounters did occur, they were dramatized and exaggerated in recorded histories. Among these conflicts was the conflagration known as the Deerfield Massacre of 1704. Although other confrontations had erupted since Deerfield's founding in 1673 which also had resulted in deaths of English-descended residents of the community, this one was exceptional.

On the morning of February 29, 1704, a group of Indians and French from Canada raided isolated Deerfield, killing 43 of its 270 residents and 7 from neighboring towns. Another 112 were taken captive and walked to Canada; 21 died on the march. Over the following years, some of the remaining captives were "redeemed," but others chose to stay with their captors. This single event has so strongly marked the history of Deerfield and its environs that it provides a grounding point for almost everything written about the area—and it is indeed a gripping story involving violent death in Deerfield.[11]

Despite such episodes of violence, however, contact between the descendants of the initial settlers and Natives persisted, most often peacefully. Although Indians had sold and quit-claimed land by treaty to agents of the Massachusetts Colony in the area that became Franklin County, they often retained fishing and hunting rights, and settlers sometimes met them in the forests and along rivers and streams. Settlers also traded with the Indians and sought them out for their knowledge of local plants and their medical uses. Like colonial physicians, Stephen West Williams collected widely from the local plant species and created a portfolio of approximately five hundred specimens. He also is believed to have consulted with local Natives in identifying plant names and traditional uses.[12]

The town of Pocumtuck (later Deerfield) was a colonial outpost, established in 1673. The land was originally granted to proprietors of the town of Dedham, Massachusetts, in compensation for land rights transferred to Indians residing nearby. Only a few English from Dedham actually moved to Pocumtuck, the others choosing to sell their rights.[13] Many of the initial settlers moved up the Connecticut River valley from nearby communities to the south. This stretch of the valley offered exceptional farmland, forests, and pasture.

At the time of Timothy Dwight's visit in 1796–97, Franklin County had not yet been delineated. By the time his *Travels* was published in 1821, the county had been established, and Deerfield, Greenfield, Montague, and Shelburne formed the center of social, agricultural, commercial, and political life in the region. Each town numbered one thousand to two thousand people in the early 1800s, and each was prospering. The naming of Greenfield as the county seat in 1811 signified its status as a commercial crossroads and up-and-coming town. Because it, like Shelburne, had been part of the original Deerfield land grant, many of its earliest settlers were regarded as Deerfield families, and its places, as Deerfield places.[14]

In his letter about the healthfulness of New England, Dwight listed the following as the "principal diseases of New-England": "the Dysentery; the Typhus, Bilious, Remittent, and Scarlet Fevers; the Pleurisy; the Peripneumony; the Croup, or Angina Trachealis; the Cholera Infantum; the Chronic Rheumatism; and the Pulmonary Consumption." "The Gout is rare," he added, "and the Stone almost unknown. Of these diseases the most extensively fatal is the Pulmonary Consumption."[15] In Dwight's list we find three major causes of death that are the centerpieces of subsequent chapters: cholera infantum, scarlet fever, and consumption. Throughout the nineteenth century they would repeatedly be identified as among the most significant causes of death in New England. Doctors in Deerfield and elsewhere in New England feared their appearance. In the middle of the century, Stephen West Williams wrote in his "Topography" that "the croup in infants, the dysentery, the scarlet fever, and other species of fevers, and the consumption, may be said to be the most prevalent complaints."[16]

Nevertheless, the predominant message from these early observers was that rural New England in the nineteenth century was generally a healthy country. David Hackett Fischer agrees, pointing out that mortality rates in New England at the time were much lower than those of western Europe or southern colonies such as Virginia. But in the mid-1600s New England's mortality rates were roughly three times those of today (25–30 per thousand compared with 8–10 per thousand).[17] Infant and early childhood mortality was always high by today's standards. For other age groups, periods of relatively low mortality were occasionally interrupted by short episodes of much higher mortality. Epidemics of smallpox, influenza, scarlet fever, and diphtheria were frequent threats in the seventeenth and eighteenth centuries. So while it was generally true that rural towns were healthier than cities, and that mortality rates in New England were moderately low compared with those of Europe and the Chesapeake region, the claims of Dickinson, Dwight, and others must be weighed against the evidence.[18]

During the later colonial period, the time of Williams's grandfather, Dr. Thomas Williams (1718–1775), doctoring was often a part-time occupation, and training was minimal. Rarely would someone wanting to become a doctor travel to Europe to study under a known physician in London, Edinburgh, or Paris. The more common practice for physicians in colonial North America was to be trained through apprenticeship with other doctors. Theories and therapies were limited; "medicines" and treatments varied little from one doctor to the next. Only two medical schools were founded in North America before the American Revolution, the College of Medicine in Philadelphia, in 1765, and Columbia College (then Kings College) in New York, in 1767, but colleges such as Harvard and Yale offered some medical training. The lessons for a doctor-in-training, whether he was an apprentice, a college student, or a combination of the two, were almost always based on the ideas and approaches of European physicians, and those ideas did not change dramatically during the eighteenth century.[19]

European medicine was still based on the Hippocratic and Galenic traditions, together with more recent theories about states of the body in illness. Doctors in North America, because of language accessibility and travel, were most familiar with British training, although that would change somewhat in the early nineteenth century. The Hippocratic tradition, or humoral theory, maintained that the body was governed by four humors—blood, black bile, yellow bile, and phlegm—and the imbalance of these humors produced sickness. Treatment was primarily a matter of determining which humor was out of balance and then restoring balance by bloodletting, blistering, and the administration of purgatives and emetics. Hippocrates also described environmental influences on health in his treatise *Airs Waters Places*.[20]

By the eighteenth century, particularly through the influence of the Scottish physician William Cullen (1710–1790), the humoral theory had been embellished with the notion that imbalance in nervous energy, or excitability, lay at the root of all disease. This new line of thinking did not entirely replace humoral theory, but it proposed nervous energy and blood as the most important life forces. Cullen published his *First Lines of the Practice of Physic* in the 1780s. It was reprinted in many subsequent editions and remained the most respected medical text in the United States well into the nineteenth century.

Cullen also proposed a system of disease classification and described what he termed "proximate" and "remote" causes of illness. The proximate causes were symptoms to be treated; the remote—in Hippocratic fashion—might include climate, bad air (miasmas) or water, and the constitution of the patient. One of Cullen's students, Benjamin Rush of Philadelphia, fostered the theory of excitability in the United States and argued that effective therapy required massive, or "heroic," bloodletting or purgatives, such as calomel, a mercury compound.[21]

Surgery was another important component of eighteenth-century medicine. Although it had suffered in the early 1700s from being regarded as a trade—often, barbers doubled as surgeons—increasingly it became a specialty and a significant part of the practices of regular physicians. In the absence of modern anesthesia and antiseptic practices, however, infection and complications from surgery were common. As a result of the increased interest in surgery, anatomy became an important part of medical training in many schools and apprenticeships. And as medical training became more formalized, cadavers for study became increasingly difficult to acquire, leading to many reports and documented incidents of body snatching in Europe and North America. Would-be doctors might procure a cadaver from a grave robber, and occasionally student doctors were caught snatching bodies themselves. This practice sparked protests and even riots in New York in 1788 and in New Haven, Connecticut, and other cities in the late eighteenth and early nineteenth centuries.[22] Considering the therapeutic regimens of bloodletting, evacuation, and vomiting and the accounts of body snatching, the public justifiably demonstrated a mixed reaction to the medical establishment at the time.

Despite the blemishes on their profession, many doctors enjoyed high status in their communities and were considered learned men and men of honor. At the same time, just as many were probably feared and disrespected. Surgical knowledge and procedures were advancing, but the same could not be said of many other areas of medical practice. Medical historians have commented on the fact that although the intentions of eighteenth-century doctors were probably mostly honorable, the theories and treatments to which they subscribed were dangerous to the patient and often complicated the course of disease or even contributed to the patient's death. Calling in a physician was, in many instances, the choice of last resort, because of both fear of treatment and monetary expense. As an old English expression put it, "God cures, and the physician takes the fee."[23] This was an age of domestic medicine, when ill health was most often treated at home, and mothers or midwives were likely to be consulted before a doctor.

Doctors on the frontier of Massachusetts were probably fewer per capita than in the urban coastal cities, but the data are not definitive.[24] Probably, proportionately fewer of these frontier doctors than their urban counterparts had any significant formal training—perhaps not a bad thing. A larger proportion of rural doctors may have combined the classical therapies with home remedies and "Indian," or herbal, medicine. Often, doctors received at least part of their training "in the field" as surgeons in the French and Indian War or the American Revolution.

In the towns surrounding Deerfield that would eventually make up Franklin County, as many as forty regular physicians may have been present at any one time between 1750 and 1830, for a population averaging about twenty-five thousand.[25] Reportedly, six doctors practiced in Deerfield in the eighteenth century, beginning as early as 1724. By the 1770s, four of them were practicing simultaneously.[26] Most notable was Thomas Williams, then approaching the end of his career. According to George Sheldon, in his 1895 history of Deerfield, Williams

> came to Deerfield in 1739; became a prominent figure as a man of affairs, as well as in his profession; was surgeon in the abortive Canadian expedition [of] 1746 and for the line of forts; he left Fort Mass. only two days before its capture in 1746; was surgeon in the regt. of his brother Ephraim, at the battle of Lake George, Sept. 8, 1755 and dressed the wounds of Baron Dieskau, the captured commander of the Fr. army; in the campaign of 1756 he was lieut.-col.; rep 2 yrs; selectman 2; town clerk 17; judge of probate and justice of the court of common pleas; and had an extensive professional practice.[27]

Thomas Williams exemplifies many of the characteristics of doctors at the time. Doctoring was his occupation, but he also owned farmland and served in several civic offices, signifying his relatively high status and the community's respect for him. He studied medicine with Dr. Wheat of Boston and received an honorary master of arts degree from Yale. No doubt he learned much of his surgery in the French and Indian War. Among his medical papers are some recipes, including one for "an 'approved medicine for the jaundice' containing earthworms, and a 'diet drink.'"[28]

Thomas Williams's son, William Stoddard Williams (1762–1829), received his medical training by apprenticeship to his father's cousin, Dr. Erastus Sargeant of Stockbridge. He studied with Sargeant for two years, 1782–84, and was then certified by Sargeant to practice medicine. Before returning to Deerfield in 1786, he practiced for a short time in the Berkshire County town of Richmond, perhaps to test his skills on patients other than family, friends, and acquaintances. While in Deerfield he traveled on at least one occasion to Northampton, the site of what was probably the nearest apothecary at the time, to buy pharmaceuticals. A receipt dated June 14, 1796, reveals that he purchased chamomile, opium, mercury, and ipecac (a purgative). These purchases suggest that he was conducting his practice in a fashion comparable to that of other physicians of his time, including those in Boston and even London.[29]

Williams's receipt reinforces the view that there was little in his black bag, or that of any other physician in Massachusetts, that had significant therapeutic value to the patient. Laudanum was an alcoholic tincture of opium in very common use by regular physicians and those who formulated patent medicines in the nineteenth century. It was used to ease pain. If a broken bone needed setting, the prognosis was good, but bloodletting and the rest of the doctor's efforts would be in vain and might only weaken the patient further. William Stoddard Williams continued to see patients into the new century, and he died in 1829, on the eve of a new era in medicine. It included the systematic search for remote causes of illnesses, the collection of facts, and some new competitors in the regular physicians' midst.

Among colonial New England households, including in Boston and Deerfield, typically 15 to 30 percent of children died in their first year of life. Cotton Mather (1663–1728), the famous Puritan minister of Boston, is reported to have had fifteen children and three consecutive wives. Seven of his children died in infancy, and only two survived him.[30] Large families with multiple child and infant losses were common in greater New England and in the Connecticut Valley. Thomas Williams, for example, who lived approximately two generations later than Mather, had two consecutive wives and also fourteen

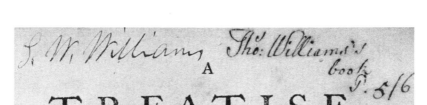

J. W. Williams   *Tho: Williams's book*   *J. 5/6*

A

TREATISE,

OR

REFLECTIONS,

Drawn from PRACTICE on

GUN-SHOT Wounds.

Wherein the Nature, Symptoms and Cure
of Gun-Shot Diforders in general are
explained, whether Contufions, Wounds,
Fractures, &c. or Complications of thefe;
as alfo, the Wounds from this Caufe,
of each particular Part, are methodically
treated of, and their Peculiarities in Point
of Cure, fully exhibited.

By HENRY FRANCIS leDRAN,

Sworn Surgeon at *Paris*, and Senior Mafter of that
Company ; Senior Surgeon Major of the Hofpital
la Charité; of the Royal Acidemy of Sciences,
and of the Academy of Surgery ; Confulting Surgeon to his Majefty's Camps and Armies.

Tranflated from the French Original.

LONDON:

Printed for JOHN CLARKE under the
Royal Exchange Cornhill, 1743.

Title page of medical text owned and signed by Thomas Ephraim Williams
and Stephen West Williams. Courtesy of HDL.

Pharmacy receipt for purchases made in Northampton by Dr. William Stoddard Williams, 1796. Courtesy of PVMA Library.

children, three of whom died in infancy. The average family might expect to lose two or three children before the age of ten years.[31]

Adults of all ages were less likely to die than were children, but adult deaths from infectious disease and accidents, as well as "old age," were nonetheless frequent. A Puritan in early New England might well have asked himself whether his moral and religious character put him in God's favor or whether he was doomed to a life in hell. Was the loss of so many children a punishment for sins committed? A test? For fatalistic Puritans, it might have seemed most often that they were doomed, although there was always hope of salvation. People's negligible understanding of contagion, infection, and disease causality at this time, combined with a strong belief in God's providence or lack thereof, amplified the connection between moral character and sustained life. The same was true of their Anglican brethren and relatives in England. To most doctors, a successful cure for disease depended on the moral character of the patient and the purity and disposition of the soul.[32]

New England Puritans came to North America to practice a faith that was stripped of many of the rituals, celebrations of holy days, and affectations and worldly ways of the Anglican leadership in England, all of which were believed to have corrupted the church. The faith required "purification." Thus, Puritans observed neither religious nor secular holidays. Sermons were often grim, meant to frighten children and adults alike regarding their prospects in the afterlife. All temptations of the flesh were to be avoided; life on earth was a matter of solemnity and hard work, based on a covenant with God to serve. No amount of effort, however, ensured a place in heaven, for Puritans believed in predestination. Repentance could help, but because God selected those to be admitted to the kingdom of heaven, believers never felt they could substantially alter their fate. This set of beliefs could lead to a dreary life of toil, often accompanied by a profound fear of death.[33]

Most Puritan burials in colonial New England were simple, with the body laid in a plain wooden coffin and little in the way of accompanying formal ritual.[34] As grave markers came into regular use, they, too, tended to be simple, made of slate, granite, or some other local material, with simple inscriptions, although early motifs engraved on the stones could be ornate. Often these motifs included a skull or a skull with wings, which gave way to more stylized versions and eventually to angels' heads, sometimes with wings. Later, in the federal period, other patterns, including urns and willows, became the fashion. All these motifs can be found in the earliest cemeteries in Deerfield. Kevin Sweeney's research on grave markers in the Connecticut Valley led him to conclude that while these broad patterns do exist, it is not as tidy as some have suggested and there are many local variations. Karen Halttunen observes that despite their apparent simplicity, gravestones and their iconography formed a close link between death and the colonial landscape during this period.[35]

In colonial Deerfield the church bell tolled every time a death occurred.[36] Death was a common topic of conversation, in the meeting house as well as at home, and no doubt in the presence of young children. Virtually everyone would witness a death at some time. By the end of the eighteenth century, the commonness and everyday presence of death had not changed substantially, but religious attitudes toward it were beginning to moderate.

By the revolutionary period, Deerfield was no longer an outpost by any measure, and despite the distances and difficulty of travel, its residents enjoyed frequent interactions with Boston, Springfield, Hartford, and other cities at some distance. The town of Greenfield was established separately from Deerfield in 1753, and Shelburne was cleaved from the northwestern section of Deerfield in 1768. Montague, across the Connecticut River, was settled in 1754 and incorporated in 1765; its origins lay not in the Deerfield deed but in the town of Sunderland to the south.

Colonial gravestone with variation on the urn and willow motif, Albany Road Cemetery, Deerfield. Photo by author.

When the General Court required that an annual reporting of births, deaths, and marriages be collected in the Bay Colony beginning in 1639, various towns and the port city of Boston initiated registration, bills of mortality, and other records, but they were of uneven quality in the colonial and federal periods. For this reason it is difficult to generalize about the overall health and longevity of the European-descended inhabitants of Massachusetts in these periods. Researchers agree that New England fared better in health than did colonies to the south, and that life expectancy at birth might have been as high as forty years, whereas it was as low as twenty-plus years in the South. The short life expectancy was due to an extremely high rate of infant mortality, which lowered the average life expectancy for the whole population. Persons surviving to age twenty might have expected to live to sixty or more.[37]

What also seemed clear to many observers was that mortality was lower and life expectancy higher in the United States than in many parts of Europe. This perception was shared by Adam Seybert, a doctor and a congressman from Pennsylvania. In 1818 he wrote:

> The causes which have checked the progress of the population in other countries have been more limited in the United States. . . . Our [American] people [are] composed of agriculturists and our commerce is supported chiefly by the surplus of their industry. Few . . . are . . . in unhealthy occupation[s]; our towns and cities are not yet so large as to endanger the health of their inhabitants; fatal epidemics have not been very prevalent; property is much divided amongst the people, and a very moderate share of industry will enable every individual to gain his support.[38]

Although Seybert exaggerated the opportunities offered to all Americans, like Timothy Dwight, he captured the advantages of a largely rural population that enjoyed greater control over its resources.

In Massachusetts as elsewhere, the most dangerous places to live in terms of the threat of infectious disease were growing port cities such as Boston—and again, southern port cities were much worse. Crowding, poverty, slavery, polluted water and food supplies, and a continuous source of fresh pathogens in ships at anchor all played their roles. In much of western Europe, such conditions excepting slavery were even more prevalent. Preventive measures were few. Appropriate public health interventions were not yet understood, let alone planned and implemented, and therapies were scarce.[39]

The most notable exception was smallpox. The efficacy of inoculating healthy people with material removed from smallpox pustules was known from at least the early 1700s and used in both Europe and North America.[40] In 1798 Edward Jenner of Gloucester, England, reported his success in using the milder, much safer, cowpox as a source of the vaccine. Because of the vaccine, true smallpox epidemics became rarer in late eighteenth- and early nineteenth-century

Massachusetts and were virtually absent in the Connecticut River valley.[41] According to an article in the *Greenfield Gazette and Courier* for March 5, 1801, "In several places on the continent, festivals are annually celebrated in honor of the discovery of the vaccine inoculation." The article continues:

> Some chiefs of the Cherokee Indians attended the presidency of the United States of America. They had heard, (as they expressed it), "that the Great Spirit had gifted a white man, over the great water with a power to prevent the smallpox." Eagerly enquiring, and being informed of the fact, they received the infection on their arms, and carried it into the midst of their tribes. It is a pleasing reflection that these untutored savages have spread it throughout their country, and that they are eminently expert in the practice of the new inoculation: They are preparing their rude but sincere presents to Dr. Jenner, a token at once of their admiration and gratitude.

Vaccination for smallpox, historically also referred to as Kine Pock, was the first preventive therapy for an infectious disease and the basis for one of the earliest public health efforts in the United States. On March 4, 1828, the *Greenfield Gazette and Franklin Herald* announced:

> It will be recollected that notice was given a few weeks since to the inhabitants of this Town, that all who wished to be inoculated for the Kine Pock, might avail themselves of the privilege free of expense—About 500 persons have been inoculated since said notice was given. The Physicians have visited most if not all the School Districts in this town three times. If there are any persons who have not attended to it, and wish to be inoculated, they can be, free of expense, by applying to Drs. Stone, Brigham, or Barrett, previous to the first Monday in March next.

Before 1840 the Connecticut Valley enjoyed low population density, productive farmland, and some isolation from the disease threats more common to the urban centers and coastal regions, such as yellow fever, a scourge of many North American port cities in the late 1700s and early 1800s that seldom reached to inland towns.[42] Malaria, too, was virtually unknown in the interior. Yet cities and coastal areas have been the focus of most mortality studies of this period. Research on mortality in towns of the central and western parts of New England before 1840 has been rare.

In the early 1970s, my graduate students and I initiated research on the towns of Deerfield, Greenfield, Shelburne, and Montague. Using the best data available, and being careful to estimate rates accurately, we concluded that life expectancy in these four towns between 1750 and 1850 was closer to fifty years than to the forty others had estimated for towns and cities along the eastern seaboard. Infant mortality was relatively high, but still only two-thirds or even one-half the rates reported for Boston.[43] Our estimates would translate to approximately 150 infant deaths per thousand births in this part of the valley, in comparison with 200–300 infant deaths per thousand births in a city such as Boston in the same years.[44] By today's standards for life expectancy at birth in the United States—close to eighty years—even fifty years suggests a relatively high mortality rate.

It also appears that we should make no simple assumptions about a consistent trend toward greater life expectancy and a decreasing death rate over the period—or the reverse, for that matter. Because the average age of the settler population was increasing from 1750 to 1840, and because incipient industrialization and significant (but difficult to measure) in- and out-migration of new populations were taking place in the region, the pattern is not simple. In addition, few improvements in the treatment or prevention of diseases were made during those decades. With the limited quality of data from this time, it is difficult to be more precise.

It is possible to say somewhat more about the sometimes fatal diseases that English American settlers contracted in the eighteenth and early nineteenth centuries, and the causes prove to be those we meet frequently in the years after 1840 as well. Some causes still pose challenges in translation to modern nomenclature, such as the meanings of "dropsy," "catarrh," and "bilious fever."[45] Fortunately, medical historians and others have decoded most of these outdated categories, so that we understand them better in terms of modern disease classification.

We cannot know whether every diagnosis in the late eighteenth century was based on a competent recognition of the symptoms and presentation of a particular disease and according to a consistent set of criteria, but on statistical grounds we can infer that most cases described by one of the old terms were, indeed, cases of what we now classify by a particular modern term. In part the limitations of the data themselves direct our focus on Connecticut Valley mortality after 1840, because by 1850 the causes identified by attending physicians were becoming more reliable, and the state was requiring more complete and consistent record keeping.[46]

Between 1790 and 1840 domestic medicine, or the informal use of folk remedies, was still the most common first line of therapy. Medical practitioners in Massachusetts and throughout the United States, however, particularly those who had received formal training or had undergone an apprenticeship in medicine and identified themselves as "regular" physicians were being challenged by an increasing number of new, "irregular" practitioners offering their "expertise" and services.

Stephen West Williams, born in 1790, exemplifies the "regular" physicians of the time. By the age of sixteen, he is said to have read Benjamin Rush's five-volume medical work *Enquiries*, Thorton's *Medical Extracts*, and Erasmus Darwin's *Zoonomia*. Serving an apprenticeship, in this case with his father, and attending a short medical course of study were not uncommon. He returned at age twenty-three to join his father's practice. He was a prodigious reader and writer and often lectured at nearby medical schools, including Dartmouth College in Hanover, New Hampshire, and the Berkshire Medical Institute in western Massachusetts.[47] He followed the medical literature closely and owned an extensive library for his time. Indeed, referring to his fellow doctors in the Franklin District Medical Society, who Williams believed were "as well educated physicians as are to be found in any part of the States," he mentioned that "many of them have medical libraries of standard merit, of from fifty, and I presume I put it at the lowest estimate, to six or seven hundred volumes."[48]

Williams maintained a wide correspondence, including with physicians in England. He took great interest in local history and wrote several essays on Deerfield and on his own ancestors. His best-known work was probably his biography of American physicians, published in 1845.[49] Williams's life and work coincided with a transformative period in American medicine. His training was traditional and from the "old school," but his interests and his medical and intellectual pursuits were contemporary and even progressive.

Regular physicians like Williams, however, did not hold a monopoly over medical practice in New England or the rest of the United States. This was the age of Jacksonian democracy, and a recently empowered American public was more inclined to take matters into its own hands. Increasingly, people distrusted so-called experts, including doctors. Self-proclaimed experts and irregular physicians were a sufficient enough threat in Massachusetts in the 1830s that the Massachusetts Medical Society passed rules barring their membership and censoring regulars who consulted with them.[50]

One self-proclaimed medical expert was the prominent Presbyterian minister Sylvester Graham, originally of Suffield, Connecticut, and, later, Northampton, Massachusetts, who thought the American diet was too stimulating and rich (by far the most common ailment being treated in the United States at the time was dyspepsia, or acute indigestion), and people were becoming intemperate in their habits. He criticized the "blood letters" and "pill pushers" and advised people to "avoid medicine and physicians if you value your life." He argued that Americans' food no longer came from a mother's kitchen but was processed in a factory, and so its purity could not be trusted. What was needed was simple, wholesome food and his "Graham bread."[51] The empiric Samuel Thomson of New Hampshire, founder of the Thomsonian system of medicine, railed against regular physicians and recommended, as alternatives to their treatments, heat and his botanical remedies of cayenne pepper and lobelia. Many other "irregulars" joined these two New Englanders in the medical marketplace, all suggesting that the citizenry could treat itself—even for the most serious diseases—using their particular "system."[52]

Almost as threatening to New England's regular physicians were a few other regulars who published medical advice books for the household. Their actions took "domestic medicine" to a new level. It was one thing for the woman of the household to seek medical knowledge from a trusted midwife or in the familiar recipe books that had been appearing for some time. It was quite another for regular physicians to publish books that were made widely available. Who were these upstarts? Dr. William Buchan's *Domestic Medicine*, published in Edinburgh in the late 1700s, achieved some familiarity in the United States. In 1830 John C. Gunn, a regular physician from Tennessee, published *Gunn's Domestic Medicine*, which he boldly dedicated to Andrew Jackson.

> In dedicating the following work, Sir, to the President of the United States, in the person of Andrew Jackson, I freely confess myself influenced by interested motives; they are not, however, such as are connected with pecuniary considerations. Every man in the community, ought to feel an honest pride in being beneficial to his country; and, if he cannot be so in *Legislation, Diplomacy, or Arms*—he may at least make the attempt to be useful in the more retired and less brilliant walks of literature and science.

"Morally and physically speaking," Gunn explained, "every man ought to be his own physician, so far as his circumstances render it possible;—and even in cases of great difficulty, and when it is essential to employ a regular physician, a partial knowledge of the science of medicine, would not only enable a man to guard against imposition and imposture, but to make a judicious and safe selection."[53]

A doctor like Stephen West Williams must have wondered whether his patients owned a copy of Gunn's book and might try to second-guess his treatments. But of greater concern to him than patients' potential to bypass doctors through home health guides were his irregular competitors. In a talk to the Franklin District Medical Society, he decried those "pretenders to the profession of medicine, under the form of Perkinism, mesmerism, homeopathy, hydropathy, [and] phrenomesmerism, . . . the Rochester rappings, and all their kindred delusions."[54]

Williams recruited other regular physicians in Franklin County to join the Massachusetts Medical Society, because it was through such associations that the regular physicians could seek legislation for licensing doctors and establishing fee schedules, in addition to sharing their knowledge. His dedication to this cause is revealed in the following letter to a colleague:

Deerfield, June 10, 1839
Dr. Bull (Shelburne, Mass)

Dear Sir—A committee of one from each county has been appointed by the Mass. Med. Society at its annual meeting, for the purpose of making such alterations in the constitution and Bye [*sic*] Laws of the Society as may be deemed necessary.

GUNN'S
DOMESTIC MEDICINE,

OR

POOR MAN'S FRIEND.

IN THE HOURS OF AFFLICTION, PAIN, AND SICKNESS.

THIS BOOK

POINTS OUT, IN PLAIN LANGUAGE, FREE FROM DOCTOR'S TERMS
THE DISEASES OF

MEN, WOMEN, AND CHILDREN,

AND THE LATEST AND MOST APPROVED MEANS USED IN THEIR CURE,
AND IS EXPRESSLY WRITTEN FOR THE BENEFIT OF

FAMILIES

IN THE WESTERN AND SOUTHERN STATES.

IT ALSO CONTAINS

DESCRIPTIONS OF THE MEDICINAL ROOTS AND HERBS OF
THE WESTERN AND SOUTHERN COUNTRY, AND HOW
THEY ARE TO BE USED IN THE CURE OF

DISEASES:

ARRANGED ON A NEW AND SIMPLE PLAN,

BY WHICH THE PRACTICE OF MEDICINE IS REDUCED
TO PRINCIPLES OF COMMON SENSE.

McC 25757

Why should we conceal from mankind
That which relieves the distresses of our fellow-beings?

Knoxville,

PRINTED UNDER THE IMMEDIATE SUPERINTENDANCE OF THE AUTHOR,
A PHYSICIAN OF KNOXVILLE.

::::::::::

1830.

Title page from *Gunn's Domestic Medicine*, facsimile ed. Courtesy of author.

The object of the mover of the resolution, a gentleman from Hampden [county], was that the society might exert as direct influence & practical an influence upon the remote counties as upon the central ones.

It is of importance that every physician of regular education in the commonwealth should belong to some association of this kind. In the centre counties almost every regular physician has united himself with the Society, and a large majority of all the respectable physicians in the state belong to it. If we can have the same benefits in the remote parts that they have in the centre there can be little doubt that all our regular physicians will want to unite with us.

I have the honor to belong to this committee, which is to meet at Worcester on the 10th of July next. & it has been thought advisable to write to most of the regular physicians in this county whether belonging to the society or not, for their opinions respecting the alterations which it would be desirable to bring about in the constitution & bye laws, in order to effect the wished for object, rather than call a county convention as they have done in Hampden.

You will confer an obligation upon me if you will suggest to me in writing, on, or before the 1st of July next such alterations as you may think desirable to effect these objects. I think you have a copy of the constitution & bye laws of the Society.

I should like your opinion upon the article relating to consultations, & upon the propriety of endeavoring to form a branch society, either in the old county of Hampshire, embracing the counties of Franklin, Hampshire, & Hampden, or in the county of Franklin. Your opinion upon any other point connected with the subject will be thankfully rec'd.

I hope, my dear Sir, you will find time & inclination to reply to this soon after the reception of it. By doing so you will greatly oblige.

Your sincere friend
Stephen West Williams"

In the decades from 1800 to 1840, while professional physicians were seeing increased competition in the medical marketplace, the older, established, agrarian families of rural western Massachusetts and the rest of rural New England were also facing competition. Western expansion and the construction of canals, roads, bridges, and turnpikes reduced the market prices of beef and grain. In addition, a new class of commercial and manufacturing entrepreneur began establishing businesses that attracted a new labor force, including the sons and daughters that farmers needed on the farm. Some of the younger generation were even leaving the area to seek their fortunes in the west, in New York and beyond. The new transportation networks also meant new opportunities for illnesses and diseases to visit towns in the valley. People could travel farther, and travelers could bring contagion.[56]

In 1830 the population of the United States was 90 percent rural. In Massachusetts the figure was probably closer to 85 percent, but even the smaller towns in western New England had been growing rapidly, through both natural increase and the arrival of newcomers.[57] Annual growth rates often exceeded 5 percent during the late eighteenth century, but between 1800 and 1850 growth slowed considerably, and the population numbers for many towns held virtually steady for many years. A physician from the hill town of Rowe, Massachusetts, remarked that "there are born yearly, not more than a third as many children now, as in the early settlement of the town. Then the people, the first settlers, were young and prolific. Now the young leave us, in the pursuit of other homes, and none but the barren and unprolific are left behind."[58] The old Yankee population was declining as a percentage of the general population. New people were coming to the region, but mostly to the valley towns and not to the hill towns. New patterns were emerging.

Deerfield, situated on prime agricultural land, continued to do relatively well even in the early 1800s, although its growth slowed slightly in the following decades. The village of South Deerfield, however, eventually displaced Deerfield village center when the railroad arrived in the 1840s. In the northernmost section of Deerfield, the village of Cheapside on the Green River gave the town a footing in the commercial and manufacturing opportunities that were developing in the region. Greenfield, also in the lowlands of Franklin County, with its origins in agriculture, was becoming the favored place for boats carrying goods up and down the Connecticut River. It promised to be the choice not only for transportation but also for commercial enterprises and small manufacturing.[59]

Greenfield's growth, too, slowed somewhat during the early nineteenth century but picked up again after 1850. Hill towns such as Shelburne showed no appreciable growth between 1800 and 1850, but the village of Shelburne Falls, because of its favorable location on the Deerfield River, became a small manufacturing center and outpaced the old Shelburne village center. Although towns like Shelburne were successful to some extent in the early 1800s because of good pasturage and orchards, their terrain was too hilly and their soil too rocky and thin to be productive for crops. In all three towns the arrival of railroad lines in the late 1840s and the 1850s encouraged people to move toward the railroad stops and water power. Montague, on the east side of the Connecticut River, remained principally an agricultural community like Deerfield until after the Civil War, when a planned industrial village, Turners Falls, was created. Investors rebuilt a canal around Turners Falls on the Connecticut River that had been used in the past primarily for log drives south from Vermont and New Hampshire. They also prepared the adjoining land for water-powered mills and worker housing.

These towns were part of the landscape that Stephen West Williams traversed in his daily rounds and on his travels. In 1842, when it took him two days to travel by carriage or coach to Boston, even more time was required to take a wagonload of goods to market or for a drover to take cattle to Boston's

Brighton market. By 1850 the same region would be served by a large network of canals, roads, bridges, turnpikes, and the newly built railroad lines going both north-south and east-west.[60]

The rural landscape of western New England in the 1840s presented a complex, diversified terrain far different from the imagined landscapes of Thomas Cole and P. F. Goist and far different, too, from the monotonous, flat, rich farmland then opening up in northern Ohio, extending as far as the eye could see. It was a landscape of narrow but productive floodplains, of hills and narrow stream valleys. It hosted a great variety of economic activity, of which agriculture, though significant, was only a part. The old Yankee families like the Williamses no longer held the power and authority they had enjoyed only a few years before, but they were still an influential presence in the politics, economies, and everyday lives of Franklin County and its citizens. Along the Connecticut River valley they were connected to a wider sphere of influence, and their names were well known among their professional contemporaries in Boston and elsewhere. But new entrepreneurs and professionals were arriving daily, and working-class families from abroad were beginning to appear.

3

CHOLERA INFANTUM

[Cholera infantum is] an acute disease of childhood, characterized by high fever, severe vomiting and diarrhea, and symptoms of collapse, due to inflammation of the intestine.
　　　　　　　　—Frederick Rossiter, M.D., *The Practical Guide to Health* (1908)

UPON RETURNING TO DEERFIELD after delivering his address to the Massachusetts Medical Society in May, Stephen West Williams hoped that the ailment known as the "summer complaint"—cholera infantum—would spare his town come August. The previous year, 1841, as he had told his colleagues in Boston, Deerfield had lost thirteen infants and toddlers (out of thirty-one deaths), most of them during an epidemic of that disease. At the time, cholera infantum was a vaguely defined set of ailments, chiefly dysentery and fever. We now include it in the pneumonia-diarrhea complex, a name that characterizes, symptomatically, a group of common respiratory and enteric infections.[1] Using infants and cholera infantum as the focal point, in this chapter I describe transitions in medical practice during the mid-nineteenth century and illustrate the ways in which treatments and mourning practices differed among families by class and ethnicity.

Williams was well acquainted with dysentery, which always seemed to take its greatest toll on the very young. In 1803, at the age of thirteen, he had watched his father tend patients during a serious epidemic in Deerfield. The outbreak was complicated by its having been preceded by a measles epidemic, and it hit mostly along the main street in the village center. About 350 of Deerfield's approximately 1,400 residents lived on the street at the time, and 65 of them died—at least 54 of them because of dysentery.[2] In his *Medical History of the County of Franklin*, Williams wrote: "It was not uncommon to see two and sometimes three funerals a day in one street, for several weeks in succession. . . . I was then a youth, and, of course, was not much acquainted with the details of practice in this complaint at that time. I understood, however, that the mercurial practice [doses of calomel as a purgative] was the most effectual."[3]

Since 1803, except for bouts of scarlet fever in 1831 and 1832, Deerfield had been free of disease epidemics until dysentery struck again in 1841. In the third week of July that year, there were several complaints of dysentery along the village street. "In August," Mary Willard recorded in her reminiscences, "a dreadful epidemic of dysentery broke out, six cases, I think, being fatal. Almost every member of our family either had the disease seriously, or threatenings of it. Sept. 4 was a day never to be forgotten by me. On that day Mary Wilson, perhaps the most brilliant girl in Deerfield, & a particular friend of ours, died. In the afternoon there was a funeral of a child."[4]

The town clerk in Deerfield recorded that nine children died in the late summer of 1841, among them the infant children of Caleb Jones and Francis Hawks, who lived across the street from each other and were Williams's close neighbors and patients. The Jones and Hawks families had both suffered dysentery, followed by cholera infantum in the young children. Williams and his partner, Dr. A. Sumner Haskell, treated the Hawks children in early September.[5] Administering calomel as a purgative was still the recommended treatment, although Williams had been experimenting with the use of astringents, particularly Cerussa Acetata, carbonate or sugar of lead, along with some opium, and he thought it to be effective.[6] Nevertheless, the Jones and Hawks infants died on the same day, September 4.[7] As the church bells rang for their funerals, Williams may have been reminded of his own son, Albert, who had died in 1822 at the age of one year.

Williams's hope for a better year in 1842 would be short-lived. As he returned to his duties after his trip to Boston, he found June and early July to be relatively ordinary—mostly routine calls, and no outbreaks of disease.[8] But then he began to hear reports of dysentery in the village center and other districts of town. The earliest death of an infant came, as in 1841, in late July, followed by the deaths of several other very young children, among them, on August 2, two-year-old George, son of Stephen West Williams's cousin John George Williams, and on August 17, seventeen-month-old Julia Lucretia, daughter of Williams's close friends David and Julia Sheldon.[9] At least fourteen infants and children under the age of two died in Deerfield between July and October 1842.[10]

At the time, medical practitioners knew little about what caused cholera infantum or how to treat it successfully. What almost everyone in mid-nineteenth-century Massachusetts—and elsewhere—knew was that the first year of a child's life was particularly dangerous. Babies were "known" to be naturally frail. Common sense, the advice manuals, and midwives all agreed that one must be particularly careful to keep a young child warm, clean, and well fed. It was also believed, by the medical community and the general populace, that certain aspects of the climate and local environmental conditions brought

Allen Sisters, *The Baby*, 1898–1900. Courtesy of PVMA.

additional risk. When these conditions—such as long stretches of hot, humid weather—were coupled with unclean privies, standing garbage, or other wastes that produced foul and putrescent "miasmas," sickness was sure to follow.

In Boston and in manufacturing cities such as Fall River, miasmas were believed responsible for the deaths of many infants and children every year. In the relatively cleaner and less crowded countryside, sickness and loss of life were perhaps rarer, but threats existed, and a few children died each year of "lung diseases" and cholera infantum. Teething infants who were being weaned from their mothers were known to succumb to the disease quickly, causing people to believe that teething itself was the cause of the illness. In the worst years, such as 1841 and 1842, the soil or weather or some combination of the two was suspected of making matters more severe.

The late summer months, as Stephen West Williams pointed out in his lecture, were particularly unhealthy for children, especially for very young children, even in generally healthy Deerfield. At these times the "summer complaint" or "autumnal fevers" took their toll. Some of the elderly and even some older children might die, but infants and toddlers were the most vulnerable. According to "Hall's Family Doctor," as a widely consulted home health manual was known, September was "the month malign."

> September gives rise to more disease in town and country together than any other month of the year. It is fruitful in diarrhea, dysentery, and fevers of every grade, from common fever and ague to the most malignant form of bilious, congestive and yellow fever. The immediate causes of these maladies are the hot days and cool nights in conjunction with the habits of people. . . .
>
> This general cause of disease existing in the atmosphere is always generated in the latter part of August and during September; it is called miasm—an emanation from decaying vegetable matter, mud, leaves, plants, roots, etc; it is distilled death, literally, because the heat of the noonday sun, acting upon matter like these, causes the deleterious agency to rise up, like alcohol or whisky from a still. When the cool of the evening comes, this air is condensed, becomes heavy, falls to the surface, and is breathed by whole communities, sometimes breaking out in a night and destroying hundreds before the morning. In such cases the temperate, plain living and industrious, are the very last to suffer, if at all, because they have good blood, which has a "power" to resist disease.[11]

Gunn's Domestic Medicine provided the following account of the summer complaint and its recommended treatments:

> This vomiting and purging of children, called *Cholera infantum*, prevails during the heats of summer; it is a dangerous and destructive disorder throughout the United States. Of all the complaints with which childhood become afflicted in its earlier stages, this is, at least amongst the infantile population . . . the most destructive. . . . Its frequency and danger are always in proportion to the heat of the weather; children are subject to it from the third week after birth, to the second summer, at which period it is the most fatal to them.

Many distinguished Physicians have been disposed to consider teething as the cause of this complaint. I am, however, convinced, that this is not the cause of *Cholera infantum*, or puking and purging. Remedies—... nothing is of greater service than a gentle emetic in the morning, followed by a dose of calomel, mixed with a small quantity of Ipecacuanha, at night.... The emetic not only cleanses the stomach, but produces a soft moist state of the skin. The Calomel and the Ipecacuanha as I have described, will greatly lessen the severity of the disease and not unfrequently [*sic*], check it.[12]

In 1841 the *Greenfield Gazette and Courier* advised adults with summer complaint to try a less drastic remedy:

People need not be long troubled with that disorder so generally prevalent at this season, commonly known as the Summer or Bowel Complaint, when the certain remedy therefore may be found on every man's dinner-table, in the shape of salt and vinegar. Two tea-spoons full of the former dissolved in half a gill of the latter, and swallowed at a draft will in most cases effect an instant cure.—The second dose, if needed, will assuredly accomplish it.[13]

Around this time Dr. Oliver Wendell Holmes began making his case that nature heals and doctors should let the first stage of a disease take its natural course. For example, in his famous critique "Homeopathy and Its Kindred Delusions," presented to the Boston Society for the Diffusion of Useful Knowledge in 1842, he argued that homeopaths were claiming a cure from their dilutions which was simply the product of nature taking its course. Stephen West Williams had heard that the Harvard-trained physician and public health reformer Dr. Edward Jarvis, who had once practiced in nearby Northfield and later in Boston, held the same beliefs.[14] This made sense, but sometimes diseases progressed rapidly. Nature was a powerful healing force, but Williams himself had observed patients make seemingly miraculous recoveries from almost certain death once he had administered the recommended treatments of purgatives or emetics and opium or laudanum drops. So many new theories were being bandied about—and those irregulars! Dr. Williams thought the homeopaths and others were quacks, dangerous to their patients and to the good name of medicine.

Cholera infantum, affecting most of all the youngest children, was sometimes accompanied by teething, and that made proper treatment all the more difficult. Should one cut the gums slightly to ease the eruption of teeth, or should one focus on the loose bowels and vomiting? Or treat both? One benefit of belonging to the Massachusetts Medical Society and the emerging Franklin District Medical Society was the opportunity to share information and knowledge of proper treatment for each complaint.[15]

A contemporary of Stephen West Williams, Lucy Buffum Lovell, of Bellingham, Massachusetts, wrote an account of her daughter's death from the disease that is as informative about medical practices of the time as it is moving. The treatments the child received were quite familiar to Williams and likely similar to those he prescribed. Lovell was one of five daughters of a prominent Quaker family and was married to the Reverend Nehemiah Lovell, a Baptist minister. The couple suffered the deaths of all three of their young children, two from scarlet fever and one, that of their second daughter, Laura Martha Ashley, from dysentery in mid-September 1840, at the age of nineteen months.[16]

Lucy Buffum Lovell's diary is an extraordinary narrative, and I rely on it heavily in this chapter and the next. "About the last of August," soon after she had been weaned, Laura, Lovell writes, "was taken sick with summer complaint." She continues:

> She had been remarkably well and her bowels seemed to be in a very good state Wednesday morning. I thought particularly of this as many children in neighboring towns, and some in this, were dying with dysentery, and I spoke of it to her father. Before night, however, a diarrhea came on, and we felt some afraid she was going to be sick. But she was very pleasant through the day and especially at night just before going to bed. (59)

Laura's symptoms came and went over the next few weeks, and her parents hesitated to call the physician. One morning she seemed to have "a better appetite than usual." But, her mother wrote,

> I . . . suppose now that it was thirst, for she very soon lost it all. I perceived she was unwell again and sent for the doctor, but he had gone to Boston. This was on Wednesday and he did not call till Friday evening. He did not think she was very sick, told me to feed her with simple food and give her a little magnesia. In the morning he called again and cut her gums. Since he had cut them before, three eye teeth had come through the gums. It was the fourth that seemed now to be the cause of her sickness, as I have no doubt her first sickness was caused by the inflammation of the other three. On Sabbath morning she seemed rather more unwell and exceedingly languid and feeble. She would answer when spoken to, but did not seem inclined to talk, or play, of her own accord. That day I took off her frock and put on a flannel nightgown, and I never dressed her afterwards.
>
> Monday she continued to grow more feeble, and Monday night her disorder assumed the form of dysentery. Then we began to feel more alarmed. Though the doctor encouraged us, and had it not been coming so gradually, we should have thought there was nothing particularly alarming in the case. Tuesday we gave her oil, and after it, opium injections to quiet the bowels—but she grew worse. . . .
>
> She seemed more comfortable Thursday than the two previous days, and we felt some encouraged, though her medicine did not seem to have a good effect. We gave her laudanum injections, and while the effect lasted, she would sleep. But the irritation of the bowels continued and we were obliged, according to the directions of the physician, to repeat the injections, and increase the dose.

We began with about twenty drops of laudanum in a little starch, and increased the dose till we got it up to fifty drops. . . .

During the evening [on the Friday of that week] she remained much as she had been in the afternoon till about one-half past ten, when her breath was suspended again for a few moments. But by raising and rubbing her, it was restored again as before, with the exception that she did not revive as before. She continued to breathe quicker and quicker ten or fifteen minutes, and then without the least struggle, or anything to show that death had done its work, her spirit winged its way to another, better world. (61–67)

Lovell's experience of medicine in this instance was typical for someone of her cultural and socioeconomic circumstances. The forms of treatment the doctor applied, and the way infant diarrhea was understood by the parents and the doctor, would change little until early in the next century. Nevertheless, physicians such as Stephen West Williams would persist in searching for answers and cures, while continuing, for the most part, to treat each disease by convention and tradition.

Lucy Buffum Lovell's diary offers insights into how parents in mid-nineteenth-century Massachusetts in her relatively well-educated and middle-class social stratum felt about and dealt with the deaths of their children. Her diary entries sometimes convey a quiet acceptance, but, as revealed in the following passage, there is nothing in them of indifference.

It is useless to conjecture what [Laura] would have been, though I find my mind is much inclined to look back and think what she was to us, or look forward to what she would have been. Better is it for me to think of her as she is—in the arms of Jesus, who said, "Suffer little children to come unto me and forbid them not." Why should we wish to hold her here? True she was a lovely flower, and we often think how pleasant would our fireside have been this winter if she could have been spared to us. I feel that I could cheerfully make any sacrifice to promote her welfare. O, may I remember that she is where she needs not a mother's watchful care, for the eye of the compassionate Saviour is upon her, and his Arms enfold her. I shall never feel anxiety on her account lest she should at last lose her soul. And if I, through grace, am admitted to the abode of the Blessed, I shall meet among the happy throng around the throne, my sweet little Laura. (67–68)

The religious faith that helped sustain Lovell in her grief also shaped the customs the Lovell family observed in conducting Laura's funeral and burial.

Laura was buried on Sabbath afternoon about five o'clock, September 20, 1840. In the morning Father Shubael Lovell preached from II Cor. 4:17 and 18. "Our light affliction which is but for a moment, worketh for us a far more exceeding and eternal weight of glory." Never did the truth of the Gospel seem more precious. We were led in our minds to look away from things seen and temporal, to those which are unseen and eternal.

Allen Sisters, *Roana Sweeping*, 1913. Courtesy of PVMA. Soon after this photo was taken, Roana Andrews died of cholera infantum, age two and a half years.

In the afternoon my husband preached from Job 5:7. "Man is born into trouble, as the sparks fly upward." I did not go out in the afternoon, but he expressed to me that he felt it a privilege to preach.

Rev. Mr. Smith of Woonsocket came over to attend the funeral. He offered prayer at our house and a few friends were present, after which we went to the meeting house wherein we heard the 103 Psalm read and remarks by Brother Smith. It was a solemn occasion, and, I hope, led some to reflect more upon eternal things than we are apt to do.

We then, after taking the last look, followed the remains of the little one [which had been laid out in a room in the family's home], beautiful even in death, to the house appointed for all living. (68–69)

Lovell told her older daughter, Caroline, who was almost four, that the grave was "dear Laura's little bed." "They will put green grass over it and in the spring we will plant flowers there," she explained to the child, "and it will be pleasant and we shall love to go there and see it." These words, she said calmed Caroline's "agitated spirit, and from that moment she has seemed to think of death only as the way to Heaven, if we are good, and the grave, only as the resting place of the body" (70).

The mourning events and the services performed would have been similar in Deerfield in 1842, though in a Congregational service the minister would likely have met the family at the entrance to the church and accompanied them to the cemetery for a short sermon and offering of prayers. In an Episcopalian service, the liturgy would have been from the 1789 edition of the Book of Common Prayer: "The Minister, meeting the Corpse at the entrance of the Churchyard, and going before it, either into the Church, or towards the Grave, shall say, or sing, I AM the resurrection and the life, saith the Lord: he that believeth in me, though he were dead, yet shall he live; and whosoever liveth and believeth in me, shall never die. St. John xi. 25, 26." Nothing in the liturgy would have referred to the infant; it would have spoken directly to the adults at the service about their own prospects after death, though Bible passages referring to children might have been read. In a Congregational or Episcopalian service, in the unlikely event that the child had not been baptized, the minister would have offered prayers but not given a eulogy. Services would have been held in the home and the body would have been kept there for visitation prior to burial.

Somewhat later, in the 1850s and 1860s, a new memorial custom gained some popularity: photographing the deceased. By this time the earlier Daguerreotype photography was giving way to wet-plate methods, and photography was becoming more affordable for family portraiture.[17] Most often the subjects of posthumous photographs were infants and children, although adults lying in state or even seated among family members were photographed as well. One example comes from J. L. Lovell, who operated a photographic studio in

Harry Judson Hitchcock, shortly
before and after death, 1867.
Courtesy of PVMA.

Amherst, Massachusetts. In 1867 he made a memorial photograph of Harry
Judson Hitchcock, the two-year-old son of a prominent doctor, Edward Hitchcock Jr., and his wife, Mary, after the child died of dysentery.[18]

By 1840 ample means for the religious and cultural expressions of mourning
existed, and with the advent of photography, age-specialized caskets and other
material culture, families had ever-increasing options for their expressions of
love and grief. Ann Douglas refers to the period between 1820 and 1875 as one
of a "magnification of mourning," for the young child's premature death.[19] I
return to this topic in Chapter 4.

The Sheldons, Willards, Buffums, and Lovells represented "old stock" New
Englanders. By the late 1840s, something had been happening recently in
Franklin County that had local people concerned about the health of their
towns. Many foreigners, primarily from Ireland and Germany, were moving
into the area looking for jobs. The experts claimed to have established that
this influx was a cause of illness, proposing that the habits of the foreign born,
who were said to exhibit lax morals and intemperance, increased the chances
of fatal disease. Perhaps their natural constitutions were weaker than those
of "native" Yankees as well. Some people feared they brought contagion with
them from their homelands, from the ships that transported them, or from
the cities where they had previously lived.[20]

A report by the Sanitary Commission of Massachusetts in 1850 recommended that "measures be adopted for preventing or mitigating the sanitary

evils arising from foreign emigration" (*sic*).[21] The Massachusetts Board of Health declared, more neutrally, in 1873 that "the seasons, local and endemic influences, and more than all, the means and manners of life in the family seem to be prominent as friends or foes, to aid or impair the infant constitution, in its struggle against the adverse influences that threaten it."[22] But the health stigmatization of the foreign born had by no means ended. In 1875, for example, the Boston Board of Health reported: "Our Irish inhabitants and their offspring, by consequence of their numbers, and of their morbid tendencies, exert a distinct influence upon our apparent sanitary condition. In the case of Boston, the influence thus exerted is so great that it becomes necessary to make allowances for this etiological factor, when attempting to make an estimate of our real sanitary condition compared with that of other cities.[23]

Deerfield and surrounding towns were changing. More businesses and small manufactories appeared, and more people arrived from other regions. While shopping in Greenfield, one might now hear an Irish brogue or English spoken with a German or French accent.[24] The writer of a letter to the *Greenfield Gazette and Courier* in 1859 offered this opinion about "Our German Population":

> Perhaps all of your readers are not aware how large a German population we have among us. There are in this village and in Cheapside, not less than seventy German families; and probably no class of our adopted citizens are more peaceable, frugal and industrious than they and, they are by no means insensible to the many material advantages they enjoy here; but the features and beauty of the country and the excellence of its products are not to be compared, say they to those of fatherland. America may and probably does possess some noble rivers, but—"What streams divine can ever match our river Rhine?". . .
>
> They have some strong prejudices besides this and one of them is their love of their favorite beverage. All the eloquence of all the temperance lecturers and any possible amount of moral or legal persuasion would fail to convince them that water is the best drink for man. It may do for women and children, but for a full grown German, nothing like "pure lager."[25]

As the epidemics of the 1840s receded from people's memories and the local population became more diverse, it was easy to forget the vulnerabilities of the "native born" Yankees in those earlier years and to focus instead on what seemed to be happening in the crowded working-class neighborhoods in Greenfield, Cheapside, Turners Falls, and Shelburne Falls and in the houses in South Deerfield that took in boarders. Children of the native born still succumbed, but in the larger picture their deaths tended to be overshadowed by the uneasiness arising from all these changes.

In the Deerfield area, the Irish and German families living primarily in Cheapside were recent immigrants, many of them directly from the old country. They came to work on farms, in the small mills, or on the railroad. Many had no trade, but a few were skilled or semi-skilled laborers who came from the cutlery centers in Solingen, Germany, or Sheffield, England. Housing was crowded, and because of recent recessions, the job market was depressed when, in 1872, another epidemic of infant and childhood dysentery struck.[26]

Between July 10 and September 25 that year, at least fifteen infants died of cholera infantum or dysentery in Deerfield. Most were under the age of one—a different pattern from that observed in 1841–42. Twelve of the infants were seven months old or younger, suggesting that mothers were supplementing their breastfeeding, possibly because they had too little milk, and possibly because they were working as wage laborers.[27] The child would be offered cow's milk, sugar water, or maybe bread soaked in milk, any of which could easily become contaminated. The surnames were different this time, too, principally Irish, a few German: Sullivan, Hess, O'Hara, Mahans, Maynard, Fritz, Wagner. Only one or two surnames in the records can be easily recognized as those of old Deerfield families. The epidemic spared Deerfield center and prevailed among the working poor of Cheapside. Unlike Lucy Buffum Lovell and the Yankee residents of Deerfield, this new immigrant population was largely mute in Franklin County of the 1870s. They are written about, but because of illiteracy, poverty, and diminished status, they seldom found opportunities to voice their own stories.[28] Drawing on the vital records of Deerfield, the 1870 federal census for Deerfield, and histories of manufacturing and industry for the area, I offer the following plausible scenario for the 1872 epidemic. The names, locations, and deaths are real.

The summer of 1872 was unusually hot, and more than a few households in Cheapside had experienced "the summer complaint" by late August. Many families were also experiencing economic difficulty because the big Russell Manufacturing cutlery factory had moved to the village of Turners Falls in Montague in 1870. The post–Civil War economic boom was rapidly deflating, and economic depression was settling in, heading toward the Panic of 1873–74. But some work was still available—the railroad yard in East Deerfield was hiring—so families were still attracted to the area by the prospect of finding jobs. Housing was scarce, such as it was in the boarding houses and small, close rooms of the homes along Deerfield Street and the surrounding streets and roads. Available housing lagged in Turners Falls, too. The so-called Cutlery Block—tenements recently erected by the Russell Company—was full. Many arriving families boarded with relatives in already crowded homes or rooming houses.

Sarah Corless, a recent immigrant from Ireland, was fretful. She was barely able to keep up with housework and cooking for her extended family and still do bits of

piecework and housekeeping when she could find the work. She breastfed her twins,
Sarah and Mary, as often as she could, but it was hard with two. Seldom could she
afford to buy milk to supplement, so occasionally she gave them a bottle of sugar water
to stop their crying. Their older siblings needed to eat, too. Keeping the children fed
was difficult enough, but Sarah also lacked enough cloth for diapers, and with only
one privy for three households and fourteen people—including her husband's brother
Thomas and his family—it was hard to keep the babies clean and dry. Even getting
water involved going to the pump near the river, with its filthy banks and terrible
odors, or all the way up to the railroad station to use the pump there, where the station
master would sometimes chase her off.

Now the twins, only a month old, had come down with the bowel complaint. Many
other infants and toddlers in the neighborhood had been sick, and several had died. The
Fritzes' newborn triplets had died in May. As triplets, they had been born without a
chance. But little Lizzie Shehan, only seven months old, had died the previous month,
and Sarah had heard the Listens had lost their boy Henry, only a year old. And there
was the O'Hara boy. Was it the soil? Or the terrible smells coming from the streets
and along the river? No one really knew. Was it some contagion that infected only the
immigrant and first-generation families, as the rich people up in Greenfield or down
in Deerfield Village sometimes claimed?

Sarah would have liked to send for a doctor and get his opinion, but she could not
afford even a tin of milk, and she certainly did not know any doctors. She remembered
her parents' fear of doctors back in Ireland, where they were called grave robbers, but
maybe in America it was different. Thanks to William's brother Thomas, William had
been able to find some work as a railroad laborer in the yards over in East Deerfield,
but it was not steady. Since the cutlery factory had moved to Turners Falls, most men
found it more difficult to keep a steady job. Even if William and Sarah had known a
doctor who would come, he would have expected a fee.[29]

On September 5 Sarah put the twins to bed, but the infant Sarah was doing poorly.
She tried to eat but barely took any water, and her stool was liquid. She shuddered
with convulsions and barely opened her eyes. By the next morning she was dead. Sarah
wanted to do everything she could to save Mary, but there was nothing she could do
except hope and pray. She knew the matter was in God's hands. Four days later, Mary,
too, passed away, in almost exactly the same way as her twin sister.[30]

The service held for the Irish children would have been different from those
conducted for Laura Martha Lovell and for the Williams and Hawks children
in the early 1840s. The Corless girls were likely baptized two or three days
after their birth, but there probably had not been time for the priest from the
Roman Catholic church up in the center of Greenfield to come and give last
rites. Perhaps a wake was held at the house. If a funeral service was held, it

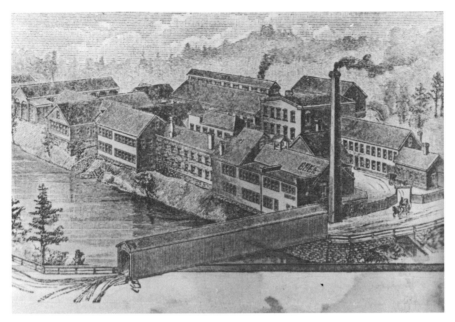

The Wiley-Russell Factory, Cheapside: a different view of the valley. Courtesy of Peter Miller, Historical Society of Greenfield.

would have been a Catholic liturgy, and the children would have been buried in the Irish section of Green River Cemetery.

For families like the Corlesses there would be no diary entries, no photographs, and little money, if any, to spend on the material symbols of the family's love and grief. Perhaps only anticipation of the hardships that would follow had the twins survived would have tempered their mother's grief. Worse still, there would be the allegations by some in high office and among the general public that these foreign-born mothers were "unfit" and ignorant of the proper care and feeding of children.[31]

In Stephen West Williams's address to the Massachusetts Medical Society in 1842 he reported that "there are about forty-four practicing physicians in this county [Franklin], who have been regularly educated."[32] Many of them were as well trained as any in New England and perhaps better trained than their counterparts in other parts of the United States. Yet in the mid-nineteenth century, although medical personnel recognized infant and early-childhood mortality as a problem, it was more the purview of statisticians, doctors concerned about health reform, and other experts than it was of the family physician. Surgical procedures and techniques for treating the diseases of adults were much more the order of the day.

Minutes for the early years of the Franklin District Medical Society reveal that dysentery was discussed on rare occasions and infant mortality was scarcely mentioned. Stephen West Williams himself makes no reference to the special risks to young children in his published writing, although in his 1842 *Medical History* he points out that a severe form of dysentery affects primarily infants and young children and that children seem particularly vulnerable to the disease in the late summer and early autumn. Certainly, by the mid-nineteenth century, medical personnel had come to recognize the existence of a high risk to weanlings in the hot months of late summer. They would link that risk, however, to the heat and foul odors, because they were not yet capable of making the broader observation that this was the time of year when food, cow's milk, and water were most likely to become contaminated. Notwithstanding the poorly understood notions of contagion, in an 1850 report, Dr. Lemuel Shattuck, of Concord, Massachusetts, and his associates on the Sanitary Commission of Massachusetts demonstrate a basic understanding that clean water is an important factor that seems to reduce infant mortality.[33]

By the 1870s, local physicians were increasingly seeing infant mortality as a problem worthy of their attention. The Franklin District Medical Society held four meetings a year, and in October 1871 the participants discussed the use of calomel in infancy. According to the society's papers, "Dr. A. C. Deane reported cases of *cholera infantum*, successfully treated by the internal administration of carbolic acid sol[ution]."[34] By the mid-1870s the society had discussed cholera infantum or infant diarrheas on other occasions, including October 14, 1874 (indigestion in bottle-fed infants), October 12, 1875 (intestinal inflammation in children), and February 9, 1876 ("autumnal fevers"). High infant mortality was reported for 1874 and 1875, with many late summer and early autumn deaths. Physicians who attended the October 1874 meeting apparently regarded the recommended feeding formula favorably: "the top of the milk mixed with water in proportion 1 to 2 of the latter with some sugar."[35] This remedy would have been fine for families with clean wells and pure milk, but perhaps not for the residents of Cheapside.

At the October 1875 meeting, each member was asked for his views on the best method of managing intestinal inflammation in children. Afterward, "the merits of opiates, calomel astringents, absorbent stimulants and dietetic management, were fully discussed and advocated, according to each ones [*sic*] views of the pathology of these cases, or as viewed without regard to pathology," and "the discussion developed much interest." In August 1876, "discussion ensued with regard to Dr. Emerson's theory of the pathology of cholera infantum, and treatment, as laid down in his address before the Mass. Med. Soc."[36]

Although the germ theory of disease was by now beginning to be known among health reformists and some physicians in the United States, it would be a long time before health professionals gained a good sense of the underlying differences between diseases such as cholera and typhoid or the ability to distinguish cases of infant diarrhea according to pathogen. The pioneering work of Joseph Lister, Louis Pasteur, Robert Koch, and others was under way in Europe by the early 1870s, but not until the 1880s were pasteurization and other bacteria-killing processes developed, the importance of aseptic and antiseptic practices in surgery recognized, and many bacterial pathogens isolated and identified.[37] Still, many regular physicians greeted the new ideas with skepticism, and several more years would likely have passed before most physicians, especially those in rural areas such as the Connecticut Valley, would have had the knowledge and skills to deploy them.

But by the 1870s, although physicians still did not know the viral or bacterial causes of infectious diseases, they were becoming increasingly interested in systematically classifying the causes of death. Local doctors might use terms such as cholera morbus, Asiatic cholera, cholera infantum, and typhoid fever without any knowledge of the pathogens involved. Cholera morbus in early diagnoses might or might not have been the result of the actual *Vibrio cholerae* bacterium.[38] Lacking knowledge of pathogens, one physician might have diagnosed infant pneumonia as consumption, and another as lung fever. Infant diarrhea might be attributed to typhoid, cholera, teething, dysentery, or the broad category cholera infantum. The symptom of convulsions, brought on by fever and extreme dehydration, might be listed as the cause of death.

By the mid-nineteenth century, when reformers and statisticians were beginning to pay attention in a new way to the toll of early childhood deaths resulting from lung fevers and diarrhea, Lemuel Shattuck had been lobbying for almost a decade for better collection of data on deaths, births, and marriages in the state. Motivated by what he saw as inordinately high mortality in the cities of the Commonwealth, he was influenced by the recent trend in England to survey the nation's districts for the causes of mortality. A founding member of the American Statistical Association, he had developed a keen interest in statistics, and although he was not a doctor, he closely followed the work of health-minded physician-reformers in England. Shattuck was instrumental in getting the Massachusetts Registration Act of 1842 passed into law, systematizing the collection of birth, death, and marriage records in each town.

In 1845 Shattuck published a report on the sanitary condition of Boston. He and Dr. Edward Jarvis of the American Statistical Association then lobbied the state legislature for a broader survey. In 1849 Shattuck was elected to the legislature and almost immediately secured an appointment, along with

Nathaniel Banks Jr. and Jehiel Abbott, to conduct a sanitary survey of the entire state. The report of Shattuck's Sanitary Commission of Massachusetts, published in 1850, was a model for its day. It recommended the creation of a state Board of Health and the passage of laws to protect the public's health.[39] By recapitulating statistics from England showing very high rates of infant and childhood mortality, Shattuck was able to draw parallels with Massachusetts, thanks to the earlier laws regarding vital registration. The commissioners also noted that the crude death rate—the expression of deaths in relation to the size of the entire population—was misleading about the effects of diseases on particular age groups and those of foreign birth. Better statistics were needed, showing the infant death rate as a proportion of the number of births.[40] (See Appendix A.)

Shattuck was beginning to look at the association of causes of death with ages in the population, and he was following classifications of the causes of death formulated in England. The first annual report of the Registry and Returns of Births, Marriages, and Deaths in Massachusetts used a nosology based on seven major categories of disease.[41] Already, the influence of William Farr, who, along with his colleagues in England, had developed a refined disease classification, was apparent. By 1850, Shattuck was extending his framework for Massachusetts to include Farr's nosology and earlier work on sanitation in England by Edwin Chadwick. Chadwick's work had been focused on the poor and the apparent association between poverty and high mortality. Shattuck believed poverty was no excuse for lack of hygiene and cleanliness, but he was interested in the relationship between birth and death rates, sanitation, and crowding and in what he thought was the need for facts and an understanding of the laws of nature.[42]

Farr's disease classification, which involved four major classes of disease: zymotic, constitutional, local, and developmental, was formally introduced in Massachusetts in the fourteenth annual report of the Registry and Returns of Births, Marriages, and Deaths in 1855.[43] Following Farr and others, the report writers placed cholera infantum, cholera, dysentery, croup, and all fevers in the zymotic class of diseases—those known to be epidemic, endemic, or contagious.

The steps taken by Shattuck and his colleagues launched an explosive growth in record collecting and recording from the 1850s into the 1870s. There was an ever-increasing call for accurate data and sanitary reform and an emerging sense that reformers would have the ability to actually prevent deadly diseases. Sufficient data had been compiled for the state that in 1897 the Massachusetts Board of Health was able to include in its annual report a summary of forty years of vital statistics, including an impressive array of tables on the relationships between mortality and age, population density, and seasonality, by city or town and by cause of death.[44]

Stephen West Williams, who retired in 1853, had been somewhat ahead of his time in his interest in statistics. While most physicians were attending to their local practices and individual treatments, Williams and a few others were captivated by the collection of reliable statistics on deaths in their respective communities. His correspondence and his actions illustrate his statistical bent and a growing awareness that disease was indeed preventable. He even corresponded with Lemuel Shattuck between 1849 and 1851. The two had been Massachusetts delegates to the National Medical Convention held in Philadelphia in 1847, where Shattuck first proposed that Farr's nosology be adopted by American doctors. They certainly met again when the American Medical Association, an outgrowth of the National Medical Convention, conducted its second annual meeting in Boston in 1849.[45] They began a correspondence in which Shattuck first sought data from Williams on western Massachusetts.[46] Williams replied by letter in 1850 with a list of the number and training of physicians in Franklin County, among other things, and in 1851, he commented favorably on Shattuck's *Report of the Sanitary Commission of Massachusetts*. Apparently the respect was mutual, as evidenced by the following letter:

Deerfield Mass[tts] April 7, 1851
Mr. Lemuel Shattuck, Esq[r]

My Dear Sir, I owe an apology to you for not in this replying to your last of February last, which was placed in my hand by our Representative Mr. Clapp. on March meeting day, together with your inestimable Report on the Sanitary Survey of Mass[tts]. . . . I have now read it with great attention, & think it the most able document I have ever seen in any language. . . .

I do not know that the bill you have presented can be amended. If it passes I should like to be a member of the Board of Health, not the Secretary, for that must devolve upon no one but yourself, but one of the physicians of it. I have for many years, had a great fondness for medical statistical inquiries, & even when I have read the works of Bisset Hawkins & Emerson on the subject, that interest has increased. Besides my address to the Massachusetts Medical Society, from which you have quoted so largely, and for which I thank you, I many years ago published an article on the climate & diseases of Deerfield, which was printed in several of our medical periodical journals, & an abstract of it was published in Holmes' prize address upon intermittent fever, which you have seen...

I am, Respected Sir, with much esteem
    Yours Most Truly,
    Stephen W. Williams[47]

Stephen West Williams is, in some ways, an iconic figure for mid-nineteenth-century American medicine. Learned and active in his profession, he seems to have straddled the chasm of change that was beginning to open in his time: he held onto traditional medical practices in his care of patients even as he became a pioneer in the emerging science of health statistics. The classification of cause of death was becoming more systematic—if not particularly accurate about cause—and knowledge was improving about the conditions in cities that were associated with high mortality. From their primarily rural, agricultural, and ethnically homogeneous beginnings, the towns of Massachusetts were being transformed by commercialization, industrialization, and immigration. They were experiencing greater ethnic and class differentiation, and some of their neighborhoods suffered from crowding, poverty, and unsanitary living conditions that fostered higher death rates.

In the decades following Williams's retirement, little changed in the way of treatment from the methods he had used during the 1842 dysentery epidemic in Deerfield. After 1880, an awareness of the bacteria involved in many diseases grew and began to affect some physicians' antiseptic and aseptic practices—but a broad range of effective interventions and therapies was yet to be realized. What had largely been accomplished was that the medical descendants of Stephen West Williams had greatly curbed their use of purgatives, emetics, and bleeding as therapies.

Shortly after Williams's death in 1855, a series of epidemics struck the Connecticut Valley that were more prevalent and more lethal among children from the ages of about two to twelve than among infants and toddlers.

THE FEVERS OF CHILDHOOD

Ring around the rosy
A pocketful of posies
"Ashes, Ashes"
We all fall down.

—Children's rhyme popular in nineteenth-century America,
once thought to have originated in medieval England
during the plague

The scarlet fever, which has very seldom prevailed in this town, is now
prevailing quite extensively among children. We hear of its prevalence
also in several of the neighboring towns.

Greenfield Gazette and Courier, December 27, 1858

AMONG THE CHILDHOOD DISEASES that tormented families, communities, and public health officials in nineteenth-century New England, the so-called childhood fevers—scarlet fever, measles, and diphtheria—worked by far the greatest devastation. They took their heaviest toll on young children who had survived the precarious first two years of infancy and toddlerhood. For "statists" such as Lemuel Shattuck and William Farr, these diseases, along with cholera infantum, fell into the zymotic order of nosological nomenclature.[1] They were listed in the miasmatic class, suggesting that they originated in bad air. We now understand that they are caused by viruses or bacteria transmitted primarily in droplets that become airborne when an infected person coughs or sneezes, not, as nineteenth-century physicians conceptualized it, from "bad air."[2]

These diseases could infect susceptible people of any age, and some infections were more indiscriminate than others. But they were called childhood fevers because they made their effects felt most seriously in young children who had previously been unexposed to the offending pathogen but who were old enough to have lost any antibodies they might have acquired prenatally through the placenta or postnatally through mother's milk. Many adults had already survived these diseases as children—the symptoms could range from a mild sore throat to the severity of rheumatic fever—and had developed effective

Allen Sisters, *A Spring Dance*, 1909. Courtesy of PVMA.

immune responses to those strains of pathogens. Then as now, however, people who contracted such diseases for the first time as adults could grow severely ill.

After 1850, smallpox became infrequent in Massachusetts, thanks to clearer notions of its contagiousness, which prompted quarantines, and also to its being the one disease for which an inoculation was by then providing immunity (see Chapter 2). For measles, diphtheria, and scarlet fever, as well as whooping cough and croup (at least some of which was diphtheria), no vaccination existed, nor did any understanding of the cause.

These diseases visited the Commonwealth and the Connecticut Valley several times in the second half of the nineteenth century. Among the worst epidemics were those of scarlet fever, or scarletina, as it was often called. Two such epidemics struck Deerfield and the surrounding towns, one in 1858–59 and another in 1867–68, local expressions of a pandemic that afflicted North America, Great Britain, and Europe between about 1840 and 1880. Typically, such fevers might be responsible for a few childhood deaths in any given year, but at certain times conditions were favorable for major outbreaks. Some combination of environmental circumstance, susceptible individuals, and a virulent strain of the pathogen converged. Such was the case in Franklin County in 1858.

In December of that year, uneasiness overtook the valley. Everyone had heard or read in the local newspaper that scarlet fever was "out there." The *Greenfield Gazette and Courier* reported that on November 8, Clarence Hawley, age two, died of the disease and that four days before Christmas, Mary Boylston, age eleven, and Lucy B. Downs, age four, died. All three children were from Greenfield. In January 1859, matters grew worse. A full-blown epidemic was at hand. At the north end of the old Deerfield village center, three boys whose families were neighbors all died that month: eight-year-old Elihu Ashley on the tenth, two-year-old Jesse Stebbins on the eighteenth, and five-year-old Frankie Sheldon on the nineteenth, just two days' short of his sixth birthday. Frankie was the son of George and Susan Sheldon; his father was a fifth generation resident of Deerfield and justice of the peace. Elihu Ashley and his parents lived next door, and Jesse Stebbins just across the street. The Ashleys and Stebbinses, too, were prominent in the community. These houses still stand near Deerfield's North Meadows, a short distance from the village common and meeting house.[3]

In April 1859, David Sheldon Jr., a cousin of George's, and his wife, Julia, who lived on the same street, lost their second daughter to scarlet fever—their first having died of dysentery in the epidemic of 1842. Similar scenarios must have played out up and down the Connecticut Valley and indeed all across New England and the nation. Death was a common occurrence, and a culture of mourning flourished in the United States in the mid-nineteenth century which often centered on the loss of children. In middle-class households, heartfelt grief was expressed openly but with constraint. It was filtered through norms and conventions to which the "proper" family was attuned.

To the residents along the main street in Deerfield, January was a cold month in more ways than one. The symptoms progressed so fast. Children were playing one day, sick the day after, and gone the next. As the days passed, several other neighbors—even some of the parents—would suffer the same symptoms, but it was the young children who were hardest hit.

Over the course of eight weeks, as scores of children died in the communities along the Deerfield and Connecticut River valleys, physicians discussed the cases and considered treatments at their county medical society meetings.[4] Some thought their poultices and concoctions were working, but others were less sure. The *Greenfield Gazette and Courier* published the death notices every week and even reported other outbreaks around the country—in Cincinnati, in Philadelphia. Out west in Illinois, Abraham Lincoln's six-year-old son, Tad, was stricken with scarlet fever that year but survived, and the future president himself became infected and symptomatic.[5]

Through the writings of Lucy Buffum Lovell, who had confronted scarlet fever two decades earlier, we can glimpse the way the Sheldons and other parents must have nursed their sick children and felt their losses. The Lovells' daughter Caroline was only three in 1840 when her younger sister, Laura, died. In May 1842, at the age of five—after a day when the family visited Laura's grave—Caroline came down with a fever, a rash, and vomiting.

> Before noon the eruption was out all over her body, and assumed a dark reddish appearance. . . . I watched by her bed during the day with painful anxiety. Though I then supposed she had the measles, and our physician had pronounced it a case of measles, yet I felt alarmed. She was so frail I feared she would not endure even an attack of the measles. If I had known it was that awful scourge, scarlet fever, I should have had still less hope for her.[6]

During the short course of the disease, Caroline's mother, father, and family friends sat and watched over her day and night. She was moved from the bedroom to the parlor, and three different doctors administered to her. On Wednesday Dr. Waterman came: "He thought it was a very severe case of measles. He advised bathing with weak lye and a poultice of slippery elm, both of which I adopted," Lucy wrote. Thursday evening, she continued, Drs. Metcalf and Stanley called on Caroline. "They gave us no encouragement. By nine o'clock a stupor seemed to be coming over her, which told us too plainly that death was doing its work."

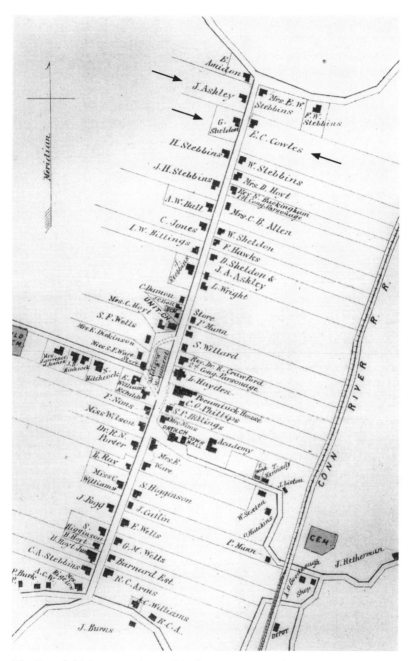

The Deerfield Street as pictured in the 1871 Beers Atlas. Arrows point to the houses of the three boys. Courtesy of HDL.

George and Susan Sheldon's house, 1889, photographed by the Allen Sisters. Courtesy of PVMA.

We stood by her bed to see the lamp of life go out. She had said nothing during the night. Her pains seemed to have left her. Surely the bitterness of death was past. There was no struggle. Nothing to indicate that death was there, but the low faint breath and the pallid countenance. Her end was peaceful. I kneeled down by the bedside and placing my ear near her mouth listened to the low breathing of the "sweet dying child." About four o'clock the sound died away and as the sun rose clear and all nature seemed to be rejoicing, her spirit was borne away to Him who gave it. O, if there ever was a guiltless soul on earth, since our blessed Saviour's passion, it seems to me hers was one.[7]

No such diary or written record exists for the death of Frankie Sheldon or his friends, but we can imagine a similar situation in the Sheldon household in January 1859. Indeed, only a few years later, after George Sheldon had begun to keep a diary himself, he wrote in a voice distinctly different from Lucy Lovell's about the death of the daughter of his friends Samuel and Harriet Thaxter Willard. Yet his entries express similarities in the cataloguing of events and the shock of confronting a fatal childhood disease. Hattie Willard was thirteen when she was afflicted with diphtheria during an outbreak in 1863. Samuel Willard, like his father, had lost his eyesight soon after his graduation from Harvard College in 1835, so when Hattie fell ill, George Sheldon was called upon to assist the family. The following account appears in his diary:

March 11—Carried 16 bush[els] corn to Mill—Evening was called to see Hattie Willard who I found with Diphtheria. Sent for Dr. Dean

March 12—Hattie very sick—I spent what time I could spare from my chores with her

March 13—Carried 14 bush[els] to Mill and bro't Amanda [probably Amanda Stebbins] up to Millers where she spent the night—I also spent all my spare time then and [two words illegible] all night. A very sick girl

March 14—With Hattie as usual. Mrs Asa Stebbins and Mrs. Nat-Hitchcock came to watch with me. Hattie had been gradually failing all day. And at 11 o'clock she gently passed away in my arms. A terrible case of a terrible disease—She has suffered very little pain. Tuesday night appeared the first symptoms—a sore throat. Next morning after a feverish and chilly night her throat was much worse, but no decided appearance of diphtheria. At night however the back of her mouth & throat were entirely covered with a silver-white coating—the real diphtheria membrane. Cauterizing did no good. She was in a sort of stupor with no pain, little external fever & only wanted to be let alone. Her throat was not sore, she said, outside or in but she "felt first rate"—she swallowed harder with great difficulty. Next Morning—Thursday—her stupor had passed away & she was cheerful & bright, in no pain, but quite horse [sic]. Quinine and brandy were administered freely from Wednesday night to the last, with what nourishment she wished. She drank freely of milk and took broth & e[illegible] Friday morning & also at night. Dr. Deane called her better. Amanda and I watched that night & found her breathing gradually becoming obstructed and her stomach was disordered, so much so that nothing could be kept down for some hours. When the Doctor came Saturday morning he removed a large piece of the membrane which had become loosened, from the back of the mouth which relieved her breathing a little. The obstruction never appeared to me to be in the windpipe, but about the tonsils & palate. Still she swallowed day by day, better & better till 5 minutes before she died. She swallowed as well, to all appearances, as ever when in perfect health. No soreness. No pain—but her throat looked entirely filled up and awfully ulcerated. Some nausea[?] today—breath gradually shorter & shorter, but very little more obstruction to the last—when one spasm, or rather shudder. Easing her in my arms her head fell back—two or three short gasps & all was over—& so did Harriet Thaxter Willard [pass], a girl at the age of 13 years, remarkable for her physical development as for maturity of character—the pride & comfort of her father & the hope of the family—In stature & maturity she exceeded the average of [women?].

March 15—Mr. Wheeler of Cambridge preached.[8]

George and Samuel were close friends, but this relationship alone does not explain George's depth of involvement in Harriet's final hour. Perhaps his earlier loss of Frankie compelled his support and care for this child and her family. As for Samuel Willard, a hint of his grief over Hattie's death appears in the will he wrote soon afterward.

Deeply impressed by judgment and constant admonitions of the uncertainty of human life, and particularly so by the recent sudden death of my beloved daughter Hattie, I Samuel Willard of Deerfield, County of Franklin, State of Massachusetts being of sound mind, deem it expedient and proper now and without further delay, to make such a disposition of my property and Estate as appears to be the good of those concerned. . . .

Sixth. I give and bequeath to my near and dear friend George Sheldon, who has stood by me in the most trying event in my life, such books as he may select.[9]

On June 8, 1863, the *Greenfield Gazette and Courier* reprinted a short column by the minister who officiated at Hattie's funeral, Rev. Mumford.[10]

Rev. Mr. Mumford, who is in charge of the Unitarian society in this town [Deerfield] during the absence of its pastor in the war, writes pleasant letters from the "valley of the Connecticut," to the *Christian Enquirer*. From one of these, we quote these interesting passages: "Village funerals continue to interest and impress me. There is an evident reality in the grief, and a perfect artlessness in the expressions of sympathy, which make these scenes very genuine indeed. One burial was that of a grand-daughter of Rev. Dr. Willard, that good and true minister of Christ, whose memory will be cherished for centuries by dwellers in this valley, which he loved and adorned so long.

Mumford went on to explain that Hattie had been a great help to her blind father and grandfather and had often been observed escorting them around the village. In this observation we see another important aspect of the loss of an older child. Not only did time within the family endear the child further to her parents, siblings, and extended family, but also the maturing child increasingly fulfilled an economic role vital to the material well-being of the household.

With so many deaths in 1859 came a procession of funerals. The *Greenfield Gazette and Courier* noted on January 24 that "Rev. Mr. Moors of Deerfield, was called upon to attend two funerals on Wednesday afternoon and Rev. Mr. Headley of this town three on Friday. In most of the towns in this vicinity the scarlet fever continues to rage among children and there are many deaths."

The Sheldon family papers do not discuss the preparations for Frankie's funeral and burial. Still, much is known about common funerary practices in the United States and in rural New England at this time, and sources specific to the Connecticut Valley offer glimpses of Deerfield in mourning in the 1850s and 1860s.

Hattie Willard died on a Saturday. On the following Monday, George Sheldon noted in his diary that he "carried Susan and Sarah to G'f'd [Greenfield], engaged Mr. Mumford to attend the funeral." The next day he "went to G'f'd to procure a coffin, brot home Mr. Mumford, assisted Frank Wright in taking a picture of Hattie.[11] On Thursday, March 19, he attended Hattie Willard's funeral and "took tea with Mr. Mumford."

Lucy Buffum Lovell's diary entry about the burial of her daughter Caroline attests to the importance of her religious faith in sustaining her:

We went for Mrs. Ellery Thayer to dress [Caroline] for the grave. I combed her hair and braided it, as I had so many times done, and tied the ends with a narrow white ribbon. I felt that it was a great privilege to do it once more for her. During the day, which was Friday, the third of June, I think we were divinely supported, and felt willing to give her back to God. One thing only troubled me, the uncertainty with regard to the state of her soul. I sought an answer of the Lord, but he doubtless, for wise reasons, withheld it. O, I thought if I could only be sure that she was happy, that her soul had been washed and made white in the blood of the Lamb, I could then be entirely reconciled to the bereavement.

These feelings continued three days. I could not fix my mind upon anything definite with regard to her. I wanted to think of her among the ransomed spirits that surround the throne and my prayer was that the Lord would be pleased to give me some assurance of her state. It seems to me now almost like presumption, but I did not realize it then. I felt so anxious for her soul. I did not think she was lost, but I could not think of her anywhere in particular. Friday night my husband proposed getting some young ladies to watch in the house, as is customary. I told him I wished he would procure those who would feel love for Caroline from having been acquainted with her, and would be very careful. Two young ladies in whom we had the most confidence, expressed that they felt it to be a privilege to sit up, and we consigned the care of the precious remains to them for the night. On Saturday afternoon she was buried. The funeral services were conducted at our house. Brother James Boomer, from Wrentham, spoke words of comfort and consolation to us.

Many of the neighbors came in to weep with us. Brother and sister Samuel B. and Elizabeth Chace, with their children, and sister Lydia Buffum Read, came from Valley Falls. On Saturday afternoon June 4, 1842, just one week from the day on which she had visited the graveyard with us, we laid Caroline by the side of her dear sister Laura.[12]

Many funerals at this time were performed in the family home, without embalming, which did not become a common practice in New England until later in the nineteenth century.[13] Other funerals took place in the church or meeting house. By the late 1840s or early 1850s, portrait photographs of deceased children, like that of Hattie Willard, were often taken and a lock of the deceased child's hair was likely saved. In well-to-do households, the child's body was laid out in the family parlor for viewing and visiting before the funeral.[14] Such families generally purchased a coffin rather than building it themselves. In 1862, the coffin makers Miles and Lyons in Greenfield advertised: "*Coffin Wareroom*. The subscribers have on hand at all times a good supply of Black Walnut and other kinds of coffins. Also,—Coffin Plates and burial Clothes of all kinds constantly on hand."[15]

According to burial records, during the 1858–59 epidemic, at least four children were buried in Deerfield's Laurel Hill Cemetery, and eighteen in the Green River Cemetery in the district of Cheapside, which served families from both Deerfield and Greenfield. South Deerfield and the other neighborhoods of the town must have accounted for additional children who died. Minnie Wise, age two and a half, was buried in Baptist Cemetery in West Deerfield.[16] The ministers of these towns visited surviving family members at home and no doubt sent members of the church to offer food and comfort over the following days and weeks.

Because Frankie Sheldon and his friends died in midwinter, burial may have been difficult, and perhaps even postponed until the spring thaw. George and Susan Sheldon gave considerable thought to an appropriate epitaph, selecting the following lines from the poem "Resignation," by Henry Wadsworth Longfellow:

> In that great cloister's stillness and seclusion,
> By guardian angels led,
> Safe from temptation, safe from sin's pollution,
> She lives, whom we call dead.[17]

The Sheldons wanted to delete the first line and begin the epitaph with "By guardian angels led," and they needed to change the child's gender reference from "she" to "he." A letter from Longfellow found in the Sheldon family papers indicates that George Sheldon wrote to the poet asking for permission to use the lines but with changes.

Cambridge, February 14, 1860

Dear Sir,

If you make the changes suggested, I think you must show that something has been left out, by some mark or other. You might, for instance, have the inscription now read:

> *He is not dead, the child of our affection!*
> . . .
> *By guardian Angels led*

Here points . . . would indicate the omission of one or more lines; and, would make the change less objectionable.

I remain, Yours with sympathy, Henry W. Longfellow[18]

Ignoring Longfellow's request, George and Susan placed the following as Frankie's epitaph:

> *By guardian Angels led*
> *Safe from temptation, safe from sin's pollution*
> *He lives, whom we call dead*

On June 22, 1860, George Sheldon entered in his diary: "Assisted in setting up monuments to J. R. Childs and little Frankie—which are the finest in the County, I think." On January 19, 1863, he wrote, "4 years today!" and sometime later added a penciled notation, "Frank died." In his scrapbook he loosely placed a couple of poems from the local newspaper. One is titled "Little Charlie, A Lament, by T.B. Aldrich": "God walking over starry spheres Did clasp his tiny hand, And led him through a fall of tears into the Mystic Land."

The 1867–68 scarlet fever epidemic affected more people in the poorer section of Cheapside than in the Deerfield town center. One monument in the Green River Cemetery was erected for two boys, Henry Vetterling, age nine, and Charles Young, fourteen, who died within six days of each other. Possibly for economic reasons, but surely because the two families knew each other and the boys were friends, the stone shows two hands in a handshake.[19] The epitaph is in German and somewhat eroded, but translated roughly it reads: "You who read this do not cry / God has done well / He is with our sons / We bid them good night."[20]

Occasionally the archives give up the transcribed or self-authored words of a young sibling, a schoolmate, or the deceased himself or herself. Children in Victorian England and the United States were well ensconced in the culture of mourning, and the loss of their peers was an all-too-familiar experience.[21] Lessons from church and school prepared children—especially girls—for appropriate behavior surrounding death, funerals, and burials. They might recite

Vetterling-Young gravestone, Green River Cemetery, Greenfield, Mass. Photo © Carol Betsch.

or transcribe poems of consolation or mourning in class and embroider them into samplers at home. Words attributed to young children often read as if the guiding hand of a parent or other adult lay behind them. An example of a poem that might indeed have been written by the deceased, but which was offered in a child's obituary by her parents, is a poem found in the writing box of Luany B. Wilcox, daughter of the Reverend William Wilcox of South Deerfield, who died in 1863 at the age of fourteen.[22]

> Mourn not for me dear mother
> I soon shall be at rest;
> My weary head I soon shall lean
> Upon my Savior's breast.

A whole genre of "weep not for me" poems existed in nineteenth-century Britain and the United States. A young child fearing death but wanting to comfort her parents might well have composed a version of this form of poetry. More original, personalized, and lengthier writings on illness and death were more characteristic of older adolescents and young adults, as I discuss in the next chapter.

The *Greenfield Gazette and Courier* was the principal source of information for the citizens of Franklin County, and its short notices of deaths in Greenfield and surrounding towns gave readers rudimentary statistics that showed when outbreaks of scarlet fever and other childhood fevers were taking place. On February 7, 1859, for example, the paper reported: "There were 15 deaths in the town of Greenfield in the month of January, 1859—3 of consumption, 9 of scarlet fever, 1 of whooping cough, 1 of inflammation of the brain, and 1 accidental." More subjective evidence was available, too—people in the affected neighborhoods, from the richest to the poorest, suddenly had more funerals to attend and more sick families to look in on or look after.

Because of the legislation passed during the preceding decade, town clerks now had ledger forms for recording vital statistics using standardized entry procedures. Local chapters of the Massachusetts Medical Society had recently advised their member physicians to adopt standardized reporting practices as well. Scarlet fever was by now relatively easy to diagnose because of its characteristic rash, or "exanthem," which accompanied the sore throat, fever, inflammation of lymph nodes, and abscessing of the throat and tonsils. Most physicians and others attending deaths were well attuned to scarlet fever and could differentiate it from diphtheria. What they were less able to realize, because they did not at this time understand the nature of the underlying pathogen, was that diagnoses such as septic sore throat, erysipelas, puerperal sepsis (childbed fever in mothers), and rheumatic fever could all be associated with the same streptococcal bacterium as scarlet fever.[23]

As with cholera infantum, the medical community at the time could offer little in the way of effective treatment to those infected with scarlet fever. Indeed many medical historians suggest that the decline in scarlet fever after 1880 was due to declining virulence of the pathogen and improved preventive public health measures, such as quarantining, instruction in better nutrition, and antiseptic practices, rather than individual treatments. The bacterium responsible for scarlet fever was identified in the third quarter of the nineteenth century and directly associated with scarlet fever in the 1920s, yet an effective treatment—antibiotics—was unavailable until several years later.[24]

Nevertheless, by the 1860s, physicians were ubiquitous in western Massachusetts. Each of the study communities had at least one doctor, and

Greenfield had several. Even Deerfield, with a population of 3,072 in 1860, had five doctors practicing between 1858 and 1870, often three or more of them simultaneously.[25] At least three of these doctors attended meetings of the Franklin District Medical Society in July 1858 and July 1859, when participants discussed treatments for scarlet fever, including the use of "tincture of veratrum viride," a common homeopathic remedy consisting of the roots or seeds, or both, of hellebore plants in alcohol.[26]

At the time of these epidemics, prescriptions were abundant but largely ineffective. Doctor's journals and home health manuals written by physicians of the period describe many concoctions available for treating scarlet fever. According to *Gunn's Domestic Medicine*, for example:

> A disordered state of the stomach, and bowels, teething, exposure to cold, striking in of any eruption, and in short, every thing which can excite an increase action in the heart and blood vessels, will produce more or less fever. . . . When these fevers take place, cleansing the stomach and bowels will be proper, for which purpose give an emetic, or puke, followed by two or three grains of calomel, to which add flour, five or six grains of rhubarb: for the dose of either of these medicines, see table; after which Bateman's drops, Godfrey's cordial or paregoric, at the same time bathing the child in warm water, will greatly assist in lessening the irritability of the system and removing the fever.[27]

The 1872 edition of *Hall's Health at Home*, another popular manual, gave slightly different advice:

> The great points to be labored for in scarlet fever are:
>
> First. Keep the bowels free by a free use of fruits, berries and cracked wheat.
>
> Second. Keep out the rash by the prevention of chilliness and looseness of bowels.
>
> Third. Keep down thirst and fever by acid drinks, lemonade, buttermilk, etc.
>
> Fourth. Keep the room cool and well ventilated.
>
> Fifth. If there is a tendency to debility, add some meat, poultry, and soups, with bread crust, to the diet.
>
> Sixth. In great heat of the skin, sponge it frequently with tepid water.[28]

Gunn called for a potentially toxic emetic followed by paregoric—tincture of opium; Hall called for the use of natural foods. Because scarlet fever was not always fatal, and because the opiates, alcohol, and other ingredients in doctors' remedies might give patients some relief from symptoms, physicians—despite their limited capacities to treat and certainly to cure—were highly valued for their efforts. An editorial in the *Greenfield Gazette and Courier* published February 12, 1859, reads: "The scarlet fever is prevailing to considerable extent, but our physicians thus far have managed it very successfully. We think it no more than a just compliment to them to say they are as good as the county affords, attending early and late and at all hours, faithfully, to their not infrequently arduous duties. Success attend them." Even so, the children of families who could afford a doctor's services might have been vulnerable to the complications of misguided treatment.

By the late 1860s, after a child died, the room where he or she had been tended would likely have been whitewashed and all linens and other objects cleaned. Such practices of hygiene became increasingly common in late-nine-teenth-century America among the middle class, although in the working-class district of Cheapside they were less likely to have been affordable, known, or deployed. In keeping with the growing understanding of the prophylactic qualities of cleanliness, predominant theories of disease causality at the time marked as most susceptible those who were deemed unkempt and unclean, who had immoral habits, and who did not have their houses "in order."[29] According to common knowledge, the cramped houses with damp cellars and malodorous privies were hotbeds of miasma. It is easy to imagine that families such as the Sheldons, Ashleys, and Stebbinses along the main street in Deerfield wondered why, despite their habits of cleanliness, their family members were succumbing to disease. Perhaps they expected scarlet fever to appear or to be more virulent in the poorer sections of town, among immigrants and those whom they perceived to have profligate behaviors.

With the advantages of modern epidemiological methods and knowledge of the pathogen responsible for scarlet fever—*Streptococcus pyogenes*—it is possible to offer an explanation for why so many children in well-to-do and poor families alike died during these outbreaks. Researchers have suggested that from time to time, *Streptococci pyogenes* evolved into unusually virulent forms, much the way antibiotic-resistant strains of bacteria evolve today. Such a strain did not respect the advantages of social class or wealth. The evidence from Deerfield is consistent with this interpretation.[30]

When Frankie Sheldon died in 1859, he had a thirteen-year-old sister, Susan Arabella (Bell), and a ten-year-old brother, John. Unlike with smallpox, most physicians at midcentury did not understand clearly that scarlet fever spread from person to person. Therefore, it is unlikely that Frankie's parents quarantined him from his siblings during the epidemic, and it is quite possible that Susan, John, or both fell ill, too. Within a few years physicians would begin to prescribe quarantining to prevent the spread of childhood fevers, and later in the century this practice would be widely adopted and institutionalized. With such changes, political forces outside the family began to take charge of disease control. The Deerfield School Committee, for example, as revealed in the following passage from its annual report for 1883, attempted to play a role in public health by cajoling parents into keeping their sick children at home. The school committee at that time did not yet have the authority to mandate quarantining.

> We feel it is to be an imperative duty to assist in guarding against the spread of epidemic diseases: measles, scarlet fever, small-pox, diphtheria, etc. Whenever we learn of a case of a family where there are school children, and school in session, we kindly request the parents of the little sufferer, if they have other children of school age, to detain them at home until the physician or the committee are satisfied that the danger of contagion is passed. We should feel ourselves guilty of a very grave offence were we so negligent or imprudent as to knowingly allow unnecessary exposure to such terrible diseases. It is with sadness that we recall the bright little faces that have so often welcomed us, that have within the year gone from our schools and homes, forever gone: little victims of some one of the above mentioned diseases. The impression deepens for while writing this, even at this moment, comes a request to asst at the funeral of one of our little scholars. Afflicted ones, you have our fullest sympathy.[31]

In the 1858–59 and 1867–68 epidemics, the residents of Deerfield, Greenfield, Montague, and Shelburne could have gained a sense of the broad effects of the outbreaks from local newspaper accounts. Probably most households unaffected by the disease knew a family that was affected. At the state level, however, the larger consequences of an epidemic were more thoroughly understood through the gathering of statistics. The seventeenth annual report of births, marriages, and deaths registered in Massachusetts reported that "scarletina produced the greatest number of registered deaths, among Zymotic diseases, in 1858." These reports, published every year beginning in 1843, detailed causes of death statewide by county, sex, age group, and month. In addition, they broke down the causes of death into the nosology and classification systems the state had adapted from William Farr's scheme.

Beginning in 1839, physicians in Massachusetts passed resolutions in support of systematic collection of vital statistics. Realizing that if this were solely in the hands of the fellows of the Massachusetts Medical Society the effort would not reach all segments of the state, they supported a statewide system of registration. In May 1842 they endorsed the new act passed by the legislature: "Resolved, That the Fellows of the Massachusetts Medical Society will cheerfully aid in carrying into effect the provisions of 'An act relating to the registry and returns of Births, Marriages and Deaths,' and by furnishing information of the deaths that may come under their observation, with their causes, and by any other means that may properly pertain to their duty as physicians."[32]

From the early 1840s on, the Office of the Registry and Return of Vital Records and Statistics used detailed summaries of data reported by the cities, towns, and counties of Massachusetts to compare annual rates of death. For example, after naming scarlet fever as the predominant cause of death among infectious diseases in 1858, the state's report for that year noted that in 1855 there were only 347 deaths recorded from this cause, but in 1857 the number was 2,013; in 1858, however, it fell to 1,051.[33] The report for 1859 stated that "scarletina produced 1,038 deaths in the year, against 1,051 in 1858, and 2,013 in 1857. It prevailed throughout the year, but less in the last than in the first half."[34]

At the same time, the members of the Massachusetts Medical Society were collecting and tabulating some of their own data, while supporting the state registration system. "At the annual meeting of the Medical Society of this State in May, 1859," it was reported, "a monograph was read by Dr. B. Cutler, one of its Fellows, upon the zymotic *diseases* which prevailed in 1858. This was founded on the returns of 13,024 cases by 117 physicians."[35] The advantages of these data, as the Office of Vital Statistics acknowledged, was that they included, along with cases that resulted in death, mild and even severe cases that had not been fatal. Throughout the 1850s and 1860s, the Massachusetts Medical Society actively promoted efforts at statewide vital registration and for creation of the state Board of Health.

The residents of Deerfield and Greenfield were made aware of the official record keeping for epidemics by the *Greenfield Gazette and Courier*, which occasionally published short synopses from the state's annual reports. For example, in March 1861 it reported: "Diptheria—We gather the following facts from the Massachusetts Registration Report, just issued, of the births deaths and marriages in Massachusetts during the year 1859: 'Diphtheria is the reported cause of 32 deaths in 1859 against 18 in 1858.'"

These examples suggest that a connection was growing between the state, local authorities, and the local medical community in their understanding of infectious disease, its distribution, and its magnitude. Their record keeping was an essential precursor to attempts at intervention. But although the groundwork was being laid for a better understanding of the complex associations between diseases and their many causes, practicing physicians for the most part probably lagged in their appreciation of these associations. A physician in Greenfield might have consulted the annual registration reports, noting the many fatalities and the way the data were organized, but the reports might not yet have provided much he considered helpful in his daily practice.

By 1869, following the two significant scarlet fever epidemics in Deerfield and the surrounding communities, what we observe in terms of institutional structures having control over the child's body in sickness and the disposition of the child's body in death was much the same in rural Franklin County and cosmopolitan Boston. As with the diarrheal deaths discussed in Chapter 3, the recognition of the relationship between a specific pathogen, an environment,

and a susceptible host still lay well outside the typical knowledge and practices of physicians and the families afflicted. The evidence suggests that care
and treatment of the child remained centered on the family, a small circle of
friends, and most likely an attending physician, who, along with his medical
society chapter, was aware of contemporary theories and treatments. If the
disease was fatal, the local religious authority likely performed the appropriate
service, and by law the town clerk recorded the death. The local newspaper
probably reported the death and often provided anecdotal information about
the progress of epidemics and about popular treatments for the prevailing
disease. The year's deaths were listed in the annual town report and also sent
to the State House in Boston. Local boards of health, where they existed at
all, provided little in the way of intervention. Selectmen and school adminis-
trators may have recommended quarantines, but they had little authority, if
any, to enforce public health measures.

Parallel to this local system of recognition and treatment was a bureaucracy
burgeoning at the state level to collect, record, and organize death data. But
like local town boards, the state had little direct authority to intervene in communities or to control the behavior of affected persons. Public movements to
create policy and actively intervene in children's health were emerging but
few were inaugurated before the 1880s. The American Medical Association
went on record as early as 1849 that its members were the "guardians of public
health,"[36] but the Office of Vital Statistics and after 1869, the newly created
state Board of Health would increasingly claim knowledge and authority over
the public welfare (see Appendix B).

Although mourning for the loss of a child might take on unique local forms
of expression, rituals of mourning and interment were becoming somewhat
standardized for middle- and upper-class families in the United States by the
mid-nineteenth century. The sources available for the four Connecticut Valley
towns suggest it was no different from other places. Yet formalized mourning practices did not diminish the genuine grief these families experienced
or the pain and guilt a parent might feel in an age when medicine was given
credence far beyond its power to cure. As Karen Sanchez-Eppler notes, for
the family members of a lost loved one, there is no "one authentic voice of
mourning and one pious and artificial voice of mourning . . . Both registers
of bereavement are available." One is distinctive, individual, and heartfelt; the
other circulates within the larger culture of mourning.[37]

Lucy Buffum Lovell, a mother who tried all measure of medical means to
treat her child, relied on her faith to carry her through. Today, as I peruse old
newspaper advertisements and advice columns claiming a cure for cholera infantum or scarlet fever, I find humor in their preposterous claims. But I wonder,

too, how Lucy Lovell, Susan Sheldon, and scores of other young mothers in the mid-nineteenth-century Connecticut Valley viewed these advertisements after losing a child. Even those literate and well-educated mothers might have paused for a moment and wondered what might have been when they were told there was no need to fear with "Dr. Fowler's Extract of Wild Strawberry in the medicine chest."

The many children who made it to their early teens, having survived infant bouts of the summer complaint and then the fevers of childhood, were on their way to being at greatly reduced risk of dying from the principal infectious diseases of the day. But there was one infectious disease that persisted at all times and threatened children and adults of all ages—consumption (tuberculosis). One age group particularly susceptible to death from this disease was adolescents and young adults.

5

DUTIFUL DAUGHTERS, PALLID YOUNG WOMEN

*More [illnesses] occur from pulmonary consumption than from any
other cause.*

—Stephen West Williams, "Medical and Physical Topography
of Deerfield, Massachusetts" (1836)

"CONSUMPTION, that great destroyer of human health and human life, takes
the first rank as an agent of death; and as such, we deem it proper to analyze
more particularly the circumstances under which it operates. Any facts regarding a disease that destroys one-seventh to one-fourth of all that die, cannot
but be interesting." So wrote Lemuel Shattuck, who had earlier lost his own
father to consumption, in his *Report of the Sanitary Commission of Massachusetts*
in 1850.[1] Throughout the nineteenth century consumption—a large proportion of which was pulmonary tuberculosis—was a major killer in the United
States and Europe. In the latter half of the century it was the leading cause
of death for both sexes, although more girls and women died of it each year
than did boys and men.[2]

Observers early on established that consumption, unlike dysentery and
scarlet fever, showed little evidence of seasonality and fluctuated less from year
to year than did the epidemic diseases.[3] In city and country it was a constant,
daily reminder of chronic illness and of the mortal self. And although it was
well known that death from consumption could take one at any age, people
were beginning to understand that a particular segment of the population
in New England, as elsewhere, was unusually vulnerable: adolescents and
young adults, especially young women—people normally considered to be
in the "prime of life."

Shattuck went on to observe, among the vital statistics he was able to gather
for Massachusetts, that for the years 1845–48 almost three times as many young
women between fifteen and twenty died of consumption than did men of
the same age group, and for those twenty to thirty, the rate was twice that of
men. Parents were losing their precious, dutiful daughters. Vital statisticians,

physicians, sanitarians, and health reformers would repeat similar statistics for most of the second half of the nineteenth century, in Britain as well as the United States. It came to be recognized that the strenuous work of girls and young women, compounded by their greater tendency to be cooped up indoors with a lack of fresh air, contributed to their vulnerability.[4]

In earlier chapters the experiences of infant diarrheas and childhood fevers was observed primarily through the eyes of parents and other adults in authority. The story of consumption in the 1870s and 1880s, however, offers voices from the afflicted themselves. Moreover, in this story the state begins to play a larger role in measuring and managing disease and health. The arena in which citizens of rural New England experienced their ills was slowly becoming enlarged, encompassing their urban neighbors and institutions of the state.

In the medical establishment, too, important transitions were taking place. With the work of scientists such as Louis Pasteur in France and Robert Koch in Germany, the third quarter of the nineteenth century saw the germ theory of disease gain coherence and some familiarity among doctors and laypersons.[5] The country doctor in Franklin County could begin to envision the infectious agents that somehow caused many of the zymotic class of diseases. In 1882 Koch isolated and identified the cause of consumption: the tubercle bacillus, a type of bacterium now assigned to the genus *Mycobacterium*. By the mid-1880s an occasional country doctor might even have possessed his own microscope and been able to observe the characteristic shape of tubercle bacilli in the expectorations of his patients.

Today we tend to regard *consumption* as an antiquated term for pulmonary tuberculosis, and indeed, it often was in the nineteenth century as well. But what was called consumption then was not necessarily a single disease. Doctors applied the term to any number of wasting diseases, including what we now know as tuberculosis. Sometimes they used the term *phthisis* (pronounced *tisis* or *teesis*) as a synonym for a wasting consumption or for pulmonary symptoms. *Scrofula* referred to symptoms of the lymphatic system now generally thought to be caused by tubercle bacilli, and these could be combined with pulmonary symptoms. Only after Koch isolated the bacillus and physicians became familiar with microscopic diagnosis was the term *tuberculosis* assigned a more objective and constrained meaning.[6] Nevertheless, consumption, whether clinical or metaphorical, provides a useful disease category in examining the deaths of young women in the Connecticut River valley during the second half of the nineteenth century.

Two archetypes dominated nineteenth-century portrayals of consumptive patients: the pallid, emaciated, yet luminous young woman and the debauched, morally weak, constitutionally defective working-class person, more likely

Illustration for William Cullen Bryant, "Consumption" (1824). From *Poems* (1876). Courtesy of Katherine Ott.

an immigrant.[7] The latter was often marked male, although working-class "girls" could share this stereotype. Similarly, affluent young men, particularly those deemed artistic or intellectual, could occupy the romanticized image of the middle- or upper-class consumptive. Perceptions of the underlying causes of the disease, its course, and even its outcome could be strongly influenced by the perceived social status and occupation of the afflicted. The "constitutional weakness" of the Irish laborer was somehow different from the "natural frailty" of young middle-class women. The idealized image of the consumptive young woman predated the stereotype of the immigrant worker and was more common in the early than the later nineteenth century. But in many people's minds these somewhat contradictory types continued to coexist.[8]

The number of Irish people afflicted, particularly Irish factory workers, was a concern of the state from about 1850. That was the year Shattuck had reported his observation that the major source of immigration was Ireland and had recommended, as quoted in Chapter 3, that preventive measures ought to be taken against "the sanitary evils" arising from immigration. Because "intemperance," "filth" (rather than poverty), poor job "choice," and an inherently weak constitution—all part of the Irish stereotype—were thought to be causal factors in consumption, it was commonplace for health officials to castigate the Irish and other recent immigrants for bringing the disease on themselves.[9] Judging from articles in the *Greenfield Gazette and Courier*, this bureaucratic sentiment about disease susceptibility was seldom reflected in the local press, although the paper certainly treated Irish and German immigrants and African Americans stereotypically. But in official publications of the state and its major city, Boston, there was little ambiguity. For example, Boston's Board of Health report for 1875 devotes many pages to the health threats of the Irish population. Among Boston's residents, it says, the Irish "exceed their proportionate tribute to deaths by all causes" and exhibit "excessive liability to consumption." It describes consumption as being among the "constitutional diseases which are transmissible by inheritance."[10]

The archetypes blurred and faded to some extent at the turn of the century, but the attribution of character defects and poor living habits to the consumptive lingered. With cholera infantum and scarlet fever, parents might have been thought guilty of improper care, but the sick child was seldom stigmatized. A person with consumption, however, could easily be deemed to have aspects of character, personality, or behavior that made him or her more susceptible to the disease. In young, working-class men, susceptibility to consumption was often attributed to weakness of moral character and uncontrolled appetites. In young middle-class women, character flaws might be attributed to accident of birth or temperament, although, as "Hall's Family Doctor" suggests, environment or bad judgment could increase the risk of disease:

From fifteen to the marriageable age of twenty or over, and better over, being a great deal about the house, [girls] are very apt to lay the foundation of lives of wretchedness by inadvertently falling into personal habits which undermine the health irretrievably. Medical books assure us that the large majority of cases of DYSPEPSIA and CONSUMPTION have their foundation laid in the "teens" of life, ailments which are easily avoidable in nine cases out of ten.[11]

These stereotypes caricatured a reality that was far more complex, and many in the nineteenth-century social welfare and health communities recognized them for what they were. Yet such images were common enough in both popular culture and medical parlance that they were accepted by the general public and professionals alike. While focusing attention on consumptive girls and young women in this chapter, I want to keep social class and circumstance always in the equation.

Even in Stephen West Williams's time, patent medicines and quack practices were available to consumptive patients who were willing to pay, and the trend continued. Years later, on March 6, 1876, the *Greenfield Gazette and Courier* published an advertisement for a typical patent potion: "Too young to Die," its headline warned: "Thousands of young persons between the ages of 16 and 25 die of Consumption, every one of whom might have been saved by using *Hale's Honey of Horehound and Tar* when the cough first set in." But the preferred treatment by the 1870s, which did seem to help in many cases, was a combination of rest, fresh air, a healthy diet, and moderate exercise.

It was a cure more readily available to middle-class young men than to young women, even those from wealthy families. Men, enjoying considerably greater freedom of mobility, might travel to the mountains of Colorado or take the invigorating air of New Mexico. Such distant travel would have been considered improper for a young woman, especially if she were single. Few women would receive such opportunities until early in the twentieth century. In the nineteenth century, the daughter of wealthy parents or the wife of a well-situated man might instead have been able to travel to Saranac Lake or Saratoga Springs, New York, to take the waters and fresh air closer to home.[12]

One of the earliest travelers from Franklin County to partake of the healthy water and bracing climate of upstate New York was twenty-three-year-old Esther Grout, from the town of Hawley, some miles west of Deerfield. Esther and her sister Sophorina were both in poor health in their late teens and early twenties, and both traveled for the rest cure to Saratoga Springs and to Hamilton, New York. On May 30, 1830, Esther Grout wrote in her diary: "I am expecting to take a journey to the springs at Saratoga for my health. I feel that I shall be placed in the way of many temptations and unless assisted by an all-mighty arm, shall be liable to forget the Lord and his mercies. Oh Lord, help me to watch and praying continually during my absence, I should [not] do something to the dishonor of thy name among those who love thee not."[13]

Over the next five years, Esther Grout was in and out of sanitaria in Saratoga Springs and Hamilton—and more often in than out. Her diary entries reveal a devoutly religious young woman who worried that she might not be worthy of God's love and attention. On her birthday in 1830 she wrote: "Lord help me to spend the ensuing year in a more profitable manner—to myself and to others." In July 1832 she prayed: "Lord, suffer me not to be a hindrance in the way of salvation of other souls as I fear I have often been, but prepare me for usefulness while I live, and for happiness hereafter." On New Year's Eve that year she thanked God for continuing the life of her sister, who had long been "in a consumption." Her father, too, was ill with a chronic disease, which she did not name.

In January 1834 Grout returned home to Hawley. It appears from her diary entries that she was no better; perhaps her parents brought her home thinking that the sanitarium could provide nothing more. In February she wrote:

> I returned from Hamilton about six weeks since, found my journey very fatiguing, took some cold on the way and added to it after I reached home, which brought on severe cough and opened the wound afresh at my lungs. It is now about five weeks since I commenced spitting blood again. I find it very difficult to do anything to check this, without my injury in other respects, and remedies for other complaints will injure my lungs. I never so much needed the services of a skilled physician as at present. I had a very good one at the west. Since I am home I have seen none, though I have had several ill turns, which have very much reduced my strength. I know of no better way for me to do than to be content with my situation and trust in the Lord. He can heal me without the aid of earthly physicians or he can sanctify my present afflictions to my soul and prepare me for a peaceful and happy death and permit me to dwell forever with him.

Grout's diary also hints at the social and emotional toll consumption might take. Although many couples married with prior knowledge of the illness of one partner and prospects for a short life, other patients were abandoned as their disease progressed. Something of the sort apparently happened to Grout, as her final diary passage, written June 28, 1835, suggests.

> Had I known two years since that the state of my health would have been such as it has since that time, and that I should have experienced other disappointments and trials, which it has been my lot to experience, the anticipation of them would probably have been an injury to my health. At that time I had reason to expect that if my life was spared I should long before this, have formed a connexion with one who professed to be my sincere friend. During my stay

in H. with my sister he was kind and attentive and often supplied my wants in sickness. He more than once proposed our union at that time, but on account of my feeble state of my health, and other reasons, I thought best to delay a few months, and return to my friends. When I left the place, he promised to visit me in a few weeks. After my return he repeatedly wrote and informed me that he should visit me soon. I had then not the least suspicion that he would prove false to me. But thus has he proved, and so be it. Since then I have heard nothing directly from him.

For many months I was kept in painful suspense and knew not what to think of this long silence. But have recently received some intelligence from my sister concerning him, and think I have no reason to expect that I shall ever see him again, unless by accident. But I think I can see the hand of God in all this and have nothing to say. I feel that I have cause for thankfulness, that I was not permitted to form an indisolvable connexion with one whose regard for me would so soon cease. From the first of our acquaintance I often sought direction of God and prayed that he would order things in such a manner as should be most for my own good and for his Honor and Glory.

Esther Grout survived for another three years and died on December 23, 1838. Her diary could have been written by any number of other middle- or upper-class women in the 1830s. Her symptoms, the treatments she received, and her experience of the illness remained typical for consumptives through the remainder of the century, even as medical diagnosis became more precise.[14]

In the years that followed, the kind of treatment Esther Grout would have received would have been augmented by prophylactic measures recommended by a growing number of physicians and public health officials. "Fresh air, by day and night, strong and nourishing food, dry soil on which to live, sunlight and warm clothing are the means of saving many lives which would have been otherwise hopelessly lost in the preceding generation . . . , and never mind the carpets; better they should fade than the health of the family."[15] But even as early intervention and efforts at prevention made headway, patent medicines and unorthodox treatments persisted. In Franklin County in the 1870s, as in the rest of the state and the country at large, citizens were bombarded with theories and self-proclaimed curatives. The treatment of consumption, was a central part of what Katherine Ott observes, as the "medical . . . free for all," of the period, and each person had to navigate a sea of often conflicting ideas.[16]

Throughout the nineteenth century, the rate of death by consumption declined slowly and erratically in Massachusetts,[17] although the barely perceptible decline was interrupted by a definite increase in the mid-1870s (see Appendix C). A few experts in the 1870s recognized the uneven decline, but much more apparent was that consumption of the lungs remained a common, persistent, and devastating disease.[18] Attempts to persuade the Massachusetts legislature to create a state board of health finally met with success in 1869. It was the first board of its kind in the United States, established in large part because of concern about consumption.[19] The 1870s became the first decade of "state medicine" in the United States, during which the state would attempt to influence sanitary conditions in cities and towns.

The early philosophy behind this state medicine was inextricably tied to the name Henry I. Bowditch.[20] A distinguished physician who advocated over many years for the creation of the Massachusetts Board of Health, Bowditch was selected to head the first board. He had undertaken a survey of the state and made a thorough inquiry into theories of the causes of consumption in other countries. He was persuaded that in New England, soil moisture was a major determinant. Bowditch had been a student of the famous French physician Pierre-Charles Louis, from whom he learned the powers of observation and the "numerical method." He undertook careful observations on the geographical distribution of consumption in Massachusetts and New England and concluded that it was highly associated with people living on damp soil. The precise mechanisms or connections that produced consumption from dampness were not elaborated on. Bowditch and his contemporaries considered their facts of association to be sufficient.[21]

Bowditch's survey took him to Franklin County in 1861. His friend Lyman Bartlett of New Bedford had written Bowditch a letter of introduction to his brother, Alfred Bartlett, of Conway, explaining that Bowditch "visits Conway & Deerfield for the purpose of investigating the causes of consumption." Lyman Bartlett asked his brother to take Bowditch to the top of "Dickinson Hill," where he would "realize what a variety of local climate rests under his eye."[22] Like Shattuck's earlier exchange of letters with Stephen West Williams, this correspondence illustrates the close connections between prominent state officials and the educated elite residing in Franklin County.

While Bowditch emphasized soil moisture as a source of consumption, other theories were being tested. As early as 1867, for example, readers of the Greenfield newspaper might have learned about the potential transmissibility of pulmonary consumption in a report on the proceedings of the International Medical Congress of Paris titled "Consumption Pronounced Contagious."

The first question discussed in the Medical Congress, was the question which reaches and interests more directly, perhaps, than any other, every family. It was the question of tubercle, its contagiousness and prophylactic. . . . Experiments have been made upon rabbits and other animals by inoculating under the skin the matter from tubercles, and those inoculated animals die consumptive in three months' time. The discussions of the Congress established no new doctrine in a positive way, but they brought out many valuable facts which will put the profession a step in advance in the right direction.[23]

Yet debate continued over whether tuberculosis is contagious, that is, caused by germs. The theory faced considerable resistance even within the medical community, in Massachusetts as well as internationally, and of all the causes proposed, received probably the least regard or emphasis from the medical establishment in the 1870s, despite the close attention many American physicians paid to the findings of their European colleagues.[24] Even after the tubercle bacillus was identified in 1882, physicians wondered why some people were symptomatic in the presence of the microorganism but others were not. Hereditary tendencies and habits of life were still regarded as strongly associated with consumption. Obvious associations between the disease and certain occupations and places of residence demonstrated that life habits must be important. The first annual report of the Massachusetts Board of Health noted that the distribution of consumption was "very unequal." The board's second report, in 1871, drew attention to the high rates of consumption among minors working in factories, although all minors seemed to be at relatively high risk. Clearly, several factors had to be involved.

During the nineteenth century, expanding industrialization and increasing immigration rapidly changed the social landscape of Massachusetts, including the Connecticut Valley. The area was still dominated by farms, but by 1870 the population of Deerfield had grown to slightly over thirty-six hundred people, and Greenfield followed close behind. Towns were becoming more diverse as immigrants moved in to take the increasing variety of jobs. Small mills and manufacturing shops lay scattered along rural lanes and the streets of Cheapside and South Deerfield, and the other three towns as well. The Wiley & Russell Company, occupying the former Russell Cutlery buildings in Cheapside, was probably the largest single employer in Deerfield, with the Arms Manufacturing Company of South Deerfield the second. Some neighborhoods or districts, including Cheapside, combined dense residential building with manufacturing. Overcrowding, substandard housing, and lack of sanitation became preoccupations in towns such as Deerfield and Greenfield, as well as Boston, Lowell, and Lawrence.

By the 1870s, the overly romantic view of the young middle- or upper-middle-class woman afflicted with consumption or tuberculosis had begun to give way to stark recognition of the multitude of working-class consumptives.[25] Proportionally, fewer women like Esther Grout and more young women of other socioeconomic classes and national backgrounds were acknowledged as suffering from the disease.

The Collins and McCarty families were among eight families occupying two adjacent dwellings in Cheapside in 1870, where housing was dense, many dwellings accommodated more than one family, and poverty was pervasive.

Their stories, drawn from the 1870 federal census, are typical of the families in that part of town for whom consumption was a daily reality. James and Margaret Collins, both born in Ireland, shared the neighborhood with other Irish immigrants as well as people from Germany, England, and elsewhere in Massachusetts or New England.[26] James Collins was a day laborer with no savings or personal property of note. He and Margaret had eight children, aged nineteen years to three months. Because so little work was to be found, the older children, including the sisters Margaret and Mary, had no regular employment and most often helped at home. Johniven, the oldest son, was only twelve.

Next door, the McCartys lived in a multigenerational household of Irish immigrants. Jerry L. and Hannah McCarty had two children, Margaret and Michael. Jerry's older brother and his wife, Julia, had six children, John, James, Julia, Charles, Ellen, and Maggie. Jerry was a railroad laborer, and his brother a day laborer, when he could find work. Three of the young sons in the extended family—Michael, thirteen, John, seventeen, and Charles, ten, found some work in the cutlery factory but were paid very little.[27] Even with the children occasionally employed, the McCartys, like the Collinses, had few assets. Between them the brothers owned less than about twelve hundred dollars' worth of real property—no doubt fully mortgaged—and no reportable personal wealth at all.

Almost everyone who lived in Cheapside knew it was an unhealthy neighborhood. Infants and toddlers often contracted cholera infantum, the "teething" disease, and nearly all the adults seemed to have at least some of the consumption. The houses were poorly ventilated in summer and cold in winter, and the cellars were always damp, because they were so near the Green River. Since the cutlery factory had moved to Turners Falls, fewer jobs were available nearby, and the men and boys who had jobs in the factory had either to walk five or six miles each way or pay to ride the livery coach or train, which they could ill afford. Nevertheless, many did. On August 1, 1870, the *Greenfield Gazette and Courier* reported: "The largest train of passengers that runs out of Greenfield runs to Turners Falls daily," and on August 8: "There are some 400 workers who daily go out from Greenfield on the work train." Several families moved closer to the Russell factory, but few could afford the newer housing there, which in any case was in short supply.

Margaret McCarty, Jerry and Hannah's daughter, who had been consumptive for some time, was the first in the extended family to die. She died on September 26, 1870, at the age of twenty. Shortly after Margaret's death, a manufacturing and agriculture slump that occurred nationwide during an economic depression in the early-to-mid-1870s began to have a serious effect on manufacturing in the Connecticut Valley.[28] By the winter of 1874, just getting

by was increasingly difficult for the McCartys and their neighbors. The following spring, in May 1, Margaret's cousin Julia, also age twenty, died of
consumption; Julia's younger sister Ellen died on January 27, 1876, and her
youngest sister, Maggie, died the following September. In the household of
the McCartys' neighbors the Collinses, the daughter Margaret died on March
25, 1876, and, two years later, in October 1878, Margaret's sister Mary died.
And there were many more in other families.

Consumption flourished in other parts of town besides Cheapside.[29] While
that area may have been the most heavily afflicted, consumption presented
itself in all the villages and districts of Deerfield. In comparison with Cheapside
economically, South Deerfield prospered in the mid-1870s. The railroad had
made it a center for the shipment of agricultural produce and manufactured
goods. Most of the small farms along Mill River and Bloody Brook were able
to grow surpluses for local and more distant markets. The Arms family had
established the Arms Manufacturing Company, which made pocketbooks and
shipped them throughout New England and New York. Other shops had been
established for the manufacture of leather goods.

South Deerfield's relative prosperity could not always, however, protect its
citizens from consumption. Three young women from interconnected South
Deerfield families illustrate the point. Nellie (known as Nettie) Wells was the

Workers outside of Arms Manufacturing Company, 1889. Courtesy of PVMA.

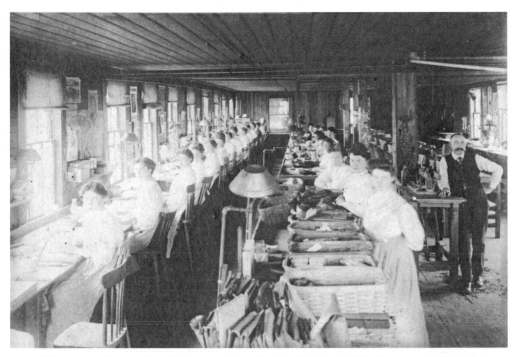

Women workers and male foreman in pocket book shop, c.1900. Courtesy of PVMA.

younger daughter of David Wells and his late wife; he was a successful South Deerfield farmer with above-average personal wealth and property holdings of considerable value. Nellie worked at the Arms pocketbook factory as a wallet maker to bring in extra income. Fannie Arms was one of four children of William and Sultana Arms, members of the manufacturing family and owners of several acres on Sugarloaf Street. Fannie worked in the Arms factory along with her father. Just up Sugarloaf Street, Hillman Thayer and his wife, Maria, lived with their five children, the youngest of whom was Stella.

In little more than a year's time, Nellie Wells, Fannie Arms, and Stella Thayer all died of consumption. Nellie, at age twenty-two, died on June 19, 1875; Stella, at nineteen, died on September 24; and Fanny, at twenty-one, died on February 3, 1876. Some speculated that the "wallet shop" was not a proper place for women; the hard physical work challenged their delicate constitutions and put them in the company of men, some of whom were coarse in their behavior.[30] The acids, glues, and other solutions used to work the hides and make the pocketbooks were thought to irritate the lungs and perhaps bring on consumption in people whose families already had a constitutional weakness predisposing them to the disease.

But young women from relatively well-to-do farming families, who worked and lived far from the noxious factory floor and damp, drafty housing, fell victim to consumption just as factory workers did. For example, William and Margaret Herron emigrated from Scotland with their daughter, Margaret, and settled on a farm just outside the village of South Deerfield, where they prospered. On May 17, 1871, when Margaret was seventeen, she died of consumption. Ellen Robbins, the daughter of one of the most successful farmers in upper west Deerfield, who helped her mother and performed the many farm chores expected of young women "at home," died of consumption on July 31, 1871, at the age of twenty.[31]

Mary and Jerusha Smith, two daughters of Robert and Filena Smith—the only African American farming family in South Deerfield and one of very few black families in the town—also died of consumption.[32] The Smiths were not wealthy, but they owned their farm outside the village on the Mill River, along with a small amount in personal assets. Mary, who at age seventeen contributed significantly to the farm and household economy, died of consumption

Gravestone of Mary Smith, an African American adolescent who died of consumption, Mill River Cemetery, South Deerfield. Photo by author.

on June 17, 1870. Jerusha, who worked in domestic service from the time she was thirteen, died five years later at the age of eighteen.[33]

Whether the person with consumption came from a middle-class family or a working-class one, from town or farm, physicians watched the disease progress in the same terrible way. First appeared a dry, hacking cough, then the slowly advancing weakness and debilitation, together with the emerging pallor and loss of appetite. Occasionally the symptoms subsided and the young person began to revive and become stronger. But when the symptoms advanced, the coughing became deeper, and the sputum contained blood, there seemed little hope. Whether one could afford to call a doctor at that stage made little difference. The Herrons and Robbinses could afford to provide their daughters with proper sick rooms; the Collinses and McCartys could not. Confinement to bed might prolong the consumptive's life, but it seldom led to convalescence and recovery. More often the outcome was death.

Obituaries published in the *Greenfield Gazette and Courier* for young women who died of consumption were usually short and simple: "In South Deerfield, Sept. 24. Estella, daughter of H. L. and Maria E. Thayer, aged 19."[34] Because of the stigma associated with consumption, most middle-class families preferred not to have this cause of death mentioned in newspaper obituaries. If the family was less well off, such mention might not be so easily avoided: "In Cheapside, May 12, of scrofula, Annie M., daughter of the late Mathew Smith, aged 18 years, 6 mos."[35] Occasionally, in an obituary for someone with some standing in the community who had died of consumption, the cause of death might be accompanied by a comment on the deceased's good character and heavenly prospects.

> DIED. In this village on the 27 inst., Miss Martha Russell of South Deerfield, Mass., aged 24. Miss Russell had spent but a few months with us, but they were amply sufficient to endear her to all who were favored with her acquaintance. Consumption ere long marked her for its victim, and her passage to the grave was rapid and attended with much suffering. But it was not a dark passage—Light from heaven shone brightly around her, and she looked with pleasure to the hour when the light of life should be lost in the clearer light of eternal day.[36]

Luany Wilcox, whose mourning poem is quoted in the previous chapter and who probably died of consumption, was memorialized in an unusually long obituary. This highly stylized, somewhat overwrought testament offers a glimpse of a mother's dashed hopes for a beloved young daughter.[37]

> In South Deerfield. Jan. 14, Luany B. Wilcox, aged 14 years, 7 months, 19 days. The deceased was born in Coleraine, Mass., May 26, 1849, and was daughter of Rev. Wm. Wilcox. Luany was a quiet and modest girl of uncommon loveliness and powers of mind. Hers was a gentle, loving spirit that ever shone with

undimmed radiance upon her calm, sweet countenance so full of expression and character, portraying a heart of the tenderest and most delicate affections and sympathies; her sensibilities were remarkably refined; she was wholly devoted to her widowed mother, ever careful to give her the least anxiety or care; in conversation she would produce subjects of the most elevating nature, and converse with marked intelligence. Although not by profession, there were strong evidences that she was indeed, a true Christian. Had her constitution allowed, she would have been an influential aid toward goodness amid the circle of youth, for she was one whom none could know but to love.—But no, she was frail; in the winter of 1862, she commenced attending school at South Deerfield, but after five weeks had passed, her health became so impaired that she was obliged to leave. Dec. 2d, 1863, she again entered the school-room with the bright hopes and anticipations so cherished in youth. But, alas! Those bright hopes were soon blighted, and the 31st day of Dec. was her last in school; during those four weeks she won the highest esteem and confidence of both teachers and scholars who tenderly watched her frail nature and favored her accordingly.

In the early 1870s, the *Greenfield Gazette and Courier* employed stereotypes and derogatory ethnic humor emphasizing Irish people's alleged love of drinking, fighting, and general rowdiness. As the decade progressed, however, and more and more death notices appeared from the Irish families in Cheapside, the paper's tone became more respectful.[38] Articles often extolled the virtues of a "good" Irishman or one who was a successful farmer or "industrious" worker, though a tone of condescension remained in the frequent references to "our Irish friends." The *Gazette and Courier*'s correspondent from Shelburne frequently used this term in reference to Irish funerals, writing, for example, on July 22, 1872: "Last Sat. Michael Meehan's child was carried to Greenfield for burial. There were 19 teams, 3 of them double, in procession. There is something beautiful in the sympathy our Irish friends have for each other in their affliction, and the zeal with which they attend funerals."

Many Cheapside children were buried in the Green River Cemetery, located on the hill behind the Wiley & Russell Company. And though death notices for these children might be brief and unsentimental, cemetery markers, when people could afford them, better reflected families' devotion and love—whether they were native-born whites, African Americans, or recent immigrants. Jane Colmey, daughter of Michael and Mary, and born in County Kildare, died of consumption in 1870 at the age of twenty-two. Her parents erected a large white stone with a cross engraved on the top. Her epitaph included another form of the "Mother, do not weep" genre: "We are not dead, we only sleep. God the father ordered it so, Your [illegible] children to him should go." Near this marker is a round-topped stone for Harriet Pierce, erected by her parents, and another, more imposing stone for Margaret Glable, who also died of consumption in 1891. The Brookside Cemetery in South Deerfield and the

Laurel Hill Cemetery next to the old village all contain impressive markers signifying parents' deeply felt loss of their young adult children.

Parents visiting the "resting places" of these girls and young women did so in pleasant surroundings. Even the names are suggestive: "Green River," "Laurel Hill," "Brookside."[39] Cemeteries that captured the peaceful landscape were now preferred over the more spare and solemn churchyard and grave-yard. Even the word, *cemetery*, derives from a Greek root meaning a sleeping room. As the old burying grounds filled up in the late eighteenth and early nineteenth centuries, relatives of the deceased were drawn to rural settings. Scholars point to such places as the very early Mount Auburn Cemetery in Cambridge, Massachusetts, established in 1831, as the origins for this prefer-ence in the United States. Mount Auburn itself derived in part from the hor-ticultural traditions of Victorian England.[40] The rural cemetery movement quickly caught on throughout New England and America. The lower part of Laurel Hill was established in 1803, but its upper part was developed decades later and is a better reflection of these cultural transitions. Green River was created in 1851, and Brookside in South Deerfield, in the 1840s.[41] Green River and Laurel Hill are each located on a hill that was, at their inception, on the edge of town. Green lawns, graveled paths, and ample shade trees enhanced the parklike atmosphere in each of the three places.

Grief sometimes led the bereaved to explore spiritualism. In the mid- to late nineteenth century, mesmerism and the consulting of spirit mediums came into fashion in the United States. Belief that one might contact a deceased family member through a spirit medium offered the prospect of consolation in learning about the deceased's fate in the afterlife and knowing that his or her soul was at peace. Mediums, often under hypnosis, claimed to be able to hear the deceased and sometimes even spoke in his or her voice. Although local ministers warned of chicanery, many grieving parents held to the belief or at least the hope that spirit communication was possible.[42]

One such parent was Dexter Pierce, who lived in Montague and later in Northfield, Massachusetts. Pierce lost at least two of his four daughters to consumption. A few years after his daughter Jane Elizabeth's death in 1855, he consulted Mrs. W. R. Hayden, a medium in Boston. Pierce prepared a transcript of the session, in which he recorded the way Hayden confirmed her contact with Jane Elizabeth by "spelling" her name out with raps on the table. Pierce then asked the spirit whether she had messages for her father, mother, and sisters. The deceased young woman, according to the transcript, spoke through the medium, telling her father that she was always hovering near and that she had a mission for her father to perform in benefiting "the

Green River Cemetery, Greenfield. Photo © Carol Betsch.

diseased portion of the human family." She encouraged her mother to look to God as the "right source of true happiness" and her sisters to "pour into [their] Souls the purest sentiments and most Holy aspirations." "At the close of the above," Pierce wrote, "I felt very thankful and spoke of leaving when the spirit of Jane rapped and the medium's hand became influenced and she wrote the following:

> Well you know my dear Father that I am always near to you and will stand near and help you sow the seeds that shall ripen for you not only in this life but will bloom in the happy life that is beyond what has been better known as the dark portals of the grave—But dear Father it is not dark it is all bright and glorious. All joy and love friend meets friend and is happy—They have none of the perplexities that overshadow their lifes [*sic*] on earth—All that is left behind with the clay while the spirit soars aloft to the mansions of love to worship the true God in Sincerity and truth
>
> Dear Father Jane loves you very much and will be a guardian angel to guide you through life."[43]

According to the criteria that Pat Jalland provides in *Death in the Victorian Family*, Jane Elizabeth Pierce's was a "good death," as were those of Luany Wilcox and Esther Grout.[44] In "polite society" the deceased would have been regarded as innocent, freed of sin. Each would have made peace with her "maker" and gone willingly in the hope or expectation of resting in the kingdom of heaven. Jane Elizabeth, her father believed, was already there.

In 1872 alone, according to an article published March 9, 1874, in the *Greenfield Gazette and Courier* on the thirtieth annual report of births, deaths, and marriages in Massachusetts, consumption "carried off 2544 males and 3012 females" in the state. For Deerfield and vicinity, data from vital records, cemeteries, and other sources for the 1870s reveals twenty-two consumptive deaths among unmarried women aged fourteen to thirty during the decade. (Married women with children who died of consumption feature in the next chapter.) Undoubtedly there were more, but for them the cause of death was either unrecorded, perhaps because of the stigma, or the cause listed is too vague to permit an inference of consumption.

The average age at death of these unmarried young women was twenty-one; eleven of them were in their teens. Twelve were the daughters of at least one immigrant parent, nine of those Irish. Of the "native born," two sisters were African American. Seventeen of the twenty-two were listed in the 1870 federal census for Deerfield. At the time of the census, one was a music teacher, one a store clerk, one a farm laborer, and one a domestic servant. Two worked in the "wallet shop," and the rest were "at home." Though the numbers are small, these cases reasonably reflect the diversity in age, ethnicity, and socioeconomic class among consumptive young women in the Commonwealth in the 1870s.

A few of the young women mentioned here would have been attended by a local physician, but most of the others would have received no regular care. As discussed earlier, however, treatments for pulmonary consumption varied little for the duration of the nineteenth century. The rest cure was augmented by the "fresh air" cure, in which patients were encouraged to live, eat, and sleep with as much fresh air as possible, including living out of doors. By the beginning of the twentieth century improvements were being seen in nursing care, management of home sickrooms, and in the regimens of sanitaria.[45] The members of the Franklin District Medical Society were surprisingly mute on the treatment of tuberculosis in the 1870s. Not a single mention was made of the disease at any of their quarterly meetings for the entire decade.[46]

By the late 1870s, physicians and sanitarians had demonstrated that mortality from consumption was highest in the dense neighborhoods of cities, among factory workers, and in places where the land was poorly drained. They had even begun to offer explanations for this pattern. But why were young women working in the fresh air on their fathers' farms and those working "at home" at such high risk? A study written by J. F. A. Adams and published by the Board of Health under the title *The Health of Farmers in Massachusetts* found that farm women's long hours and inadequate diets made them prime candidates for exhibiting active tuberculosis.[47]

In a survey of physicians, the board elicited remarks about the overall good health of farmers but concluded that women and children on farms were less healthy than men. Some physicians commented on the tendency of farm women to die young, whereas farm men had above-average longevity. Those conducting the survey felt that overwork was responsible for weakening the health of farm women. Many farm children suffered from inadequate diets, and one physician noted that girls suffered the most.[48] Girls and young women on farms and "at home" performed farm chores, domestic work, and other demanding labor in support of the household economy. They cared for younger siblings and for the sick of all ages, increasing their chances of repeated exposure to the tubercle bacillus.

Many healthy young people who contracted tuberculosis in the nineteenth century—if they were well nourished, had strong immune systems, and lived in sanitary conditions—were able to encapsulate the bacillus in the lung and remain asymptomatic and noninfectious indefinitely.[49] In contrast, frequent exposure to infected persons in close quarters, together with poor nutrition, overwork, and air polluted with particulate matter, increased a person's chances of a serious and even fatal outcome. The most privileged young women had a reasonable chance of recovery if they were able to rest, eat well, and remain in hygienic surroundings. Young women from poor families, often those of immigrants, faced higher odds. If these dutiful daughters were primary care-givers for sick family members, their risk was that much greater.

Thousands of older women and men also lost their lives to pulmonary tu-berculosis, and in the next chapter, in which I examine the mortality of adult men and women, the scourge of tuberculosis reappears But there were other causes of death to which older adults were also vulnerable—related to the risks of childbirth, accidents in the workplace, and the violence of war.

6

REPRODUCTIVE WOMEN, PRODUCTIVE MEN

There are few cases in the practice of our profession which cause more
anxiety and alarm . . . and none that are attended with more real danger,
than puerperal convulsions.

—Stephen West Williams, "Puerperal Convulsions" (1846)

A SIMPLE ENTRY by the Reverend Edgar Buckingham, a Deerfield Congregational minister, in the First Church's book of baptisms, marriages, and
funerals for 1870 reads: "April 19, Mary E. wife of John H. Stebbins. Age, 34,
cause *premat: Confin't.* [premature confinement]."[1] Mary E. Stebbins had died
from complications in childbirth, apparently with a premature infant, her
fourth child. In the town's vital records, her death was listed as having been
caused by fever—most likely what is now called puerperal fever. She was one
among many.

The members of the Franklin District Medical Society had almost nothing
to say about the treatment of women with consumption in the 1870s, but they
had much to say about the uterus. During the decade, morbid conditions of
women's reproductive organs came up at least sixteen times at their quarterly
meetings and were the most frequent topic of case histories. Specific issues
included hysteria, puerperal convulsions (eclampsia), puerperal flooding,
puerperal fever, puerperal peritonitis, metritus (inflammation of the uterus),
and the use of forceps in delivery. In one case a physician recommended
"pregnancy" for a particular "uterine condition."[2]

As medical historians have noted, the latter half of the nineteenth century
was a time in which regular physicians were competing with midwives over the
authority to manage childbirth, especially in the United States, where licensing
of midwives was neither common nor encouraged and where obstetrics was
becoming a standard component of surgical and general medical training.[3]
National patterns reverberated in Massachusetts, the Connecticut Valley, and
Franklin County. Problems of childbirth were a real concern for physicians,
but the care of pregnant and delivering women was a site for the politics and
economics of medicine as well.

Paul Starr and others have recounted how physicians involved in midwifery and, later, formally in obstetrics were able to displace traditional midwives in attending to middle- and upper-class women.[4] This transition began fairly early in the nineteenth century. John Gunn's 1830 home medical manual advised that childbed fever was "extremely dangerous and requires the immediate attention of an able physician."[5] Of all the "female complaints," childbed fever, or puerperal fever, was among those most often fatal. Its symptoms, including fever, headache, sepsis, and discharge from the vagina, might develop at any time from a few hours after delivery to a few days.

Not until well into the twentieth century would physicians realize that the "germ" causing puerperal fever was most frequently the same bacterium responsible for scarlet fever—*Streptococcus*.[6] What they had begun to recognize years earlier was that childbed fever could be spread by midwives, doctors, and other birth attendants. Doctors often failed to observe antiseptic practices as they moved from one patient to the next or even from an autopsy to a patient. Pelvic inspections and the delivery of babies ran exceptionally high risks for the transfer of bacteria from the doctor's hands to the mother's body. Some observant practitioners suspected contagion as early as the late eighteenth century. Oliver Wendell Holmes made the first strong case for contagion as a cause of puerperal fever by investigating the reports of physicians whom he queried.

Holmes published his observations in 1843 in a short-lived medical journal of small circulation, the *New England Quarterly Journal of Medicine and Surgery*. He republished the article in 1855 in his *Medical Essays*, motivated partly by the desire to reach a larger readership and partly by a challenge from two eminent obstetrical physicians in Philadelphia who disputed his findings. Shortly after Holmes's original publication, Ignaz Semmelweis of Vienna conducted more thorough epidemiological investigations of puerperal fever and published his findings.[7] To what extent Holmes's and Semmelweis's pioneering work was familiar to the members of the Franklin District Medical Society in the 1870s and 1880s is unknown. Minutes of the meetings in this period did not report extensively on the discussion of cases and specific treatments—often listing only the topic. It is reasonable to assume, however, that even by this time, few physicians in Franklin County, as elsewhere, were adhering strictly to antiseptic practices. That number would change dramatically by the mid-to-late 1880s.

In his *Report of the Sanitary Commission of Massachusetts* in 1850, Lemuel Shattuck noted that approximately 1.1 percent of all deaths annually from 1842 to 1848 were caused by diseases of the "generative organs."[8] The great majority of these were deaths in childbirth. The percentage seems small until one considers that it is a proportion of deaths among people of both sexes and all ages. If data were available solely for pregnant women who reached term in a given year, the percentage of deaths due to complications of childbirth would undoubtedly be greater. Precise numbers for specific causes of death, however, were difficult to obtain, especially for Shattuck. Puerperal fever was sometimes identified simply as "fever" or "septicemia." Deaths several days or a few weeks after delivery might be dissociated from childbirth as a contributing cause, and a consumptive woman whose condition was further weakened in childbirth might be classified as having died only from consumption.

As the century matured, so did record keeping and statistics. Samuel Abbott, in a summary of forty years of vital statistics for Massachusetts published in 1897, reported that in 1876, for every one hundred births, approximately one mother (0.885) died. By 1895 that number was reduced to 0.549—closer to one woman in every two hundred births.[9] In a review of all causes of death for married women residing in the four Franklin County towns between 1855 and 1905, 5.5 percent are listed as having died of causes related to childbirth.[10] By the late 1800s, doctors and nurses in Massachusetts had become much more vigilant about antiseptic practices. Still, childbirth carried risks, and many more mothers became ill or suffered from complications than actually died.

Deaths of women of reproductive age provide an opportunity to explore interactions, not just a single cause of death within a single age group. The deaths of mother and child could be intertwined. For example, frequent pregnancies with short birth intervals could endanger both mother and child. Mary Stebbins bore two daughters, one in 1861 and another in 1864. In May 1868 she delivered a son, who survived less than four months, dying in September from cholera infantum; then, records show the deaths in April 1870 of Mary Stebbins and a premature child, another son. Normally, an interval of twenty-three months between births would not threaten the health of the mother or child, but in this instance, the physical and emotional stress of losing her first son may have contributed to the deaths of Mary and her second son. Women who experienced a succession of short birth intervals increased their chances of infant loss and endangered their own health.[11]

A further complication was introduced when the mother was consumptive. Marietta Hoyt Ashley of Deerfield, for example, was consumptive at the time her son, and second child, was born in early August 1849. He died quickly of "marasmus" (wasting or starvation), and twelve days later she died from her consumption. The two most common causes of death for women of child-bearing age in the nineteenth century were consumption and complications of childbirth, and they were not necessarily independent of each other. An otherwise healthy woman who might normally have recovered from exposure to tuberculosis could be weakened by multiple or difficult childbirths and therefore be more likely to succumb to tuberculosis. Conversely, a consumptive mother, already weakened, was more susceptible to physical stress, infections, or the trauma of a difficult birth.

Consumptive women were often well aware of these complications, feared pregnancy, and worried about the fate of their newborns, whom they might be unable to feed and care for. Such interactions are exemplified in the life and death of Deborah Vinal Fiske, who in 1828 moved to Amherst, Massachusetts, when she married the Reverend Nathan Fiske, a teacher of rhetoric and languages at Amherst College. Deborah, who had been a sickly child whose own mother died of consumption, became seriously ill with the birth of her first child in 1829. Symptoms of severe fatigue and fever were consistent with consumption in her case as well. Her physician advised her not to breastfeed, and her infant son died of "bowel complaint" at one month. She later bore another son and two daughters; the second son also died after a wet nurse was hired because Deborah's health was so depleted.[12]

Deborah Fiske fretted about her declining health and her duties as wife, mother, and household manager. During a respite from house and children in 1836, she wrote to her husband: "I am in a strait betwixt half a dozen, whenever I think of the children. I want to see them, and yet fear the care of them and want to keep house again and yet I know I have no strength for anything."[13] Despite occasional stable periods, her health continued to deteriorate, and she died on February 19, 1844, at the age of thirty-eight.

Roughly sixty years later, at a time when middle-class women with serious consumptive symptoms often traveled to a sanitarium or retreat such as Lake Saranac, New York, Agnes Gordon Tack recorded her fears for her children, whom she missed while she was away from home receiving treatment. Her first diary entry, written in November 1908, reads: "It is a gray morning with snow on the ground and more now over head getting ready to fall. The red roof of the house against the sky is covered with snow. . . . I often think of living in it with my children and Augustus—What a nice time we would have. How I wish we had money enough to live together. It is really hard to think of the children so far away and miss so much of their coming years."[14]

Agnes Tack lived in Boston but had close relatives in Deerfield and was a frequent visitor to the town. At "Dr. Trudeau's institute" in Lake Saranac, the doctor advised her that a cure could well take five years. She noted later: "Dear little Agnes, she needs a most delicate hand to develop such a sensitive mind and heart without throwing it back upon itself and making her secretive which must be so hard for a nature like hers. My little Robert is made of firmer stuff and will get on more easily in this world. Dear little boy. I should love to see him."[15] Agnes Gordon Tack was a lucky one. After repeated stays at the sanitarium, she returned home in 1912, "cured."

As it was for adolescents and reproductive-age women, consumption was the leading cause of death for working-age men in the latter half of the nineteenth century. Another statistic that caught the eye of Samuel Abbott, among others—and that concerned state health officials—was the figure for homicides, suicides, and accidents for the second half of the century. Unlike the slow decline for tuberculosis, rates of death by these causes were apparently increasing, especially deaths due to accidents or negligence. Men were far more likely to die of such causes than women. Abbott noted: "Out of 9,022 deaths by accidental means, 4,179 were railroad accidents, including those which occurred on street railways, the number of which was considerably increased since the introduction of electricity as a motive power. There were 3,169 by drowning, 1,456 by falls, blows and falling bodies, and 218 by poison."[16]

In the early nineteenth century, ever since the coming of the industrial revolution, innovations and new technologies had been changing the pace of working life in New England and the rest of North America. The man who drove a horse-drawn wagon or walked behind a horse-drawn plow in the 1820s was being pulled inexorably onto mechanized farming equipment, onto the factory floor with its powerful machinery and drive belts, and onto steam-powered trains traveling at speeds only imagined a few years before. In the maturing industrial economy of the 1870s, 1880s, and 1890s, increasing numbers of men worked in, on, and around these fast, complex, and dangerous machines. Tolerances for error were strikingly diminished; a moment's lapse in judgment could prove fatal. And the machinery was not necessarily designed with worker safety in mind. American factories were said to be even more dangerous than those in Britain.[17]

By 1846, a north-south railroad came up the Connecticut River valley through Deerfield. The train stopped in Greenfield at the end of its completed run. Alvah Crocker, a Fitchburg (Massachusetts) textile mill owner and venture capitalist, saw opportunities in expanding the railroad westward and increasing industry in the Connecticut Valley. By 1851 an east-west route had been completed from Boston to Greenfield. Agricultural produce and manufactured goods, as well as passengers, could now move in and out of Franklin County much more easily and inexpensively.[18] This ease of transportation would prove both a boon and a burden as competition increased from the east and south in manufacturing and eventually from the west in agriculture.

Farther west, expansion from Greenfield and this part of the valley was halted by the impediment of Hoosac Mountain, where the Deerfield River valley turned northwest. Crocker and others had for many years envisioned a tunnel through the mountain, but because it would have to be more than four miles long, it posed a considerable challenge for the engineering expertise and construction techniques of the day. In the late 1850s, Crocker finally hired a brilliant young engineer named Herman Haupt to oversee the project. But the challenges of construction and, more important, the coming of the Civil War delayed expansion along this route for more than twenty years. The economic losses caused by the stalled project were offset somewhat by the increased business and agricultural opportunities the war effort brought to the residents of Franklin County.[19]

George Sheldon's diary entry for April 13, 1861, reads: "A rainy day. News came to us that war had commenced between the North and South—that Fort Sumter had been fired upon by the batteries that surrounded. The action continues all day. . . . Fort Sumter taken by the rebels."[20] The Civil War, or the "War of the Rebellion" as it was more commonly known at the time, merits attention here for its role in mortality in the Connecticut Valley.

It is generally estimated that during the Civil War, which lasted from 1861 to 1865, approximately 620,000 soldiers died. The total for Union soldiers was approximately 359,528, of whom 67,058 were killed in battle and 43,012 died of wounds, giving a total of 110,070 Union deaths from battle casualties. The number dying of disease is estimated at 224,586. In other words, about two-thirds as many men died of wounds as were killed in battle, and twice as many men died of disease as from battle wounds.[21]

Although many deaths during the war were due to infectious diseases—dysenteries and fevers were major problems in encampments—my primary focus here is on violent deaths, though the causes can at times be difficult to separate.[22] A new form of bullet, the minié ball, was developed during the war. The minié ball, made out of soft lead in a conical-spherical shape, did more damage than the ammunition used in previous wars. When it did not kill, it left shattered limbs and devastating wounds. Amputation and field surgery took place under difficult battlefield conditions, and many soldiers on both sides died of secondary infections and gangrene as a result. Prisoners of war were dealt with harshly and often died of diseases stemming from a combination of malnutrition and physical mistreatment. For these reasons, deaths on the battlefield were only a fraction of the total war-related deaths.

In Franklin County, Deerfield contributed 303 soldiers to the war effort; Greenfield, approximately 477; Shelburne, about 200; and Montague, about 150.[23] In the first two years of the war, these and most other New England towns met their quotas by the voluntary enlistment of their own "native sons" and other residents. Often the towns offered bounties to be paid to the volunteers and voted to provide additional sums of money and certain provi-

Timothy H. O'Sullivan, *Union Dead at Gettysburg*, July 1863, stereograph. Courtesy of Library of Congress.

sions. These practices encouraged enlistment by many working-class young men who otherwise might not have volunteered.

By 1863, volunteers were increasingly hard to find throughout the Union states. Men had witnessed the high casualty rates and the many deaths from disease in the first two years of the campaign and were reluctant to enlist.[24] The Union Army was forced to institute a draft, with quotas expected from each town. Draftees could enlist, send a substitute, or pay a commutation fee of three hundred dollars. Increasingly after 1863, people sought alternatives to serving. Many of those who declined military service were older, married and with children, and were engaged in farming or other occupations.

In the first two years of recruitment, Deerfield sons and other residents averaged more than 70 percent of the total number of men credited to the town. In 1863 the figure was closer to 50 percent, and by 1864–65, Deerfield residents made up less than 30 percent of the total enlisted. In the 1863 draft, Deerfield was expected to provide 83 men. Forty-six of the town's residents were exempted for medical or other reasons, and 16 were aliens. Of the 20 considered eligible, 17 paid the three-hundred-dollar commutation fee, 2 furnished substitutes, and only 1, Lorenzo Brizee, enlisted.[25] Of the 303 men credited to Deerfield for the entire war, 167 were actually native sons or residents of the town. Such proportions were not unusual for towns in the Connecticut Valley and elsewhere in New England.

When too few local citizens signed up, quotas were met by recruiting recent immigrants and working-class men from neighboring towns, from cities such as Lowell and Boston, and even from as far away as New York City, Washington, D.C., and French Canada.[26] The town of Deerfield raised money to pay for such outside recruits in each of the war years. One writer observed that Deerfield's patriotism shifted from contributing sons to appropriating funds with which to recruit outsiders.[27] My concern here, however, is in the perceived value of individual lives lost by soldiers who were "credited" to a given town.

Forty-two soldiers from Deerfield died, forty from Greenfield, and twenty-five each from Shelburne and Montague. The mortality rates for these communities averaged roughly 12 percent of those who served, equivalent to the average for all those serving in the war.[28] Similarly, most of the war-related deaths in Franklin County were the result of disease or from wounds. Colonel George Duncan Wells of Greenfield "came back home in a pine box."[29] But because embalming was in its infancy, few bodies were returned home.[30] Some may have been buried among the unknown at Arlington National Cemetery. Most were buried on the battlefield or in unadorned cemeteries near the hospitals or prisons where they died.

Among local families, no other was harder hit than the Stowells of South Deerfield. Three sons of the Stowell family volunteered—Myron, Charles, and Cyrus. Only Charles returned home alive. Cyrus enlisted in the 52nd Regiment with the nine-month volunteers of Company D, made up largely of Deerfield residents. He died in battle at Port Hudson, Louisiana, on July 6, 1863. Myron, of the 21st Massachusetts Infantry, was killed while serving as a medical assistant, removing the wounded by stretcher at Spotsylvania, Virginia, May 18, 1864.[31]

All four towns constructed monuments to commemorate their Civil War dead. Most towns did; the Civil War sparked a proliferation of monuments not seen after previous American wars.[32] These stone edifices, with their obelisk or columnar forms, their statuary and iconography, were erected by communities, not by states or the nation. They honored multiple deaths and told multiple stories, yet they displayed common conventions and themes.[33] Many of them identified battlegrounds where men had served or fallen; some made sentimental connections with the town's founding fathers or between soldiers who had fought in the American Revolution and those who served in the Civil War.

The Deerfield town monument, claimed to be one of the earliest in the country, captures these themes well. George Sheldon observed that such a monument was envisioned as early as 1864, to honor "those soldiers who had died *for* Deerfield."[34] Early in 1866 a war memorial committee was formed, chaired by Cyrus A. Stowell, father of Myron and Cyrus. Later in the year

Soldiers' Monument on the Deerfield Common, 1880. H. J. Davis stereograph.
Courtesy of PVMA.

the committee commissioned Batterson Monumental Works of Hartford,
Connecticut, to erect a "soldiers' monument" out of Portland brownstone.
It was to be an obelisk with an overall height of thirty-five feet, topped by
the figure of a soldier in "parade rest" position with a coat over his shoulders.
Batterson Monumental Works reproduced this style and theme for Granby,
Connecticut, in 1868, as well as a grander version for the Antietam Battlefield
in Maryland, which was dedicated in 1869.[35]

The Deerfield memorial was dedicated on September 4, 1867, with a ceremony that included the singing of an ode (to the tune of "Auld Lang Syne")
written by local resident Maria B. W. Barnes. One stanza went: "Old Deerfield's

sons are scattered wide / Throughout our favored land / God grant they all may meet above / An undivided band."

Although soldiers from other places might have been credited to a town such as Deerfield when they mustered into service, only native sons or full residents of towns tended to be acknowledged locally as veterans and to have their names appear on monuments. Of the forty-two names engraved on Soldier's Monument in Deerfield, thirty-four were residents listed in the 1860 census.[36] Most of the names belonged to familiar Deerfield families. Two relative newcomers were John Zimmerman, a resident of Deerfield who had emigrated from Germany, and Michael Glassett, a Cheapside resident born in Ireland. Edward J. Hosmer was from Buffalo, New York, but as the brother of the Reverend James Hosmer, minister of the First Church of Deerfield, he had volunteered in Deerfield along with his brother. It is not hard to surmise that when George Sheldon referred to "those who died *for* Deerfield," he was also referring to men of Deerfield.

As the names on the Deerfield monument suggest, to townspeople in the Connecticut Valley, the value of a life lost in combat during the Civil War was measured in part by the person's birthplace and place of residence. This emphasis on place has probably been true of all wars and most local monuments. The deaths of one's own sons and daughters makes distant wars intimate, and honoring them restores a feeling of community. During the Civil War, however, people seem to have felt a stronger sense that sons were fighting and dying for the town as much as for the union or the nation. Because the bodies of so few soldiers were returned to their communities, individual burials and their accompanying rituals were impossible for many. Thus, the few funerals that were held no doubt enhanced a community-wide response of shared identity and commemoration.[37] Everyone knew someone who had fallen.

After the national Memorial Day was established in May 1868, Deerfield embraced the annual ritual. After the war Nathaniel Hitchcock, whose only son, James, had died at Andersonville Prison, arrived every year to supervise decoration of the monument.[38] In later years the town's schoolchildren walked to Soldier's Monument to join their parents and other townspeople for the memorial observation. One student recited the Gettysburg Address, and the children then continued to the "Old Burying Ground" to place handpicked bouquets on the graves of Deerfield's ancestors.[39] At the time, townspeople commented on the fact that Rev. Hosmer marched to war with an Irish laborer whose wife did the minister's washing.[40] One can imagine times, during the decades following the war, when family members of those named on Deerfield's memorial also came as individuals to mourn their sons, brothers, husbands, and fathers. The parents of Cyrus and Myron Stowell might have

James Hitchcock, died in Andersonville Prison, 1864. Courtesy of PVMA.

met there the wife or friend of John Zimmerman or Michael Glassett—people of different neighborhoods, classes, and ethnicities, who perhaps found some sense of community in their shared loss and remembrance.

With the advent of the Civil War, Herman Haupt, construction manager for the Hoosac Tunnel, had been diverted to working on railroads for the Union Army. As the war wound down, however, serious work on the tunnel and the rail line that would run through it recommenced. Men returning from the war expanded the labor pool, as did a steady stream of new immigrants, who brought skills in stone and brick masonry, construction, and metal fabrication. Improved technologies for rock drilling and the development of nitroglycerin sped up the work pace but also heightened the risks.

Construction of the Hoosac Tunnel had taken lives before, but on October 17, 1867, a major catastrophe struck. A gas explosion in the hoist house above the central shaft sent equipment and burning timbers down the shaft. All thirteen men at the bottom were killed, by asphyxiation, by injury from falling debris, or by drowning when water filled the shaft. Their names suggest their largely Irish ethnicity: Patrick Connolly, James Bennett, James Fitzgerald, Thomas Mulcare, John Harkness, Thomas Collins and his brother Patrick, Michael Whalen, James Carvenough, John Curran, Thomas Cook, James McCormick, and Joseph Messier (described in the local paper as "a Frenchman").[41] The tunnel was aptly named the "bloody pit."[42] During its construction, 195 men lost their lives. The Hoosac Tunnel finally opened for train traffic in 1875. People and goods could now travel by rail northwesterly up the Deerfield River valley and on to Troy, New York, and beyond.

Construction of the railroads was fraught with hazards, but so was working around the rolling stock. Collisions and derailments endangered workers and passengers alike, but many men lost their lives performing day-to-day tasks involving tons of moving iron. Brakemen jumped from one car to the next, coupling and decoupling; mechanics moved and repaired equipment in the yards in East Deerfield and elsewhere. Such jobs took an all too frequent toll. A jumped track could mean instant death by crushing; an overheated boiler could blow and cause a slow, painful death by scalding.

The railroads posed a threat also to passersby. Rodolphus Sanderson of Whately, for example, died in December 1867 when he failed to hear the train whistle while crossing the tracks along South Deerfield Street with a load of milled grain in his buggy. He was thrown several feet in the air and died about an hour and a half later. His buffalo robe was found on the flag mast of the engine, a bag of meal on the cow-catcher.[43]

Probably the most bizarre set of events to occur locally was captured in a letter by Agnes Higginson Fuller to her husband, Stephen, in August 1862.

> Our [railroad] cars yesterday began with cutting off a man's leg at Bernardston, kept on to our station killing instantly poor old Aunt Dolly Smith coming out of the grave yard. On to S. Deerfield where they killed a child, & report this morn'g says another at North'n. Was there ever such a career in an hour or little more?
>
> Miss Smith, you know is entirely deaf—and could not have looked round at all. It was a great shock to her friends in the village.[44]

One of the worst railroad accidents for workers and passengers took place in April 1886. Express train number 35 of the Fitchburg Railroad had exited the Hoosac Tunnel heading east toward its next stop, Greenfield. At Bardwell's Ferry it was traversing a steep slope heading into West Deerfield when the track gave way, sending the engine off the track and the cars about two hundred feet down an embankment to the edge of the Deerfield River. There the cars caught fire from their stoves. Of the thirty-seven passengers and eleven railroad workers on board, eleven people died in the wreck or from their injuries and thirty-six were "wounded." Only one person escaped injury. The cause was determined to have been an undermined track bed weakened by recent heavy rains.[45]

The local newspapers were filled with articles about the accident for several days, and residents of Franklin County were absorbed in the story. On April 11, the Reverend P. V. Finch of St. James's Church in Greenfield devoted his sermon to the tragedy, melodramatically describing how the accident happened "just where the turbulent rapids of the tortuous Deerfield cease their roar, and begin to flow with gentle murmur into the expanding bosom of Stillwater, ... scene of a catastrophe that sent a thrill of horror though our entire community."[46]

Two of the eleven who died were railroad employees—the engineer, Herbert P. Littlejohn, age thirty-two, whose death resulted from severe burns and scalding from steam, and his brakeman, Spencer Waltham. Nine of the wounded were also workers, including another brakeman, the conductor, the fireman,

Bardwell's Ferry train accident, April 1866. Courtesy of Historical Society of Greenfield.

the baggage master, and the "colored" porter, Aaron Lewis. The passengers had included only three women; nearly all the others were men traveling on business. Herbert Littlejohn's brother and sister-in-law were on the train; they survived but their two young children did not. Among those dispatched in a special train as a rescue team were Drs. Deane, Small, and Severence. They pronounced the deaths, treated the injured, and arranged for those who could be moved to be taken to nearby homes or removed to Greenfield.[47]

The railroad commissioners found that the Fitchburg Railroad Company was not negligent in its operation or its equipment. The railroad right of way was owned and maintained by the state, with which liability resided. Establishment of negligence and liability became important as the damages and injuries mounted. Some estimates of the costs for equipment repair and replacement, lost property, and damages to those killed and injured ran as high as $250,000—at least $5 million in today's dollars. At a time when accident and life insurance were still in their formative years, paying for funerals and settling claims involved a variety of cobbled solutions. Workers who were members of the Brotherhood of Railroad Trainmen could expect some assistance and compensation for funeral costs and even lost work. Compensation to the permanently disabled or to widows and orphans of passengers and crew was less straightforward, a topic I return to later.

The increasing mileage of railroad tracks accelerated the forces of industrialization after the Civil War throughout the Connecticut River valley. The cutlery industry already had some history in Franklin County, where two major cutlery manufacturers, the John Russell Company of Cheapside, Deerfield, and the Lamson and Goodnow Company of Shelburne Falls, dated to the 1840s. By the end of the Civil War, the two companies together were producing half of the nation's cutlery. As the major postwar industry in the four Franklin County towns, cutlery employed more men than any other. In addition, many small shops specializing in the machining of tools, bolts, and other metal goods began to spring up in Greenfield and the surrounding towns.[48] By the late 1860s these enterprises, too, employed significant numbers of men. Pocketbook shops, paper manufacturing, and some textile manufacturing rounded out the major sources of nonfarm jobs and employed many women and children as well.

Each industry had its own occupational hazards, but the cutlery operations were noteworthy. In addition to belt-driven machinery, these factories used powerful trip-hammers, grindstones, and emery wheels. Even their products were potentially life threatening. Cuts were routine, and local newspapers frequently told of losses of fingers and of other serious wounds.

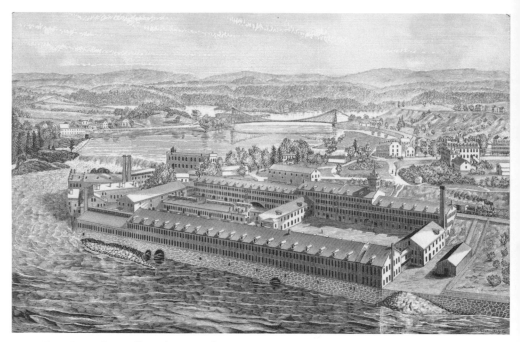

P. F. Goist, "Russell Cutlery-Works, Turner's Falls, Mass." From Everts, *History*, vol. 2. Courtesy of HDL.

Many of the accidents arising in cutlery work temporarily diminished a worker's productivity or even led to permanent disability. But severe cuts and mangled hands were seldom fatal, nor were the common injuries to eyes from flying pieces of metal and grindstone. Occasionally a man got an arm or leg caught in one of the large drive belts and suffered severe injuries.[49] One type of accident that could easily prove fatal, however, and that involved neither inattention nor negligence was the bursting of grindstones, which resulted from weaknesses or defects in the stone itself, flaws that likely were not apparent to the workers. On December 9, 1850, the *Greenfield Gazette and Courier* reported:

> Mr. Cheney Kenney, employed as a grinder in Messrs. Russell's Cutlery establishment in this town, was fatally injured by the bursting of a grind stone at which he was at work about 11 o'clock a.m. on Monday last. The stone was a new one and weighed about a ton. One piece passed up and struck the floor of the second story with such force as to upset a stove standing over where it struck. Another piece was thrown against the heavy stone wall of the building with such force as to bulge it out three or four inches where it struck. Mr. Kenney was struck under the chin by the iron of the housing over the stone with such force as to badly fracture both of his jaws and knock out most of his teeth. He lingered in an unconscious state until Friday, when he died.

This accident took place at the Russell Company's original location, on the Green River in Cheapside. Two fires, one in 1865 and another the following year, destroyed portions of the factory, and the directors looked at the possibility of rebuilding elsewhere. Alvah Crocker and B. N. Farren, who had teamed up with some other investors to finance the Hoosac Tunnel project were about to rebuild an old canal in the town of Montague and establish the new, planned industrial village of Turners Falls. The falls and the canal would generate considerable power for a series of factories. Crocker and his associates persuaded the Russell Company to purchase the first lot, move to Turners Falls, and build a much larger works along the canal.

Many Irish men who had come to the area to work on the railroad were also involved in reconstructing the canal, and many more recent immigrants were recruited for canal and factory construction as well. Like railroad work, canal building posed risks. Eugene Sullivan, for example, died in a "melancholy accident" in February 1869. He tripped and stumbled while trying to escape from a blasting site and was crushed to death by the falling, frozen chunks of earth, leaving a wife and two children in Ireland.[50]

On completion, the new Russell works was a state-of-the-art factory complex. Covering two hundred thousand square feet, it was designed to accommodate as many as twelve hundred workers, although the annual work force averaged

Men working in polishing shop, Russell Cutlery, c. 1890. Courtesy of Historical Society of Greenfield.

much less. Its equipment was of the latest design and brought mass-production techniques in cutlery manufacture to the highest level. A ventilation system was installed, and firewalls were constructed to prevent the spread of fire.[51] But these measures did not necessarily reduce the risk of accidents. Bursting stones remained an ongoing threat. As late as 1920, Jacob Stotz was killed by a bursting grindstone he was testing in the factory at Turners Falls.[52]

Even with the ventilation system, a longer-term risk to cutlery workers was the large quantity of silica, dust, and other particulate matter in the work areas. "Cutler's lung" afflicted many long-time employees and eventually took lives. Workers who also had tuberculosis were greatly affected; the polluted air hastened the progression of their symptoms and even their deaths.

State officials, too, were beginning to take notice of these industrial dangers, and life insurance companies were becoming attuned to the patterns of risk in a variety of occupations.

Premature and unexpected losses of productive men and reproductive women in the nineteenth century were accompanied by economic and emotional costs not readily comparable to those associated with losses of children. In the second half of the nineteenth century, many young women were employed in the Connecticut Valley, and their wages were important, sometimes essential, supplements to the household economy.[53] Women who died in childbirth—primarily homemakers and caregivers—were economically vital to the household as well, although men were most often the primary sources of income for their families.

I am drawn back to the case of Mary Stebbins and her husband, John Henry, a descendant of one of Deerfield's most prominent families. John and Mary were married in 1858 when Mary was twenty-two. That same year, Henry, John's father, built a large, Italianate house for them on the south portion of the lot he owned on the main street.[54] Thus, the couple began their marriage in a fine new home in a prosperous part of town. John Stebbins is listed as a farmer by occupation in the 1860 census.

As described, on September 6, 1868, the couple's third child, "Henry W.," died of cholera infantum, at age three months, twenty-three days.[55] Then, in 1870, Mary and her infant died in childbirth and a few weeks later her father-in-law died. With the loss of his wife, father, and two children, things seem to have unraveled for John Stebbins. He mortgaged his house and four and one-half acres in 1873 and was declared bankrupt in 1875. These were economically hard times in New England, but perhaps more was at work here. A young family might well rebound from the loss of one infant child—indeed, losing one child might even be expected—but the loss of two infants and a wife must

John H. Stebbins's Italianate house on the Deerfield street, photographed by the Allen Sisters, c. 1900. Courtesy of PVMA.

have been too much. Four years after Mary's death, John Henry remarried, and in 1892 his second wife, Jane Amelia Wells, purchased the property, but it was necessary for her to take in boarders to support the family.[56] The loss of a mother and caregiver, or of a breadwinner, could easily set off a cascade of emotional and economic hardships from which a family could not recover.

Industrialization and commercialization of the more agrarian parts of New England, along with an increase in immigration, upset the web of traditional links that provided care for the sick, managed funerals, and supported widows. The Irish or German wage worker could not depend on the generosity of his employer, of shopkeepers, or of the doctor in the event of a death or disabling accident. His social connections consisted mainly of his fellow workers, his neighbors, and other, equally poor families of the same ethnic background. Even many Yankee families, as they became more mobile and sought jobs in the nonfarm economy, became less secure. Farmers, too, increasingly dependent on distant markets, found their economic security less predictable. The loss of a productive son to war, the death of a wife in childbirth or of a husband by accident—all could spell economic ruin.

Several companies offered life insurance in the early nineteenth century in New England and the rest of the United States, though few policies were written. After the Civil War, life insurance became a more common option as perceived risk increased and became commoditized. The sacred life of a loved one was becoming clearly understood in terms of economic value as well.[57] The thirteen men who died in the Hoosac Tunnel accident, mostly in their twenties and early thirties, left at least three wives and ten children among them.[58] It is doubtful that any of them had insurance. In contrast, Rodolphus Sanderson, who fatally attempted to cross the tracks with his grain in South Deerfield, had recently purchased two thousand dollars' worth of life insurance.

For men working on the railroads and in the manufacturing shops, fraternal organizations and unions offered burial insurance and support of widows and orphans. As the German population in Franklin County increased during the 1870s, German immigrants established their own church and fraternal and death benefit organizations.[59] In addition to those organized by German immigrants, fraternal organizations offering sickness or accident support also included the Independent Order of Odd Fellows, the Knights of Pythias, the Improved Order of Red Men, the Loyal Order of Moose, the Fraternal Order of Eagles, and the Ancient Order of Foresters.[60] The Brotherhood of Railroad Trainmen and eventually other workers' unions also assumed some role. Life insurance companies such as the John Hancock Company and the Prudential Insurance Company flourished in the last quarter of the nineteenth century.[61] Rather than burial insurance and short-term assistance to loved ones, the life insurance companies promoted longer-term benefits to survivors. These efforts at protecting families from the loss of wage earners signify the greater economic value being attached to the lives of productive, working-age individuals.

In the late nineteenth century, just as a minister might have reminded his congregation to "lay a strong foundation" of spiritual preparedness in case they were "hurried into eternity"—as Rev. Finch did after the Bardwell's Ferry train accident—so the life insurance agent was there to remind men of their duty to their families. Equipped with brochures and pamphlets, the agent counseled husbands and fathers that it would be selfish indeed to "leave helpless widows and destitute children to face alone the miseries of starvation." The good husband and father confessed his sins, was ready for the appointed hour, and had invested in the security of his wife and children. The minister might well have agreed with the agent that it was the duty of a Christian man to make proper provision for his family.[62]

In 1900, Deerfield, Franklin County, and the Connecticut Valley looked and felt very different from the way they had in the 1840s. The pace of life had picked up, daily life was becoming more secular, and agrarian rhythms were increasingly giving way to factory and marketplace. In matters of health, the state was becoming increasingly involved. The same year in which Massachusetts created its Board of Health—1869—it also created a Bureau of Statistics and Labor to track wages and monitor working conditions. The Massachusetts Industrial Commission published a report on factory conditions in 1872, and in 1877 Massachusetts passed the nation's first factory inspection law, requiring the guarding of belts, shafts, and gears, protection on elevators, and adequate fire exits. By the late 1880s an act of the legislature had authorized expanded powers for factory inspectors in reviewing workplace conditions.[63]

The following letter to the editor of the *Greenfield Gazette and Courier* published on March 1, 1880, suggests the kind of grassroots pressure put on legislatures to mandate safety: "Protect the Workmen. Mr. Editor: The sad event chronicled in your last issue of the death of Jesse Whitmore, killed in a paper mill at Turners Falls has raised the question in many minds, 'Why [is] not the ... machinery so protected as to render such an accident impossible?' ... Every man's life is too valuable to be put in jeopardy to save one minute of time or a few dollars in money. ... They are entitled to protection."

People attending a lecture presented to the D. S. Simonds Lodge of the Brotherhood of Railroad Trainmen in 1917 learned that a new safety coupler had brought the number of railroad accidents due to coupling cars down from 44 percent of the total in 1893 to just 6 percent by 1916. The speaker, J. P. McArdle, was the federal railroad inspector for the Interstate Commerce Commission.[64] Increasingly the statist, the insurance agent, and the regulator were overseeing the health and safety of the valley's workers.

As the funeral business and the practice of embalming grew after the Civil War, the conduct of funerals began to change. Funerals were still most frequently held at home in the parlor, but they began increasingly to include a stop at the church for a more public viewing. The intimate setting, with the recently deceased laid out in a pine box, surrounded by a small number of family and friends, was giving way to commemoration in a more public sphere. An undertaker might well be employed to provide a casket and services. A few furniture stores in Franklin County, such as J. L. Lyons in Greenfield, according to their advertisements, provided more ornate caskets than the earlier pine coffins and undertaking services. The body might be displayed in a drawing room for a viewing by family and friends, and then in front of the chancel in the church during the service. The undertaker's services expanded to include carriage rental, garments, furnishings, and more. The Knights of Pythias or the Brotherhood of Railroad Trainmen might share a role with the minister

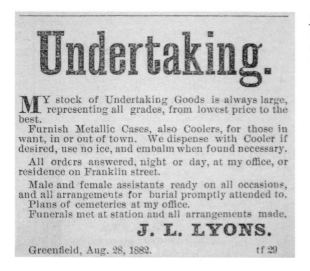

J. L. Lyons, Undertakers, advertisement in *Greenfield Gazette and Courier*, October 30, 1882.

or priest at the graveside. At the same time, mourning clothing and overly sentimental rituals were giving way to "respectful" clothing, secular practices, and a shorter period of formal mourning.

By the end of the nineteenth century, the fathers and mothers of the productive men and reproductive women met in this chapter had outlived some of their own children and were entering advanced stages of their lives. In the next chapter I examine the health issues of this generation and practices surrounding their deaths.

7

SURVIVING THE ODDS
The "Privilege" of Old Age

*Nothing is more remarkable or more interesting than the present status
of medical sciences. I think pure air & water & plenty of them, with
simple & unadulterated food seem to be the requisites for a long life.*

—C. Alice Baker, age seventy-three, to her cousin Winthrop Arms (1906)

AT THE CLOSE OF THE NINETEENTH CENTURY, Dr. Samuel Abbott, secretary
to the Massachusetts State Board of Health, took a keen interest in the long
series of vital statistics available to him through the Registry of Vital Records
and Statistics. In a report published in 1897, he noted that whereas in 1855
approximately 6.2 percent of the people alive in Massachusetts were age sixty
or older, by 1895 the figure had risen to 8.2 percent. Five years later, in 1900,
only 3.6 percent of the state's population was over the age of sixty, the result
of high immigration rates of younger individuals. In rural Franklin County,
however, 12.5 percent of residents fell into this older age group. Abbott also
published tables showing a larger proportion of females in the population
overall between 1855 and 1895, and a higher death rate for males than for
females in each decade between 1855 and 1895. Patterns were emerging that
would continue as the new century dawned. Proportionally, more people
were reaching old age, and the number of women who did so exceeded that
of men.[1]

In 1850, life expectancy at birth for the white population of Massachusetts,
male and female, was about forty years. By 1900, it had increased to about
forty-eight years for men and fifty-one for women. Contributing significantly to
these low figures were relatively high rates of infant mortality, which lowered
the arithmetic average age at death. Males who survived to age ten could have
expected to live on average an additional fifty-one years, to the age of about
sixty, females to sixty-two.[2]

Among people who survived to at least the age of sixty, the more interesting segment is the very long-lived. At a time when those who survived even
beyond fifty were a relatively small percentage of the total population, the

long-lived exceptions became persons of note. In this chapter I look at illness and death among the elderly and at the ways in which they survived and dealt with events of illness, death, and loss during their long lifetimes.

Dysentery and consumption were significant killers of the elderly throughout the nineteenth and early twentieth centuries. Diminished immune systems and constitutions weakened by age made older people vulnerable to such infections as long as they were prevalent. Pneumonia and other secondary infections took their toll as well. Then as now, however, the diseases typically associated with old age were those referred to as chronic and degenerative. They included heart disease, strokes, liver and kidney disease, pulmonary failure, and all classes of cancer.

In 1900, virtually no nursing homes existed. There was no commission on aging, no geriatric medicine, and certainly no Medicare. Massachusetts was the first state to create a commission on aging, in 1909.[3] Geriatric medicine dates its origins to the 1930s, and the federal Medicare program was created only in 1965. Because the elderly represented a relatively small proportion of the total population in Massachusetts and the rest of the United States in 1900, specialization in diseases of the elderly was rare, though not entirely unknown.[4] Public health officials at the time were preoccupied, as they had been in the last years of the previous century, with finding associations between younger people and the ubiquitous infectious diseases that caused their illnesses and deaths. Preventing infant and childhood mortality seemed, legitimately, more urgent than preventing the deaths of old people.[5] Simple numbers were partly responsible for this preoccupation. Whereas each year in Massachusetts thousands of children died of infectious diseases, the numbers for those over sixty were in the hundreds.

Still, the frequent incidence of heart disease and cancer in the elderly did not escape the notice of public health officials.[6] Moreover, by the twentieth century, experts recognized that profiles of death among older people could be quite different from those among younger people. Death among the elderly was typically preceded by a fairly long period of debilitating conditions or symptoms, and many elderly people lived with several conditions at once. Someone might have arthritis, tuberculosis, and a heart condition, for example, which might act independently or in concert to hasten death. Attending physicians often listed both primary and secondary causes on death certificates in Massachusetts.[7] But because of the limited diagnostic capabilities of the time, physicians were sometimes unable to provide a specific cause of death, particularly for the elderly, and so they simply attributed deaths to "old age."

Vital statistics for Massachusetts in 1910 show that heart disease, stroke, pneumonia, and cancer were the four major killers of people sixty years old and older. Nephritis (kidney failure, then known as Bright's disease), pulmonary tuberculosis, diarrhea, and "old age" were the next four.[8] For Deerfield between 1900 and 1910, the list is similar, but old age replaces cancer in the top four (see Appendix D).[9] Today, the use of this designation as a cause of death is much rarer than it was a century ago, although the International Classification of Diseases used by the National Center for Health Statistics still lists "old age" under "797—Senility without mention of psychosis."[10]

Life for many elderly people in turn-of-the-century Massachusetts featured slowly declining health, but old age also held positive status simply for one's having lived a long life well.[11] In addition, the elderly, then as now, had considerably more agency than the young in reflecting on their lives, writing their last wills and testaments, marking losses of others, and planning their funerals. A long life had its privileges and its costs. A look at a few examples of long-lived men and women in and around Deerfield yields insights into their life experiences as well as the events surrounding their deaths. For many of these people, as for many of their counterparts today, death became an increasing preoccupation as they advanced in years, but that preoccupation was shaped by specific contexts and historical circumstances.[12]

George Sheldon was one among several octogenarians in Deerfield in 1900. In middle age Sheldon had become increasingly concerned with the way industrialization, urbanization, and immigration were replacing the "old ways" and changing the face of his and neighboring communities.[13] The Civil War and its aftermath made Sheldon and other New Englanders nostalgic for what they perceived as a quieter, more ordered, if not more peaceful time in the past. Rapid social change and a devastating war seem to have made Sheldon's generation feel older and more reflective than their ages at the time might imply. I believe that this constellation of historical events shaped Sheldon and many others of his cohort in old age.

George Sheldon was born in 1818. As an adult he suffered the deaths of his son Frankie in 1859, his father in 1860, his close friend Edward Hitchcock in 1864, and his mother in 1865.[14] On the day of his mother's death, December 1, Sheldon wrote in his diary: "Rainy. At $\frac{1}{2}$ past one today mother passed on to her final rest. Her end was peaceful. Yesterday she fell asleep as an infant in its mother's arms. 'The Lord gives a good many things twice over, but he don't give ye a Mother but once. You'll never see sich another woman Mas'r George if ye lived to a hundred years old' (Uncle Tom)."[15]

Exceeding all expectations of the times, George Sheldon lived to the age of ninety-eight. It is reasonable to assume that in his lifetime he suffered at least one serious bout of infant diarrhea; virtually all infants did. Most likely he survived a childhood fever as well. He apparently avoided tuberculosis, but at the age of twenty-one he was seriously injured in a farm accident, a fall while

Allen Sisters, *Cronies* (George Sheldon and Mark Allen), 1898. Courtesy of PVMA.

harvesting chestnuts. He was said to have suffered sunstroke in 1853, and in 1857 an accident involving a train on which he was a passenger left him badly injured and requiring a period of convalescence.[16]

In his later years Sheldon complained of any number of aches, pains, and ailments, including that "great torment of civilized life" for the middle and upper classes, dyspepsia.[17] He had chronic back trouble. Yet by dint of economic security, good judgment, comparatively healthy living, and, most of all, chance, Sheldon survived for nearly a century, outliving a great many of his friends and family members. As a formula for a long life, he claimed "obedience to three simple rules: (1) always have coffee and a doughnut for breakfast; (2) never worry about the weather; and (3) never open any windows, summer or winter."[18]

On November 30, 1899, George Sheldon celebrated his eighty-first birthday. A historically minded person such as he must have looked back and reflected on his life and the lives of others. If we follow his gaze into the past, we can perhaps add to the detached orderliness of demographic events a notion of how someone like Sheldon actually lived those events.[19]

George Sheldon was twenty-three and still single in 1842 when the dysentery epidemic hit the infants and toddlers of Deerfield. His friend and cousin Dr. Stephen West Williams treated its victims. Among those who died was Julia Lucretia Sheldon, daughter of George's first cousin David Sheldon Jr. and his wife, Julia. In 1859, George's son Frankie died in the scarlet fever epidemic. On his mother's side George was related to the family of two-year-old Jesse Stebbins, who died just a day earlier. Toward the end of that epidemic, in April 1859, as mentioned earlier, David and Julia Sheldon lost their second daughter.[20] Three years later, when George was forty-three, he assisted his close friend Samuel Willard during his daughter Hattie's losing struggle with diphtheria.

In 1864, George comforted his good friend Nathaniel Hitchcock over the loss of his son, James, in the Civil War. He later worked with Hitchcock on the Deerfield Soldiers' Monument and in co-founding the Pocumtuck Valley Memorial Association in 1870, the year Mary Stebbins, wife of John Henry Stebbins, and their stillborn child died. John and Mary lived just two doors down from the Sheldons, and John Henry was George's second cousin once removed. George's wife, Susan, died in October 1881, when he was sixty-three and she sixty-one.[21]

These were the sorts of networks of lives lost over the years, whether to disease, accident, or war, that George Sheldon and other older citizens of rural New England— including recent immigrants with memories of lives lost in their native countries—could conjure up when they reviewed their long lives. The inevitability of witnessing the passing of close family members, distant relatives, friends, and contemporaries, with its attendant emotional cost, is an important aspect of surviving to old age. For the elderly, death was, and is, a part of everyday life. In some ways nothing has changed in this regard, but in other ways much is now different. Certainly death visited more frequently and people knew it more familiarly in turn-of-the-century New England, and it took proportionally more children. Among working- and middle-class New Englanders, including recent immigrants, the prognosis for a serious disease was generally poorer, therapies were more limited, and the handling and burial of bodies were more direct and immediate. A few examples of the way people wrote about illness and death at the time illustrate these generalizations.

Franklin Hubbard Williams was a successful farmer in Sunderland, Massachusetts, just south of Montague and across the river from South Deerfield. He began a diary in 1852, when he was eighteen, and maintained it with some regularity until his death in 1891. Into his early twenties he wrote most often about his farmwork: "July 10—Got all the hay at Deerfield & hoed 1 and 1/4 acres of beans. Mike and William finished up the job. I plowed out corn & potatoes. It is dry. Hope it will rain." He also frequently mentioned meeting with friends and the young women in whom he was interested: "July 29—Miss Martindale, Abbie Crowell & myself at 5 o'clock started for So. Hadley. Arrived at 8 1/2. Address by Dr. Stearns, Amherst. Had a pleasant day. Like Miss Martindale. Have asked to correspond with her. Has accepted. Got home 8 PM."[22]

In 1867, Williams married Jane Sanderson. As the years passed, he continued to describe his routine of farm chores but turned increasingly from friends and social life to topics of loss. In 1884: "Mike died April 2. took body to Northampton and buried it. Snowed hard all day. Could but just get home. I went with the hearse. About six teams went down." In 1888: "Aug. 22—Our dear Arthur went to bed sick. Never went out again . . . was dreadful sick with Typhoid fever." Sept. 8: "at 5 A.M. Arthur died. It seems we could not have it so." In 1890: "Mrs. Dea. Dickinson was buried in our yard. Took charge of the funeral. Was in the Church." 1891: "Amelia died at Henrys old place, has run right down. Was not confined to bed a week. Had Consumption we think."[23] Williams's engagement with the deceased was direct, with little of the involvement of hospitals, funeral homes, and other institutional structures that we would expect today. On July 6, 1891, Williams died from a fall off scaffolding while repairing his barn.

Agnes Higginson Fuller was in her early sixties during the first decade of the twentieth century. Her diary illustrates both her preoccupation with illness and death and the frequency with which her older friends fell ill or died. For example, between February 1908 and December 1910, at least twenty entries concern serious illness or death. "Ellen Emerson died today after a long illness" (January 14, 1909). "Julian Yale died of apoplexy—at last buried in Shelburne

Falls" (March 5, 1909). "Spencer has nervous dyspepsia—he is in a bad way and needs advice and care" (March 23, 1909). "Miss Alice Baker is lying at death's door from a stroke in Boston" (May 18, 1909). "Miss Baker died in Boston. Church bell at Deerfield was tolled" (May 22, 1909). "Miss Taussig died at Saranac Lake of TB" (April 15, 1910) "Mary Baker Eddy head of Christian Science Church died age 89 of pneumonia" (December 5, 1910).[24]

Like diaries, letters written by middle-aged and older persons in nineteenth- and early twentieth-century New England—at least by those of the literate middle and upper classes—frequently dwell on issues of health. Writers recount their own health problems, report on who is sick, and notify friends and family of recent deaths. A letter from Elisha Wells to the Reverend James Hosmer during the Civil War reports on the deaths of Hattie Willard and other residents in Deerfield.

> Everything moves along in the customary channels. No great changes have taken place as to worldly affairs. Several deaths have occurred in our village since you left. Henry Wells was the last he died Tuesday of this week, and it is perhaps well that he is gone those of that class seldom live to old age, and it is best on the whole that they should not, perhaps.[25] Hattie Willard died week before last. That is a hard strike for her parents, especially her Father, as she had arrived at such an age that she was of great service to him. Orrin Hawks has been very sick with lung fever. . . . Mr. Charles Williams our Postmaster has been laid up the last month with his yearly attack of rheumatism. . . . I have just heard of another death in our Company. Alonzo T. Dodge. He was a stout, hearty looking man.[26]

C. Alice Baker, one of many older women who resided on the main street in Deerfield for all or part of the year, wrote to her cousin Winthrop Arms in 1906, recounting how the mother of one of her students, having been diagnosed with tuberculosis, slept "alone in a room with every window open summer and winter—and makes her children do the same." She also describes her visit to an exhibition in Horticultural Hall on "the prevention and cure of tuberculosis," which included "microscopic exhibits of the terrible disease."[27]

Another aspect of concern with illness—one's own and that of others—was the preparation of wills and instructions about events to take place after one's death. Recall that Samuel Willard, near the time of his daughter Hattie's death from diphtheria, willed his library to George Sheldon. Some people made simple provision for funeral expenses or for the erection of a proper grave monument. Esther Dickinson stipulated in her will of 1875 that her trustees "erect a suitable and becoming Monument to the memory of myself and my husband, and I earnestly request that no ostentatious or extravagantly expensive structure shall mark our final resting place."[28] A few went to considerable lengths to choreograph the details of their last rites. James Freeman Bush, for example, was a wealthy paper manufacturer from Portland, Maine, who had frequent business dealings in Greenfield and Turners Falls. As reported in the *Greenfield Gazette and Courier*, September 27, 1913, he instructed his wife to cremate his body after he died, place his ashes on the table in the main cabin of his luxury yacht *Lydia*, and scuttle the boat in Portland Harbor. His wishes were honored as family members and two of his western Massachusetts friends looked on.[29]

William Stoddard Williams, son of Ephraim and grandson of Deerfield's famous physician of the same name, died in Greenfield in 1911. Some years before his death, he took his funeral into his own hands.[30] His instructions merit a full recounting.

Whenever I die, I wish these requests to be faithfully complied with.

It is my earnest desire to be laid in the old burying ground at the end of Hitchcock lane, on the Old Williams lot, near my honored Great Grandfather Dr. Thomas Williams and Great, Great Grandfather Col. Ephraim Williams. I think there is room at either end of the lot, I should prefer the south side. Yet, as there is a chestnut tree near there, and it would be hard preparing a place there, you can do as it seems best.

I wish to be prepared for the ground by a professional undertaker, not by persons who are not used to the business, neither do I wish my body to be frozen in an artificial manner.

I want the Rector of St. James Parish Greenfield to read the service over me, and if it is pleasant weather the whole service to be at the burying ground, the clergyman meeting the procession at the entrance. The choir of St. James to sing the anthem "Lord let me know my end," and a respectable hymn to be selected by any one who wishes so to do.

Major Henry G. Nims to have charge of the services, and to be consulted on all necessary arrangements—I wish Mr. Fred Clapp Geo. M. Willard, F. G. Fessenden, John S. Aiken, Wm. G. Hack[illegible], Henry F. Nash, Lucius Nims, & Geo. E. Rogers to be bearers. In case of any of the said gentlemen being dead or unable to attend the vacancies to be filled by Henry G. Nims, but no person living in Deerfield to assist, not from any disrespect to my native town or acquaintances, but for reasons best known to myself.

I wish these gentlemen to remain till the grave is filled, and after then return to the house, to be invited into the Library, when there is to be placed a decanter of whisky, one of gin, and one of Medford rum—some cigars, and a plate of crackers and cheese, with the understanding that they remain, and smoke, as if I were with them.

Cephas Smith must be asked to drive the choir to Deerfield, and he must be invited into the house, together with the clergyman and the choir.

I should prefer not to have a hearse used but if it is thought best Mr. Nims can use his usual good sense in the matter, neither do I want any carriages, I do not want any extravagant expense in any of the arrangements, of course, you will see that the minister and choir are at no expense in coming to Deerfield.

Greenfield, Mass.

February 13, 1880 Wm. S. Williams

According to Williams's obituary, the service was held at his house. The Reverend G. E. Schultz officiated, and none of the appointed pallbearers served. The burial took place, however, in the old burying ground on Albany Road, as Williams had wished. The obituary added that Williams "possessed a unique personality."

In the late eighteenth and early nineteenth centuries, women served decidedly and perhaps even predominantly on the treatment side of medical practice, as mothers, midwives, herbalists, and dispensers of home remedies. By the mid-nineteenth century, with the professionalization and masculinization of medicine, they had shifted profoundly to the patient side. Victorian-era women of Britain and America, especially middle-class women, were no longer seen as healers. They were characterized as frail, ruled by the demands and constraints of reproduction, and as having no business being in "business" or in becoming overeducated, overly physically active, or engaged in pursuits of a political nature. As Edward Clarke of the Harvard Medical School and the Massachusetts Medical Society pointed out in his 1873 book *Sex in Education; or, A Fair Chance for the Girls*, too much education for developing girls could produce dire consequences. Indeed, too much use of the brain or too much exercise was said to deflect the limited vital energy from the reproductive organs, causing atrophy, further disease, and nervous exhaustion of already frail bodies.[31] Because the female body was created for conception and reproduction, menstruation was the failure of reproductive ability and thus a sickness that taxed the body and sapped vital energy.[32]

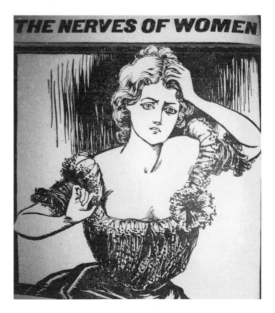

"The Nerves of Women," advertisement in *Greenfield Gazette and Courier*, October 29, 1883.

There was nothing unique in the Franklin District Medical Society's focus on the uterus where matters of women's health were concerned. Physicians regarded the womb as a major source of female sickness, and female functions such as menstruation as inherently pathological. The American Gynecological Society was established in 1876 by specialists who were among a broad range of late nineteenth-century physicians who "knew" that the source of most health problems for women emanated from the womb. The society's president, George J. Engelmann, wrote in 1900: "Many a young life is battered and forever crippled on the breakers of puberty; if it crosses these unharmed and is not dashed to pieces on the rock of childbirth, it may still ground on the ever-recurring shallows of menstruation, and lastly upon the final bar of the menopause where protection is found in the unruffled waters of the harbor beyond reach of sexual storms."[33] Dr. G. Stanley Hall, in his famous book *Adolescence*, published in 1904, updated these arguments.[34] Local newspapers in the early 1900s ran advertisements almost weekly for treatments and patent medicines for "women's complaints."

Male doctors were confident that they knew these things, but many women were less sure. Women did know that the tightly laced corsets fashionable at the time were uncomfortable and could even do harm to their internal organs.[35] They knew that the many layers of heavy clothing they wore constrained their movement and caused aching backs and sore legs. They might have worried that too much work or stimulating intellectual activity would compromise their health, but they longed for these challenges just the same. And while the medical community and popular culture were telling women that their bodies were inferior to those of men, something odd was happening as they aged: many of them were outliving their husbands, brothers, and male cousins. Except for the gender disparity in deaths among young adults due to consumption, women were surviving at a higher rate than men at every stage in the life course. If they truly were more fragile, the condition was hardly fatal.

It has been estimated that in 1900 in Massachusetts and throughout the United States, women enjoyed approximately a three-year advantage over men in life expectancy at birth. By 1950 that advantage had increased to almost seven years. Consequently, proportionally more women than men survived to age sixty-five in 1900 and thereafter.[36] Even in the early 1900s, old age was increasingly becoming marked as female. The headline to an article published July 23, 1898, in the *Greenfield Gazette and Courier* put it simply, "Men Die Faster than Women." By virtue of longevity, older women played a significant demographic and social role in rural New England towns such as Deerfield and Greenfield.

Allen Sisters, *A Link with the Past* (the Stebbins sisters), c. 1895. Courtesy of PVMA.

Crowning examples of New England's hardy women were the Stebbins sisters, five of whom lived into their eighties or nineties. They were the daughters of Dennis and Lois Stebbins of the main street in Deerfield, who had eleven children between 1802 and 1821. Two died, but the others survived well into adulthood, and the daughters were destined for long lives. Leonora (1807–1898) reached nearly ninety-one, Maria (1809–1890), eighty-one, Louisa (1811–1900), ninety, Lucy (1815–1904), eighty-nine, and Mary (1819–1903), eighty-two. Mary, Maria, and Leonora married; Louisa and Lucy did not. In 1847 Louisa, Lucy, and Mary purchased the old family home, where Louisa and Lucy spent the rest of their lives, joined by Leonora some years after the death of her husband in 1851.[37]

In 1894, when Mary Stebbins Allen became the third sister widowed, she moved with her two daughters to the Allen family house, just two doors down from the Stebbins house. Four of the five sisters were now living together or close by. They were also becoming increasingly dependent and in need of care.[38] Mary's daughters, Frances and Mary Allen, both in their forties, had never married, and it fell to them to take responsibility for their aging mother and aunts. The two had taught in the local schools but then turned to photography after severe hearing losses limited their ability to teach. By the 1890s they were

recognized photographers with growing reputations.[39] In letters Mary Allen
sent to Frances Benjamin Johnston, a mentor and prominent photographer,
she mentioned more than once her mother's and aunts' growing infirmities,
"feebleness," and need for care, with which she and her sister struggled.[40]
Such accounts remind us of the great responsibilities shouldered by younger
women in the care of sick and elderly relatives.

In some rural districts of the Commonwealth of Massachusetts, elderly
widows and single women formed a defining demographic cohort, residing
in the larger, stately homes that had once housed youthful, energetic couples
with large numbers of children. The family home in which Lucy, Louisa, and
Leonora Stebbins lived in the 1890s was one of these. As the nineteenth century
drew to a close, many other homes along the main street in Deerfield could
claim a similar history. Besides the aging group of women who were native to
the village, there were older widows and single women from elsewhere who
found the town a quiet and appealing place to spend their remaining years,
especially their summers. Deerfield had already established itself as an attractive
rural destination set apart from the hectic world of industry and commerce
during the Gilded Age. Some of the newer residents could trace their ancestry
to Deerfield families and, as children, had paid visits to relatives in town. Others came from other towns in the valley or from the Boston area.[41]

In 1884, Catherine Yale, the widow of Linus Yale, founder of the Yale Lock
Company, bought the old Samuel Willard house as a summer residence for
herself and as a year-round residence for her daughter Madeline Yale Wynne
(1847–1918). They were soon followed to the town by C. Alice Baker (1833–1909),
who in 1890 purchased the Frary house. A descendant of the Deerfield Catlins,
Baker had spent many summers there and took a keen interest in colonial
history, particularly as it related to the village. Julia Whiting (1843–1916), the
daughter of a Holyoke industrialist, purchased the Russell house, across and
down the street from the Yales, and lived there with her sister Margaret.[42]

As these and other women joined the Stebbins sisters, the Allens, and those
who had long resided in the village, the effects were profound. It has been
estimated that by 1904, women controlled more than 40 percent of the real
estate and personal wealth along the main street.[43] Nor did this older cadre
of women consist of the frail and wilting flowers alleged by doctors of the
time. After Alice Baker and her female companions restored the Frary house,
including its ballroom, it became a center for parties, meetings on colonial
revival, and readings and intellectual encounters. These women evinced no
pining for male companionship but instead showed considerable interest in
women's rights and independence. Catherine Yale, speaking on the absence
of her right to vote in local elections , proclaimed: "A woman is taxed without
power to cast a vote as to how her money shall be applied, paying her money

as a respectable citizen then standing aside with criminals, lunatics and idiots at the ballot box to see every man however mean, ignorant, or corrupt, exercise his male prerogative of ownership."[44]

C. Alice Baker had strong words for Dr. Clarke's claims that women's health would be compromised by the "study of geography and arithmetic, of Latin, Greek, and chemistry." She said, "This physiological scare is the most insidious form under which the opposition to the higher education of woman has yet appeared" and challenged Clarke's assertions for having no basis in supported facts.[45] Women who survived their husbands or other male relatives found their places along the main street, and their voices as well.

Yet as this generation of older women began dying, their deaths were mostly attributable to the same causes as those of men, which continued to be listed in the vital statistics records as "old age," "dropsy," heart disease, cancer, apoplexy, lung congestion, and a few other conditions. Kidney failure was increasingly referred to as Bright's disease. The term *dropsy*, which historically referred to renal disease, congestive heart failure, or some other cause of fluid retention, was slowly giving way to more precise terms by the early 1900s. *Apoplexy* was gradually being replaced by the more precise reference to cerebral hemorrhage, or stroke. Nevertheless, as Abbott noted in his summary of vital statistics for Massachusetts, vagueness or imprecision in listed causes and even failure to cite a cause persisted as significant problems.[46] Louisa Stebbins died of a probable stroke, and Lucy Stebbins of pneumonia, but Mary Stebbins Allen and Leonora Stebbins Russell were recorded as having died simply of "old age."[47]

Like members of other age groups, the older citizens of Franklin County probably fared neither better nor worse than their counterparts elsewhere in the country in the treatment of diseases common to them. Aside from the hysterectomies, ovariectomies, and other surgeries advised for some menopausal and postmenopausal women, as well as doctors' tendency to prescribe prolonged bed rest more often for women, most treatments were the same for men and women. Even into the early 1900s, doctors still sometimes prescribed the age-old emetics and purgatives, but increasingly they were recognizing the inefficacy of these prescriptions and the limits of their own abilities.

Popular medical treatises now recommended lifestyle changes as treatments for Bright's disease and heart disease. "Avoid hurry, straining, . . . worry, alcohol, tobacco, and meat, and live a moderate life," one doctor cautioned in reference to symptoms of heart disease. For Bright's disease he advised that "rest in bed is imperative," coupled with a "light and stimulating" diet.[48] In 1914, another doctor advised that chronic Bright's disease could be fatal, especially in the presence of "unhygienic imprudences," but that living "a quiet life"

C. Alice Baker, photographed by Emma L. Coleman, 1894. Courtesy of PVMA.

with tepid baths and "bowels kept regular" could help forestall one's fate.[49] Breast cancer and other cancers producing obvious tumors were being treated surgically by physicians in the late 1800s and early 1900s, and those surgeries included radical mastectomies.[50] Medical texts cautioned that the prognosis for cancer patients was poor.

A modestly expanding older population during the late nineteenth century provided a target for doctors' specialization. The women and men of Deerfield and Greenfield could now avail themselves of advice and treatment by "experts." One such person, by his own description, was Dr. R. C. Flower, "the famous Boston specialist." On March 31, 1893, Flower appeared at the Mansion House hotel in Greenfield during one of his New England tours. "Dr. Flower has attained such eminence in his profession in the treatment of chronic diseases," the *Greenfield Gazette and Courier* announced, that he is regarded as the highest authority in his specialties [which] are cancer, consumption, tumors, paralysis, nerve and heart troubles." The newspaper copy, no doubt provided by Flower, touted his lecture by reporting that the "terrible chronic diseases when given up as incurable by ordinary practice are by his methods

The Mansion House, c. 1879, the location of Dr. Fowler's presentation and the Franklin District Medical Society's quarterly meetings. From *The Recorder,* successor to the *Greenfield Gazette and Courier.* File photograph.

successfully treated and cured."[51] It seems unlikely that Flower's audience in fact gained much insight into its afflictions, for as John Warner and others have noted, few effective therapies yet existed for these and most other diseases in the last decades of the nineteenth century.[52]

Medicine was changing, however. One positive trend was the increasing awareness by physicians in medical schools and in practice that value could be gained from experimental medicine. Recall that until the mid-nineteenth century, most doctors had steadfastly followed the traditions of an even earlier time, adhering to the belief that sickness was the result of imbalances in the four humors. In the later part of the century, as bacteria were identified and the germ theory of disease took shape, physicians increasingly recognized that observation, experimentation, and scientific procedures held promise for unraveling the mystery of disease. Regular doctors no longer regarded empiricism as the illegitimate practice of quacks but increasingly embraced the approach themselves. With the advent of scientific medicine and of specializations within medical schools, the country doctor was starting to be complemented by specialists, both legitimate and illegitimate. R. C. Flower's method of advertising and attracting patients through public lectures likely placed him in the latter category.

Another important progressive trend lay in improvements in surgical intervention, resulting partly from the discovery of anesthetics. Anesthesia and antiseptic practices meant that doctors could more easily explore the bodies of the living, remove diseased organs, and repair or remove damaged tissue. The first demonstration of the use of general anesthesia in the United States was performed at Massachusetts General Hospital in Boston in October 1846. James Deane, a practicing physician in Greenfield, reported on his own use of ether during the summer of 1847, revealing how quickly the procedure disseminated among attentive physicians.[53] Surgery became increasingly effective as a therapy for trauma and repair during the late nineteenth and early twentieth centuries. It also affected the way the human body was imagined.

The human body had been compared to a machine at least since the Renaissance, with references to the heart as a furnace, the gut as a manufacturing plant, and the parts as fitting together, each doing its "job." In the late nineteenth century, as industrialization and manufacturing took center stage in the American economy, the metaphorical comparison reached new heights. Physicians and health educators frequently referred to the body as a miraculous machine, built by divine intervention and, unlike machines of iron and steel, capable of healing and self-repair. Detailed knowledge of anatomy and the functions of the various organs and muscles enabled people to make this comparison forcefully, if not accurately.[54] For a long life, tracts of the day exhorted, one must treat the machine well by following the "laws of health and physical hygiene." Disease was the result of failure to observe these laws. Even death by infectious disease could be avoided if one consulted a physician and followed the proper regimen. Bodily perfection and long life could be realized, but eventually all machines break down. Death in old age was the machine broken, either through failure to observe the laws at an earlier age or through simple wear and tear.[55]

The old men and women of Franklin County, of course, were not machines. Their bodies had received a good deal of wear and tear, and they suffered their aches, pains, and ailments. George Sheldon was hardly the only one to complain of dyspepsia, back trouble, and a host of other conditions. Anyone who had arrived at the age of sixty without benefit of antibiotics, analgesics, good dental care, labor-saving devices, and the other benefits of modern life could have provided his or her own list.

In a study to determine why older men in the United States in the early twentieth century were in such poor health, Dora Costa found that physical and joint stress and exposure to infectious diseases were major contributors to chronic and degenerative problems in older survivors. An infectious disease contracted in one's youth could have repercussions years later.[56] Reducing exposure to infection in childhood, combined with effective treatment and the lessening of wear and tear, apparently leads to a better prognosis for improved health in old age.

In 1909, the *Boston Post* introduced the Boston Post Cane, to be given to the oldest resident in each of seven hundred selected towns in New England. Deerfield was one of them. The canes were made by J. F. Fradley and Company of New York and consisted of an African ebony shaft and a 14-carat-gold head inscribed with the town's name. The newspaper specified that upon the death of the current holder of the cane, it was to be transmitted to the next oldest resident.[57] Those hardy and independent women of Deerfield surviving in 1909 were ineligible to receive it; not until 1930 did the paper decide to include women as recipients. George Sheldon, age ninety-one in 1909, was a prime candidate.[58]

In awarding these canes, the Boston Post company was observing a turn-of-the-century fashion of sorts that venerated the largely white population of men—and to some degree women—who had reached old age and experienced a significant portion of the previous century. Though perhaps only a publicity stunt, the tribute might well have tapped into social and political tremors of the day as well. The growing immigration of non-English, non-Protestant newcomers, dating from the mid-nineteenth century, fueled a sense among some that the old Yankee stock was diminishing. Its numbers were fewer as a result of an aging population, low birth rates, and new waves of immigrants.

Blanche Hukowicz, of Deerfield,
holding the Boston Post Cane. She
celebrated her 100th year in 2007.
Photo by Paul Franz, courtesy of
The Recorder.

The fiftieth wedding anniversary of "Mr. and Mrs. Zebina Stebbins, . . . prominent amongst the elderly and excellent citizens of Deerfield," occasioned an expression of such angst, as well as of appreciation for the elderly. The *Greenfield Gazette and Courier*, in a report of the event published January 25, 1869, observed: "The number of gray-headed kindred present betokened the kind of fibre that is in the race for weathering life's journey; and the range of ages—from 2 to 84—gave pleasant encouragement that the race is in the way of continuance. Long may it run." In another example, C. Alice Baker, participating in the dedication ceremony of some tablets commemorating those who died or were captured in the raid of 1704 for the new Memorial Hall Museum of the Pocumtuck Valley Memorial Association in 1883, declared that the assembled guests were "perpetuating . . . the institutions of the old Aryan stock from which we are sprung." Lamenting "the degenerate age" of the present, she voiced her passion for the colonial past but perhaps also the tension she felt regarding the new faces of Massachusetts and perceived loss of "the general institutions of the English people."[59] Baker's close friend, cousin, and PVMA colleague George Sheldon personified that old Yankee stock and shared those feelings.

After his election to the Massachusetts General Court in 1867 and 1872, as a representative then a senator, George Sheldon began spending more time in Boston, but he always returned to Deerfield. In 1896, though his eyesight had begun failing a few years earlier, he completed his two-volume history of Deerfield. The following year he married Jennie Arms Sheldon, his son John's sister-in-law, who was interested in Deerfield's past and had assisted Sheldon as he prepared the history for publication.[60]

As the nineteenth century ended, Sheldon had been devoting more and more attention to the PVMA museum, to maintaining the character and traditions of Deerfield, and to enjoying his reputation as a historian. In 1896, he and others lost a hard-fought battle as the Cheapside neighborhood of Deerfield was annexed to the town of Greenfield. He opposed the electric trolley system proposed for Deerfield's main street but lost that battle, too, in 1900. In 1910, however, at the age of ninety-one, he was cajoled into taking an automobile ride to observe a biplane demonstration.[61] He had witnessed the transition from horseback travel to "aeroplanes."

Along the way, Sheldon had endured the passing of many friends and relatives. Now, increasingly blind and requiring considerable care from his wife and others, he managed to continue working until his death. Reportedly, he arose on the morning of Saturday, December 23, 1916, and announced to Jennie that he was going to die. And so he did that very afternoon, in his ninety-ninth year.[62]

Perhaps it is telling that some of the last pages of Sheldon's *History of Deerfield* were devoted to cemeteries and funerals. He probably completed these pages shortly before the book was published, when he was in his late seventies. Sheldon commented that in his early days, the meeting house bells had tolled nine times for the death of a man, six times for a woman, and three for a child. Then "a succession of short strokes gave the age in years of the departed." Upon Sheldon's passing, the church sexton, Lou Brown, rang the bell for more than an hour to chime a full count of ninety-eight.

In his book Sheldon describes the spare traditions of Deerfield funerals in colonial times, observing that "no heavy financial burden was laid upon the survivors by costly and fanciful exhibitions of floral art. No pride-fostering show cases, called caskets. A receptacle for the dead made in advance would have been considered presumptuous and impious. Each coffin was made on the emergency from actual measurement and made to fit."[63]

Considerably more was made of Sheldon's death, although the service itself, on December 26, was pronounced "simple, as he would have wished." Funerals in turn-of-the-century Connecticut Valley towns were still most often held at home, although they could be held formally in churches, such as the one held for Rev. Buckingham when he died in 1894. Sometimes a service was

Funeral of the Reverend Edgar Buckingham, First Church of Deerfield, photographed by the Allen Sisters, 1894. Courtesy of PVMA.

observed in both places.[64] Funeral "homes" or "parlors" were not yet a part of
the rural New England landscape, and traditional conventions persisted longer
in rural towns than in cities. When holding a funeral at home, the family of
the deceased, if they could afford it, hung black crepe bunting on their front
porch and a black wreath or ribbons on their front door.

Under the Massachusetts general statutes, a death certificate was required
when someone died, as was a burial permit, but embalming was not. Family
members and close friends were usually still intimately involved in preparing the body for burial. For example, when Elsie Putnam's close friend Belle
Dodge died in South Deerfield, Putnam came to the Dodge house and helped
"fix" the body, no doubt washing and dressing it and helping to lay it out in
the casket, which was lined with "white brocade velvet." Dodge's robe was
"cream colored albatross trimmed with lace and swans down." Putnam also
assisted in purchasing flowers and making bouquets.[65] If a family hired the
full services of an undertaker, then care of the body might fall to his hands.
If the service was to be held a few days after death, and embalming was not
performed, undertakers had commercially available contraptions in which to
store bodies on ice.

Undertaking still rested largely in the hands of furniture manufacturers, who also made what were increasingly referred to as caskets. In Greenfield one could turn to the J. L. Lyons Furniture Company or the Green Furniture and Undertaking Company, in Turners Falls to the A. W. Goodnow Company, and in Shelburne Falls, H. S. Swan's. All these firms advertised coffins, caskets, and burial robes and frequently other services.[66] Those planning or attending a funeral but unsure about proper attire or protocols could consult Richard A. Wells's *Manners, Culture, and Dress of the Best American Society*.[67] In 1910, C. H. Walker, the undertaker in Warren, Massachusetts, billed Mrs. O. W. Rice sixty-three dollars for her husband's funeral, equivalent to a little over fourteen hundred dollars today. The fee included a casket, an outside box, care of the body, chair rental, wheat, and a hearse driven to the nearby town of Brookfield.[68]

Green Furniture & Undertaking Co. advertisement, paper and ink print, c. 1910. Courtesy of PVMA.

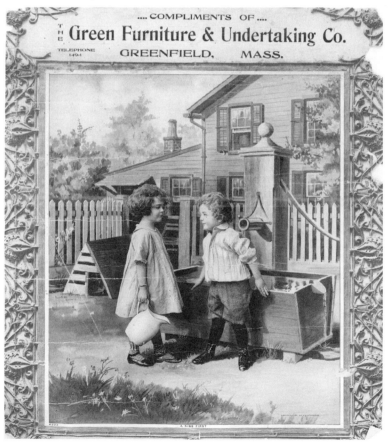

George Sheldon's funeral was held at the house he shared with his wife, Jennie, with the Reverend Cyrus A. Roys, pastor of the First Church of Deerfield, officiating. Thomas Franklin Waters, a member of the Ipswich Historical Society, delivered a lengthy eulogy in which he referred to his deceased friend as "the sage of Deerfield."[69] The room was said to have been stiflingly warm, and a dog wandered through during the long service. Sheldon's obituary described "a large display of beautiful floral tributes."[70] Six pallbearers delivered Sheldon to the family plot in Laurel Hill Cemetery. More than a life had ended: an era had closed for the town of Deerfield and its part of the Connecticut River valley.

8

MANAGING DISEASE IN THE LONG NINETEENTH CENTURY
Numeracy and Nosology, Nature and Nurture, 1840–1916

There are probably few features more characteristic of modernity than the notion that we can know ourselves through numbers. Statistics, averages, and probabilities permeate our ways of talking about ourselves and the social world we inhabit.

—Jacqueline Urla, *Cultural Politics in an Age of Statistics*

ON THE STRENGTH of a compendium of data remarkable for its time, the *Report of the Sanitary Commission*, Lemuel Shattuck and the commission concluded in 1850 that "causes exist in Massachusetts, as in England, to produce premature and preventable deaths, and hence unnecessary and preventable sickness; and that these causes are active in all the agricultural towns, but press most heavily upon cities and populous villages." In their report the commission named suspected causes and conditions they believed required immediate attention. Further, they recommended that the state create a board of health, initiate uniform vital registration, implement the system for classifying deaths adopted by the National Medical Convention of 1847, sponsor periodic sanitary surveys, and work to prevent the sanitary "evils" that arose from overcrowding and the unhygienic living conditions of foreign immigrants.[1]

People's lives, especially their aging, illness, and death, were filled with imprecisely categorized events and causations that invited standardization, greater precision, and greater scientific surveillance at the end of the nineteenth century. By 1850, the management of illness and death was already becoming increasingly scientific and secular, shifting from falling primarily within the purview of home, family, and church to being part of a more public and medicalized sphere. Throughout the second half of the nineteenth century and into the early twentieth, the General Court gave increasing authority to state bureaucracies and to people in the medical profession. A discourse about the management and control of illness evolved, as well as one about

147

the perceived threat from immigrants, who were suspected of bringing disease to America's shores and whose habits allegedly imperiled the health and well-being of the "native white" population of New England. Public health reformers argued that the state needed to invest more in preventing diseases, not just in treating them. Simultaneously, the emergence of the modern science of biology and the theory of evolution steered experts and laypeople alike in new directions.

In 1840, the population of the northeastern United States was estimated to be a little under seven million. By 1910, it had grown to a little more than twenty-five million. The foreign born made up approximately 15 percent of the total in 1850 but close to 26 percent by 1910.[2] Accompanying the growth of the population and its diversity were increased mobility, urbanization, and commercial and industrial development. As the previous chapters bear witness, small-town New Englanders experienced these changes, too, though perhaps less intensely than their urban counterparts.

In the 1840s in Europe and the United States, Enlightenment assumptions of unified ideas, single right answers, and only one "right way" were beginning to disappear. Modernism was on the rise, and it accelerated rapidly between about 1890 and the beginning of World War I.[3] Science and medicine shifted to a greater emphasis on empiricism. The theory of evolution profoundly influenced ideas of progress. Some mathematical "certainties" gave way to statements of statistical probability. Ian Hacking has referred to this trend as a move from searching for natural laws to the "taming of chance."[4]

The rise of manufacturing technologies and industrial capitalism also meant an unprecedented increase in the number of goods and services available. This change in turn relocated a good deal of capital and political influence away from the rural agricultural sector to commercial business and industry. Concomitant transformations took place in the institutions surrounding illness, death, and loss. Medicine became more scientific and experimental; public health and medicine became more authoritative and influential. The institutions involved in death and mourning also became more commercialized, and the providers of insurance and patient care, more institutionalized.

Yet what some researchers have characterized as a unified trend of modernization had its tangents, steps backward, and idiosyncrasies. Every region, state, community, neighborhood, and even individual experienced a distinct version of events and responded differently to change. George Sheldon, for example, embraced the workings of the state as a legislator and census taker but maintained somewhat anachronistic conceptions of his own hometown. He was one of many people caught between two visions of place, and Deerfield was one of many towns that held onto its past as it grew economically and ethnically more diverse. Nevertheless, the fact that we can speak of medical culture, death culture, and, for that matter, American culture means that we can identify and reach consensus about shared patterns of behavior, practices, and rituals.

In this chapter I look at three interrelated processes that bore directly on cultural patterns of state medicine, on understandings of causes of death, and on perceptions of the sick between 1840 and 1916: the rise of public health and the use of statistics, foreign immigration to the northeastern United States, and the acceptance of evolutionary theory in the United States, with particular reference to immigrants and germs. These processes were both products and shapers of modernism in the country at the time.

Paul Starr has drawn attention to an early period, from about 1760 to 1850, when competition for medical authority existed in the American democratic marketplace.[5] "Regulars" and "irregulars" jostled with each other and with laypersons for the right to treat the sick. Between the Jacksonian era and the Progressive era (circa 1850–90), Starr recognized the formalizing of training and professionalization of allopathic physicians and a commensurate increase in the authority of mainstream medical doctors. This period culminated in the systematic licensing of doctors by state boards or medical societies and in the accreditation of medical schools. Changes in public health paralleled these developments from the end of the Civil War through the Progressive era.[6]

Henry Ingersoll Bowditch, a true Victorian-era progressive, was asked to give the centennial lecture at the International Medical Congress in Philadelphia in 1876.[7] His assigned topic was public hygiene. He identified three historical epochs in American medicine. The first, from 1776 to 1832, was filled with "an overweening confidence in our art." It corresponds to the age of heroic medicine described in Chapter 2 and to notions that each person's illness was a distinct case of imbalance and excitability. The second, from 1832 to 1869, began "with the rise of more exact and scientific methods of study" and the "accurate recording of facts and subsequent analysis of them, with an extreme confidence in Nature's Power of curing Disease." This was an era of numeracy and nosology, when Massachusetts state officials began amassing vital statistics, census data, and data on causes of deaths—efforts that signaled a profound shift to thinking of disease and death in terms of a new biomedical framework. Disease was something to be measured and observed in a new culture of human science.[8]

Bowditch's third epoch, beginning in 1869 and reaching into the "Far future," was the era of "State Preventive Medicine." It was inaugurated with the founding of the Massachusetts Board of Health and saw a gradually expanding legislative authorization for the state to intervene for the public welfare.[9] One can imagine Bowditch, positivist that he was, thinking into the next century and visualizing a citizenry in perfect health, with all disease prevention and care supported by the state.

By the beginning of the nineteenth century the collection of vital statistics was commonplace on the European continent and in Britain, and it was extending to the states and colonies. Indeed, as noted in Chapter 2, the General Court of Massachusetts instructed its citizenry to record such facts as early as 1639. Although death and disease were always subjects of interest, the earliest vital statistics collected were primarily for purposes of inheritance, taxation, and military recruitment. Between 1820 and 1840, however, during an explosion of data collecting of all kinds by Western nations, documenting and assessing the health of citizens became a common preoccupation. This was no less true for the Commonwealth of Massachusetts.[10] The cholera pandemic of the early 1830s in Europe and North America is a good marker of the beginning of the statistical tradition in public health.[11]

Cholera first appeared in Britain in 1831, and France and the United States in 1832.[12] In London and other urban centers in England, experience with epidemic disease fostered the growth of statistical inquiry. The Statistical Society of London and similar societies in other cities were founded at about the same time. William Farr was one person heavily engaged in this inquiry. Farr studied briefly with the famous physician and early epidemiologist Pierre C. A. Louis in Paris, as did several other pioneers in medicine and public health, including George C. Shattuck, Oliver Wendell Holmes, and Henry I. Bowditch.[13] Through Louis a cultural network was formed involving health and medical specialists in France, Britain, and the United States.[14]

By the 1830s, Farr had achieved recognition in England and elsewhere for his studies in vital statistics. He was hired as a staff member by the General Register Office of England in 1839, and from this platform he lobbied for the improvement of registration laws and effectively disseminated his statistical methods and his theories of disease and causes of death. An active member of the Statistical Society of London, he was able to influence many people in the medical world, at home and abroad. At about the same time, Lemuel Shattuck was pursuing his interest in collecting and improving vital statistics in Massachusetts, and he corresponded with Farr about a nosology for classifying causes of death in the United States.

Farr's work is the quintessence of the numerical method advocated by Louis. He referred to his combining disease categories with statistical frequencies of cases as "nosometry" and believed, as did many other pioneers of his day, that the systematic collection of such data could reveal the true underlying causes of illnesses and deaths. Certain "districts" in England appeared to

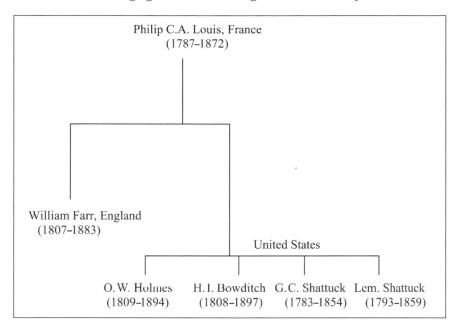

Philip C.A. Louis, France
(1787–1872)

William Farr, England
(1807–1883)

United States

O.W. Holmes
(1809–1894)

H. I. Bowditch
(1808–1897)

G.C. Shattuck
(1783–1854)

Lem. Shattuck
(1793–1859)

Chart showing the influence of C. P. A. Louis on the development of statistics and epidemiology in England and the United States. Modified from Lilienfeld and Lilienfeld, "French Influence," 33, 35.

have much greater mortality from disease than others.[15] The differences in disease rates between healthy districts and unhealthy districts were believed to be a reflection of excess and presumably preventable mortality, if only the underlying factors could be exposed. We have seen how efforts to expose those factors played out with respect to the diseases and causes discussed in previous chapters. What I want to highlight here is the profound difference between the local physician engaged in administering care to his patients in the community and people like Farr and Shattuck who developed a "statist's" view of illness and mortality. The local doctor focused his attention on the sick person and his or her immediate family, contacts, and surroundings; the statist subsumed and to some extent erased the complicated individual, replacing him or her with a statistic.

A physician or health practitioner might well have had a foot in both realms when considering a patient's disease and making his report to the town clerk or some higher authority. He was likely to be administering care and at the same time thinking about the larger causal relations he suspected were involved. One such physician was Stephen West Williams, who incorporated the concept of "healthy districts" into his treatise on Franklin County, published in 1842.[16] He

was concerned with individual deaths. But when Farr, Shattuck, and others
assumed the role of statistician, or "nosometrist," they focused their attention
on whole classes of morbid or mortal events. Accurate counts and reliable
categories held sway over individual differences in symptoms, conditions, and
patient histories. This shift in perspective was essential to the development
of the modern, numerical, epidemiological approach to disease and death.
And this approach is a part of statecraft and a fundamental component of
what has come to be considered one of the most important functions of the
modern state.

Two passages, one by Farr and the other by Shattuck, exemplify the two
men's self-perceptions and their understandings of the roles they needed to
play. First, Farr:

> How the people of England live is one of the most important questions that can
> be considered; and how—of what causes, and at what ages—they die is scarcely
> of less account; for it is the complement of the primary question teaching men
> how to live a longer, healthier, and happier life. Armed with this golden bough,
> we may enter the gloomy kingdom of the dead, whither have gone in twenty
> years nine thousand thousand [sic] English children, fathers, mothers, sisters,
> brothers, daughters, sons . . . each having left memories not easily forgotten;
> and many having biographies full of complicated incidents. Here, fortunately
> for this inquiry, they appear divested of all colour, form, character, passion, and
> the infinite individualities of life: by abstraction they are reduced to mere units
> undergoing changes as purely physical as the setting stars of astronomy or the
> decomposing atoms of chemistry; and as in those sciences so in this, the analysis
> of the elementary facts observed in their various relations to time and place will
> shed new light on the more complicated phenomena of national life.[17]

And now Shattuck:

> We are not a theorist—an experimentalist. We have no sympathy with the
> opinions of some modern reformers, who seem to be governed by theories
> founded on uncertain and partial data, or vague conjecture. We are a statist—a
> dealer in facts. We wish to ascertain the laws of human life, developed by the
> natural constitution of our bodies, as they actually exist under the influences
> that surround them, and to learn how far they may be modified and improved.
> This can only be done by an accurate knowledge of the facts that are daily oc-
> curring among us.[18]

In both passages we see an appeal to natural laws, the reification of facts, and
the erasure of the individual in deference to a larger, more important class
of truths. It is not that individuals are unimportant, as Farr notes, but that
if one is to understand the underlying laws of mortality, one must eliminate
the complexity of individual lives and deaths and reduce them to their most
fundamental attributes. In doing so the statist may uncover larger, "more
complicated phenomena of national life." Farr and Shattuck were at the fore-

front of the tradition of data collection but not yet in the era of measuring chance and probability.

Between 1832 and 1869 the stage was set for new understandings of illness and death and for new institutional frameworks within which public health could be administered. These changes represent a cultural transformation in ideas about disease and the roles of health practitioners. Because literate citizens of the United States were familiar with demographic statistics, many of them could readily accept the emerging practice of collecting data on sickness and causes of death. Such statistics quickly became embedded in the popular culture of the day, as is evidenced by the frequent references to them in local newspapers such as the *Greenfield Gazette and Courier*.[19] The following report, for example, appeared April 18, 1870: "Births and deaths in Massachusetts for the year 1868 show a considerable increase over the previous year."

Susan Greenhalgh, Jacqueline Urla, and Sylvana Patriarca, among others, have pointed out that statistics that describe populations, communities, diseases, and other categories under which people are classified also are constitutive of those groups.[20] A descriptive statistic is an abstraction subsuming all the underlying variation which actually exists among those counted. Age and sex may be fairly stable categories, but what about race, ethnicity, and religion? What about one of Farr's infectious cause-of-death categories, generated before anyone understood bacteria and viruses? The Victorian positivist in Europe or the United States trusted his senses and his methods of inquiry to provide unambiguous observations—facts. The statistical abstraction became the fact. The coupling of categories was a judgment based on observed or suspected associations, but it frequently led to causal assumptions, only some of which were valid, even though many statists cautioned against assumptions of cause.[21]

When Farr observed that people living farther away from the Thames had lower rates of cholera, he assumed that it was because they lived at a higher elevation than people crowded into the dense housing along the water's edge.[22] When Bowditch observed that consumptives often inhabited low-lying neighborhoods with damp soils, he made the association into a cause.[23] More problematic was the observed association of consumption with the Irish and some observers' tendency to leap to the inference that the Irish therefore had inferior "constitutions." Statistics offered the power to identify associations between a disease and a host of risk factors, but they also underpinned false assumptions. Statistics enabled health officials to more easily investigate the homes of the foreign born and the working class, and they gave officials the power to stigmatize, marginalize, and discriminate against those who were deemed most vulnerable.[24] The label assigned to a category became a proxy for a host of relations implied by association with other categories.

The people who first became statists in Europe and the United States were frequently from the economic and social elite. In Massachusetts they were mostly affluent, educated, Protestant Yankees whose ancestors had arrived in North America in the eighteenth century or earlier.[25] Vital and health statistics methods and categories that were not adopted directly from Europe were developed according to their perspective. Much later in the nineteenth century this would begin to change, but for several decades statistical authority rested with this elite group. When statistics were collected ultimately for purposes of policy, as they almost always were, the primary subjects of classification were usually those other than the classifiers, or else the classifiers became the standard, the ideal, the "healthy" norm from which other groups deviated.

Bowditch saw public health as "dedicated to improving the intellectual, moral, [and] physical condition of the population."[26] In a discussion of the rise of classification by numbers, Theodore Porter notes that "numbers have been the preferred vehicle for investigating factory workers, prostitutes, cholera victims, the insane, and the unemployed," and those doing the investigating "used statistics to learn about kinds of people whom they did not know, and often did not care to know as persons."[27] Statistics allowed the clutter and complications of the "infinite individualities of life" to be removed as the statists distanced themselves from their subjects.

Porter, Hacking, and others have drawn attention to the authority and power that derived from people's ability to define statistical norms and deviations from them. When categories of class, ethnicity, or race were measured with respect to disease, as they so often were, and when moral authority was coupled with the authority to make or implement policy, the result was the targeting of specific groups or individuals in ways that might or might not have reflected their actual circumstances. This coupling influenced immigration policy as well. As Hacking puts it: "We obtain data about a governed class whose deportment is offensive, and then attempt to alter what we guess are relevant conditions of that class in order to change the laws of statistics that the class obeys."[28] He points out that liberal government in the nineteenth-century United States took this approach and that although its intentions were benevolent, the state thought it knew best how to proceed. This was one of Michel Foucault's major criticisms of the way modern social science is used in the biopolitics of the state.[29]

The beginning of Bowditch's third epoch, that of state preventive medicine, marks the moment when the statistical sciences merged with sanitary science. In the 1870s and 1880s, a sustained decline in mortality from infectious diseases began in Massachusetts, including the Connecticut Valley.[30] Medical therapies contributed relatively little to this trend, save for improvements in

Franklin County Hospital, c. 1910–1914. Courtesy of PVMA.

antiseptic and aseptic practices. Instead, sanitation measures lobbied for by the state Board of Health helped reduce mortality from infectious diseases. Clean water, effective sewage removal and drainage, and preventive measures related to hygiene, quarantine, and housing were positive outcomes originating in the new culture of statistics, numeracy, and nosology. As new technologies in water filtration and sewage management were developed, the slope of the decline in mortality steepened. The large and medium-size cities of Massachusetts benefited most from the measures implemented in the late nineteenth and early twentieth centuries, but smaller cities and towns such as Greenfield and Deerfield implemented public water and sewer works for at least some parts of town between the 1880s and the early 1900s.[31] Despite their rigidity, Bowditch's epochs resonate well with the history of the public health movement in the United States. By the time of George Sheldon's death in 1916, this new culture was fully in place.

At home in Franklin County, local physicians, like others around the state, worried that too much state control of the public's health might mean a loss of their own authority and a dilution of their fees. Yet the topics they selected for their quarterly meetings clearly reflect a growing interest in public health measures. They discussed the public milk supply in 1896, Louis Pasteur and bacteria in 1899, hospital versus home treatment in 1902, and the reporting of infectious diseases to the Board of Health in 1905. They held their first meeting in the new Franklin County Public Hospital in 1910 and talked about the need for a contagion hospital in Franklin County in 1912, physicians' responsibility for protecting infants against disease in 1914, and the possibility of a county tuberculosis hospital in 1915.[32] The practicing physicians of New England were being drawn from treating only the individual patient to taking an increasing role in public health.

Accompanying the rise of statistical thinking was a public fascination with and adoption of the theory of evolution, which took a distinctive form in American science and popular culture. Evolution was thought to explain how germs changed in form and variety, to account for perceived differences among "races," and perhaps also to point the way to a more perfected human race with increased vigor, better health, and greater longevity. A useful approach to understanding these developments and the way they affected the people met in earlier chapters is to return briefly to the mid-nineteenth century and examine some of the ideas floating about in George Sheldon's cosmology and in those of his contemporaries, including the famous preacher Henry Ward Beecher (1813–1887).

Son of the famous evangelist preacher Lyman Beecher and brother of the author of *Uncle Tom's Cabin*, Harriett Beecher Stowe, Henry Ward Beecher counted many of America's most prominent people among his friends. Beecher was born in Litchfield, Connecticut, and educated at Amherst College and then at Lane Theological Seminary, founded by his father in Cincinnati, Ohio. In the late 1840s he became minister of the new Plymouth Congregational Church in Brooklyn, one of the country's largest churches. As many as three thousand people attended his standing-room-only services. Politicians, artists, and dignitaries visited his church when they were in New York, among them Abraham Lincoln and Mark Twain. Beecher also traveled widely and collected handsome fees for his lectures.[33] He might not have known of George Sheldon, but Sheldon certainly knew of him, and their politics and ideas followed similar lines.[34]

Beecher embraced a contemporary theology that, unlike his father's, endorsed the moral improvement and salvation of the well-intentioned. He was an outspoken opponent of slavery, advocating from his pulpit the freeing of slaves. Sheldon, too, was described as a "vigorous" abolitionist.[35] Beecher was concerned about immigration and the growing number of Roman Catholics coming to the United States, and especially about the influx of Irish immigrants, just as Sheldon was. Sheldon joined the Free Soil Party and then the American Party, or Know Nothings, in the 1850s.[36] Beecher too had been a Free Soil Party member and supported American Party candidates. The American Party embraced these seemingly disparate views and was popular enough to control the Massachusetts legislature in 1855 and to win individual elections in New York and several other states. The party's members—who were antislavery, opposed to immigration, and fearful of the potential influence of Rome and the rising number of Catholics in America—tended to be Protestant, "native" white Americans concerned about the heterogeneous, urbanizing tendencies they were witnessing in the 1850s and 1860s. They were also part of the core of the emerging Republican Party, with its antislavery platform.

Although Sheldon is perhaps the most prominent example, many of the old Yankee citizens of Deerfield and the surrounding towns expressed in one way or another their pride in their Anglo-Saxon heritage and their concern about the more recent, non-Protestant immigrants. The Reverend Frank Pratt, C. Alice Baker, and the Reverend James Hosmer can be included among the Deerfield friends, relatives, and acquaintances of Sheldon's who shared his beliefs. But this belief system was not a local phenomenon, as Beecher's involvement attests, nor was it exclusively of New England and the northeastern states; it was a national movement.

After the Civil War these ideas became associated with a new social theory that seemed to reinforce the entitlements of the old Yankee stock, whether Boston Brahmin or rural elite. That theory was Social Darwinism. In the late 1860s and early 1870s, Beecher and many other prominent, white, Protestant Americans became enamored of the ideas of the British philosopher Herbert Spencer. Spencer's theory of social selection postulated that the strongest survive and the weak and unfit are eliminated by "the survival of the fittest." Spencer's theory of evolution differed from Darwin's in fundamental ways, including an emphasis on the evolution of society rather than of species, a Lamarckian belief in the inheritance of acquired characteristics, and a prostitution of Darwin's idea of the "struggle for existence" into a winner-take-all competitive individualism. A certain segment of America's intellectual elite found it a seductive concept. Between 1860 and 1903 Spencer's books sold more than 350,000 copies in the United States.[37] His reputation in the United States probably exceeded that in his native Britain.

From his pulpit and with his publication of the *Christian Union*, Beecher reached tens of thousands. Other prominent American supporters included the industrialist Andrew Carnegie, William Graham Sumner of Yale, and Charles Sumner, the legislator and statesman from Massachusetts.[38] With the large Irish Catholic population in Massachusetts, it was most often the Irish who were maligned as less fit, although Italians, Germans, and eastern Europeans received their share of taunts and accusations. The Irish were singled out by people of Protestant English ancestry, whose forebears had predominated among the state's original settlers. American Social Darwinists were primed to adopt the anti–Irish Catholic and strongly hereditarian views prevalent in England.

The high fertility rate and large family sizes of Irish Catholics were seen as threats to the smaller families and declining numbers of New Englanders. The combination of Social Darwinism and hereditarian notions of racial and class inferiority permeated social and political discourse but also seeped into the discourse on health and disease. Intemperance, immorality, and a lack of control over appetites, it was thought, impaired the health of the Irish.

Spencerian thought also held that although people inherited negative traits from parents and earlier ancestors, those traits were not all locked immutably in the life-giving forces that we now call genes. They might be hereditary, but they were not entirely irreversible. With proper supervision, education, and hygienic practices, the Irish and others could be retrained in their habits to be more fit—that is, more Yankee-like. This idea may have been what Rev. Pratt was referring to when he wrote, "There has often been the danger, in some sections of our country, that instead of that foreign element being transformed in the characteristics of American citizens, that the foreign element should transform our national life."[39] The issue was whether the immigrant working class and "ethnics" would degrade American culture or whether the foreign element could be made into proper American citizens.

In his quieter way, George Sheldon adopted a Social Darwinist viewpoint in his interpretation of early American history. To his mind, the defeat of the Indians by colonial Americans was a case of a superior race defeating an inferior one.[40] Perhaps, like many other Americans, he was influenced by the writings of Lewis Henry Morgan, who proposed that humans passed through the evolutionary stages of savagery, barbarism, and civilization. Some societies, Morgan believed, did not advance to the next stage, and American Indians were an example.[41] Sheldon's involvement in the American Party is compelling evidence of his "nativist" leanings.

After Rev. Hosmer left Deerfield, he became a professor, librarian, and well-known author of popular books on American history. His most celebrated work is *A Short History of Anglo-Saxon Freedom*, more than four hundred pages long, in which one of his major themes is the value of local self-government as practiced in a "New England town meeting." Hosmer also expressed concern over the diminution of Anglo-Saxon purity from the "Celt, Frank, Scandinavian, Hollander and Huguenot." But he believed the essence of the English stock would persist, absorb the newcomers, and even expand. Of the Irish he noted that the "public schools [would] finish the work of the factory and the newspapers," and the immigrants could not have too much influence because the "native type" was so strong.[42] For some people, immigration was a concern, but their faith in a "superior race" suggested that the native, white American character would ultimately prevail. Nurture could work with nature. Others were not so sure.

Although colonial settlers brought disease and destruction to the American Indians, a strong tradition existed in American writing that the Yankee homeland was relatively free of disease. This tradition celebrated "the purity of our air and waters, the health and brawn of our people, and the vigor of our native institutions. In this light, health is regarded as indigenous to our soil; disease, as an odious alien."[43] Timothy Dwight, Stephen West Williams, Rodolphus Dickinson, and others echoed this article of faith in their narratives of a healthy and bountiful Connecticut River valley. It followed that contagion and disease had to have been introduced from the outside by foreigners. From there it was easy to tie the 1849 American cholera epidemic directly to the Irish, whose immigration to New York and New England was at its peak. And after all, the immigrant neighborhoods in New York and Boston exhibited the highest rates of infection.[44]

In 1875, the year before Bowditch's centennial address, a medical commission appointed by the Boston Board of Health published its findings on the "sanitary condition" of Boston. The report was stimulated by the very high death rates of the preceding years, particularly those having to do with the so-called zymotic class of diseases and with consumption. It was found that cholera infantum, other enteric diseases, consumption, and pneumonia-bronchitis were the most serious killers, and all were deemed amenable to preventive measures. The commission also found that deaths among the "foreign races" exceeded those of native "British Americans." Among the foreign element, the Irish showed the highest rates. Indeed, the commissioners pointed out, although Irish people made up 33 percent of the foreign population in the United States, they accounted for 41 percent of all deaths. And in Boston, where they made up 65 percent of the foreign population, they accounted for 76 percent of deaths from consumption. The message was clear: the Irish were responsible for an excess of total mortality. The report detailed "the diseases to which our Irish inhabitants are particularly liable."

> a. They comprise those affections which, in our community, are at all times the most destructive to life, namely, consumption, bronchitis, pneumonia, and the diarrheas.
>
> b. They include constitutional diseases, which are transmissible by inheritance, such as consumption and cancer.
>
> c. They include affections which are strongly significant of defective sanitation, and of a widely spread prevalence of habits destructive to health, namely, various 'filth diseases,' cholera infantum, Bright's disease of the kidneys.[45]

Throughout the nineteenth and well into the early twentieth century, immigrants would be associated with the introduction and spread of infectious diseases and chastised for their high rates of tuberculosis and infant mortality.[46] In Boston and in mill cities such as Lawrence, Lowell, Fall River, and Holyoke, the Irish were the most dominant and visible foreign-born group in Massachusetts. In Deerfield's Cheapside neighborhood, on the railroad, and at the Russell Cutlery, they were a large presence. German, Italian, French Canadian, and eastern European (Catholic and Jewish) immigrants coincided with the Irish or followed them in large numbers into the mill towns and port cities of Boston and New York. Before the 1890s, however, the Irish were most singled out for their negative effect on the "real sanitary condition" of Massachusetts cities and towns.

When the second cholera epidemic struck U.S. cities in 1849, many physicians accepted the notion of contagion, but primarily for a select set of diseases that included smallpox, rabies, and syphilis. The prevalent idea about the cause of epidemic diseases continued to be that they originated in unsanitary local conditions. Poisons produced by the putrefaction of organic matter produced miasmas, which made people sick with diseases such as yellow fever and cholera. In England, Sir Edwin Chadwick pronounced, "All smell is disease."[47] The "filth diseases" were those promoted by some people's unsanitary habits, and the Irish of Boston and the mill cities, forced by extremely low wages to live in extraordinarily poor conditions, were ripe for being targeted as an "immigrant menace."[48]

As Nancy Tomes has noted, the germ theory of disease was not a neatly packaged truth delivered on the heels of Louis Pasteur's and Robert Koch's discoveries but rather a slowly emerging set of concepts that came together in a somewhat coherent theory relatively late in the nineteenth century. Physicians and scientists on both sides of the Atlantic struggled to reconcile this theory with a long-held body of knowledge that named fermentation and putrefaction the sources of many diseases.[49] Farr's nosology, despite its internal logic and seemingly meaningful categories, created its own inertia as evidence began to mount that diseases might be caused by organic particles rather than by poisonous products of putrefaction. Farr himself, however, was slowly persuaded that his zymotic category included several diseases that might be caused by microscopic particles like those identified by Pasteur. He first proposed that these particles be referred to as "biads," then as "zymads," which he then acknowledged, in the mid-1870s, equated with disease germs.[50] By the 1880s, most American physicians recognized that specific bacteria were responsible for a number of infectious diseases, including scarlet fever and tuberculosis.

Whether they spoke about bacteria, zymads, fomites, seeds, spores, or germs, the medical scientists of the Progressive era in the United States and Europe were quick to adopt an evolutionary narrative for the "struggle" between man and microbes. Accounts of the contest were embellished with adjectives that described germs as "foreign," "murderous," and "cunning."[51] The experts painted a Social Darwinist gloss on germs, much as they had on the immigrants assumed to carry them. The devious germs inhabited the dwellings and bodies of the unscrupulous and unhygienic people who brought them. The so-called filth diseases no longer originated simply in the garbage and bad air emanating from dangerous neighborhoods. Now they were infinitely small and unseen animalcules that lived in the water, soil, filth, and air. They were everywhere, poised to infect the unhygienic. Prescriptions for prevention changed subtly from eliminating the sources of miasma to eliminating the sources of germs.

The growing understanding of disease causation and the pathways to infection meant that public health interventions could become increasingly effective, but in Massachusetts it was necessary first for the Board of Health to be granted broader authority and to be freed further from private interests and political entanglements. Beginning in the late 1880s, with recruitment onto the board of men like William Thompson Sedgwick, a period of active state preventive medicine became a reality. Barbara Gutman Rosenkrantz credits Sedgwick's pioneering epidemiological studies with combining "methods of the biologist, the sanitary engineer, and the statistician."[52] By 1891, only seven Massachusetts towns with populations of more than four thousand lacked public water supplies. Annual reports of the Board of Health noted a decrease in deaths from zymotic diseases, and state laboratories were available to test municipal water sources. Within the first decade of the twentieth century, the state had authorized laboratories for the production of smallpox vaccine and diphtheria antitoxin.

In 1914, the state elected its first Irish American governor, David Ignatius Walsh, who energetically supported a campaign to prevent tuberculosis and to build tuberculosis hospitals in Massachusetts.[53] Meanwhile, Boston had elected its first Irish mayor in 1885, and in 1906, it elected as mayor John Fitzgerald, grandfather to President John Fitzgerald Kennedy. The stereotype of the unhealthy and unfit Irish immigrant was eroding rapidly—although on occasion shifting to new immigrant groups—as stereotypes of the Irish politician were simultaneously emerging.

The conjoining of heavy immigration, a popular and vulgar understanding of evolution, and the rise of statistics and sanitary science had made for a heady brew of differing rationalities and logical leaps. Hereditarian notions of constitutional diseases were coupled with unwarranted racialized assumptions about immigrants' susceptibility to and responsibility for infectious diseases. Many people still considered the Irish or immigrant body inferior to that of the Anglo-Saxon, but there was hope. Through proper training and education, as Hosmer and others intimated, the Celt could be improved; a higher state of fitness and health could be achieved. In addition, the success of many individuals who rose from their humble immigrant origins or from the "poorer classes" confirmed that at least some fit men and women resided in all races, all classes. What was called for was betterment of the whole human race.

Despite high rates of infant mortality, many Americans in the early decades of the twentieth century thought the unrestrained fertility of immigrant families was creating far too many unfit children. They were deemed an added and costly burden to progress and a threat to public health. High rates of alcoholism and tuberculosis among adults confirmed that moral weakness and susceptibility to infectious diseases still prevailed. What had begun as a nativist, targeted, anti-immigration movement in the mid-nineteenth century had grown to nothing less than a call for improving the quality of the American people. In its shrillest form this call was for restrictions on immigration, the encouragement of fit and healthy couples to produce fitter families, and the discouragement of the unfit from reproducing their defective and unhealthy characteristics. For all the many positive changes brought about by state preventive medicine, an ugly outcome also appeared—eugenics. The eugenicists assured people that through proper physical hygiene, physical education, and proper selection of mates, America's birthright of perfect health could be restored.

From our twenty-first-century perspective, it can be difficult to appreciate how widespread and commonplace eugenic thinking was in the first decades of the twentieth century. It was not the official language of the Massachusetts Board of Health, but it was popular in the highest scientific circles and with laypeople as well.[54] "Better baby" and "fitter family" contests were held at expositions and state fairs. In 1914, *Women's Home Companion* claimed that better baby contests had been held in every state except West Virginia, New Hampshire, and Utah and that a hundred thousand children had been examined.[55] In 1910, Dr. Charles Davenport established the Eugenics Record Office at Cold Spring Harbor, New York. By 1914, thirty states, Connecticut and Vermont among them, had enacted new marriage laws or amended old ones to restrict the marriage of those deemed unfit. Some states had statutes permitting the sterilization of "unfit" citizens.[56]

In January 1914, the First National Conference on Race Betterment was hosted by J. H. Kellogg in Battle Creek, Michigan. Among the Massachusetts delegates attending were Dudley A. Sargent, professor of physical hygiene at Harvard University, Charles Eliot, president emeritus of Harvard, and

"Yea, I have a goodly heritage," Fitter Family medal. Photo by author.

Robert J. Sprague of the Massachusetts Agricultural College in Amherst. Approximately four hundred persons attended the conference, where the more than fifty presentations included "The Importance of the State of Eugenic Investigation" by Charles Davenport, "Race Betterment and Our Immigration Laws" by Robert DeC. Ward, and "Deterioration of the Civilized Woman" by Richard Root Smith.[57] A year later Charles Eliot would deliver an address to a conference of Massachusetts public health officials on his view of the most critical health issues: tuberculosis, venereal disease, alcoholism, and prostitution. Eliot saw the job of public health as that of teaching "the poor and the ignorant how to resist the temptations of alcohol." Others saw their mission quite differently.[58]

I do not claim that the early twentieth-century topic of health and illness in the United States or in Massachusetts was dominated by the discourse of eugenics, only that it was heavily inflected with eugenic thinking. What is more, this thinking filtered down to the everyday lives of the residents of Franklin County. In 1903 the *Greenfield Gazette and Courier* ran the headline "Race Suicide in Franklin County?"[59] Later in the decade the *Gazette and Courier* for August 2, 1911, reported a warning by Professor Farrabee of Harvard University that "Americans have been lax not only in allowing unfit immigrants to come here, but also in permitting unfit natives to marry." Readers would be informed that, in general, the "business girl" had better "eugenic ideals" than the factory girl. With regularity they would see articles on topics such as the number of insane in Ireland and the numbers of Italian and Polish people immigrating to the state. They would also read that "fortunately" in 1910, "118 polygamists, two anarchists, 156 idiots, imbecile and feeble-minded, 160 insane, nine professional beggars, 11 paupers, 2471 with loathsome diseases, 12,632 persons likely to become public charges, and 1365 contract laborers were debarred from all ports."[60]

The *Gazette and Courier* also carried articles and advertisements about the proper care of farm animals kept near the home, sources of the tubercle bacillus, including cattle, and home economics hints for the proper care of food and household sanitation: "Modern ideas of cleanliness call for the cleaning out of germs as well as dirt. . . . The modern way to scrub a floor is to put a little Carbonol in the water."[61] Prompted by state statutes, in the 1880s the Greenfield Board of Health required householders to report cases of infectious disease among family members and boarders, restricted the disposal of slops and offal, and made it illegal to sell diseased or unwholesome meat, milk, or provisions of any kind.[62] The residents of Franklin County were bombarded with messages from the public sphere to maintain a healthful and hygienic body, a clean house, and a sanitary community.

Despite the nativist and class prejudices that vital registration, disease classification, and the emerging public health movement inspired, these trends also reflected the good intentions and altruistic motives of the majority of its practitioners. More important, the combined efforts of statists and sanitarians produced results. Before the 1870s one is hard pressed to find significant reductions in mortality rates in Massachusetts. Indeed, during the 1870s, rates for infant mortality and several infectious diseases may have risen over the previous decade.[63] Yet even with high rates of immigration and the density of the urban poor, by at least the 1880s developments in statistics, sanitary science, and germ identification had reduced rates of infectious disease mortality. The decline was real and measurable if not always steady.

By 1915 the Massachusetts Office of Vital Statistics had compiled a long series of annual deaths by cause.[64] These figures revealed that beginning with 1870, the first full year after the founding of the Department of Public Health, infant mortality dropped from 162 deaths per thousand births to 102 by 1915. Combined deaths due to measles, scarlet fever, and diphtheria-croup dropped from 147 to 34. Deaths from pulmonary consumption–tuberculosis dropped from 339 to 114. The results represent a 37 percent reduction in infant mortality, a 77 percent reduction in childhood fevers, and a 66 percent reduction in pulmonary tuberculosis.[65] The trends were not entirely smooth, occasionally rising slightly or falling more abruptly, but overall each major infectious cause of death declined. In contrast to these declines, deaths from cancer rose from 29 to 100, and deaths from nephritis, or Bright's disease, from 49 to 94.

The 1915 Office of Vital Statistics report notes that the substantial reductions in infant mortality were effected by improvements in Boston and other large cities. "The decline in infant mortality in recent years in this Commonwealth has been due in great part to the reduction in the number of deaths from diarrhea and enteritis . . . especially during the summer season, and due in large part to methods of feeding . . . and the living and social conditions of the parents. With hygienic care . . . and careful feeding, many infants are able to pass through hot weather without serious diarrheal disturbances." Improved drinking water, improved garbage and sewage disposal, and better regulation of the milk supply came about under Board of Health authority. The report also pointed to the baby-saving campaigns of infant welfare agencies. Groups such as the largely Protestant-church-sponsored Associated Charities and the United Hebrew Benevolent Association drew on the state's expertise to launch successful campaigns that augmented public efforts.[66]

With regard to childhood fevers, the state legislature passed a key law in 1884 requiring the "family and physician of any person sick with small pox, diphtheria, scarlet fever or any other disease dangerous to the public health to give notice to the selectmen or local board of health." A sick child was restricted from attending school, and the family or physician could be fined for noncompliance.[67] Quarantine, disinfection, and other sanitary measures produced significant effects well before the development of antitoxins, antibiotics, and vaccines. As early as 1894 diphtheria antitoxin was becoming available, and subsequently a state laboratory was created to produce the antitoxin and eventually to distribute it.[68]

Several writers have credited the decline of deaths from tuberculosis to an overall improvement in the standard of living and general health in Massachusetts and elsewhere, coupled with the fresh air and rest cures and improved knowledge of nutrition in the treatment of that disease.[69] For tuberculosis, as for infant diarrheas and childhood fevers, the major changes were primarily the result of improved prevention rather than of specific treatments before 1916.[70] One vector involved in the spread of all three disease categories was milk. Bacterial contamination of milk resulting from its improper storage and handling between the dairy and the consumer was a significant problem in Massachusetts and the United States throughout the nineteenth and early twentieth centuries. Even after the identification of several disease-causing strains of bacteria in the milk supply, dairy farmers resisted pasteurization. Many physicians and public health experts considered sterilized milk harmful to children, and many dairy farmers in the Connecticut Valley and elsewhere wanted to avoid the extra labor and expense involved in pasteurization. Nevertheless, the state Board of Health promoted safe and pure handling of milk with some success during the 1890s and afterward, although laws requiring pasteurization were not passed in Massachusetts until 1921.[71]

The state's influence reached the Connecticut River valley in a variety of ways during the decades from 1840 to 1916. Public health statutes and scientific expertise quickly found their way to small cities and towns throughout the state. World War I and the influenza pandemic of 1918 brought new regimes of illness and death, but at the time of George Sheldon's death in 1916, people felt great optimism regarding the power of state preventive medicine and science to further improve health.

What also remained was a powerful ideology about the sick body that was yet to be seriously challenged. A strong association of race with national origin persisted. The Irish and the southern European body continued to be considered different and more susceptible to failure. Women's bodies, despite their longevity, were frailer and so more prone to sickness. It was only the male, white, Anglo-Saxon Protestant body that never seemed to be marked with inherent weaknesses.[72] Sometimes one sees evidence of the apparent contradiction that immigrant women were sturdier and immigrant men more capable of long hours of hard work, but the counterpoint of a body more susceptible to disease existed nonetheless. This ideology permitted the state to intervene more aggressively in the homes of immigrant families and enabled more invasive modes of treatment for women under the care of their physicians. The Anglo-Saxon male, standing before his doctor, was the "normal," average, or even ideal form of the human race, from which others deviated.[73]

Numeracy and nosology, nature and nurture had combined to produce genuinely successful efforts at improving people's health but had also contributed to stereotypes of statistical deviancy and susceptibility to illness. From the dysentery epidemic that took so many infants and toddlers in 1842 to the passing of nonagenarian George Sheldon in the winter of 1916, many transformations had taken place in Americans' understanding of illness, of primary causes of death, and of the means for disease prevention, and in some cases, even treatment.

9

BODIES OF EVIDENCE
Death, Loss, and The Search for Meaning

ON A BEAUTIFUL, sunny Memorial Day shortly before I finished the book, I walked into Deerfield's Laurel Hill Cemetery to revisit the resting places of Frankie and George Sheldon, Hattie Willard, and the other people I had come to know during my research. I wanted to take a final look at the gravestones and epitaphs of those whose names fill these pages, and I had brought my camera to rephotograph the grave markers. Flags adorned the markers of veterans of many past wars. During my visit maybe a half-dozen other visitors came. Most of them quickly planted a geranium or placed a potted plant near a gravestone, stood for a moment, and left. Only one woman lingered at a graveside.

I was reminded that the seeds for this book had been planted when, several years earlier, I had entered a local cemetery to hastily verify some names and dates for a more statistically oriented study I was then carrying out on infant and childhood mortality in nineteenth-century New England. Like Lemuel Shattuck and William Farr before me, I was interested in the data, the statistics. But on this occasion the names, dates, causes of death, and other facts I had collected and abstracted over the years suddenly took on a deeper meaning. Standing in the cemetery provoked in me a deeper awareness of lives once lived. The individual names, the interconnections revealed in family plots, and the sad, sometimes even tragic circumstances of death became important to me. I remember particularly the stone of a young woman, a Sheldon relative named Marcy, who died of tuberculosis in 1806. Her epitaph begins, "This treasure lost." The objectified and distanced pursuit of facts begged for augmentation with the more subjective, personal, and particular. Complete emotional detachment no longer seemed necessary or even desirable.

This recollection in turn reminded me of another cemetery experience involving my daughter several years earlier. When my wife and I first moved to New England with our then young children, I was struck by the lack of easy access to public land, something we had enjoyed in the West. Often when traveling or sightseeing we would eat a picnic lunch in a cemetery we passed. I appreciated the cemeteries' rural, parklike settings and the opportunity to peruse the engravings on the stones. Our older daughter never seemed bothered by this, but about the time our younger daughter turned ten, she confided that being in a cemetery made her feel strange and uncomfortable, even "creepy." She could not understand why I chose to picnic in these places.[1] From that point on we switched to eating our lunches on town commons or school playgrounds when school was not in session.

To me cemeteries had been neutral or even positive in affect; they were informative and often inviting. That human remains lay a few feet below the surface hardly crossed my mind. My daughter's reaction reminded me of the obvious—that cemeteries are by no means neutral landscapes for everyone. Together these two earlier events made clear to me the more nuanced story I could tell if I investigated the people behind the statistics. The stones with their engravings signified that death was the culmination of a biological and

James S. Smillie, "Mother Bringing Children to Rev. William Ellery Channing Monument, Mt. Auburn," engraving, 1847. Courtesy of Mt. Auburn Cemetery.

social process rather than simply a single event. The grave markers evoked many connections and many layered meanings.

As I drive by cemeteries in New England today, I seldom see anyone visiting a grave or strolling or picnicking among the stones, lawns, and graveled paths. Reading about the nineteenth and early twentieth centuries, I gain the impression that cemeteries were much more active and interactive places then—that relatives and descendants visited more frequently and that other people used the spaces much the way my family had in the late twentieth century. Mount Auburn Cemetery in Cambridge was a destination for mourners and families alike on Sunday outings. The rural cemetery movement, coupled with the cult of mourning that prevailed for much of this period, made cemeteries physical and social landscapes in which people enacted both ritualized and heartfelt performances and communed with an idealized "nature." On Memorial Day, crowds surrounded the Civil War memorial on Deerfield's town common, but one can also imagine that when George and Susan Sheldon visited their son Frankie's grave privately throughout the year, they met other parents who had lost children to scarlet fever or dysentery. A Sunday afternoon's walk or ride to the cemetery might have led to exchanges of sympathy and chance socializing with friends visiting their own departed at Green River or Laurel Hill.

In this chapter I turn from the science and public policy attendant upon illness and death between 1840 and 1916 to look at the social practices surrounding death and dying. Bereavement and commemoration were intertwined in complex ways as personal emotions and social conventions came together. Funerals and mortuary practices transcended the intimate, private sphere of friends and family; they were cultural events, usually staged in accordance with commonly accepted customs. In the 1840s Victorian mourning practices were at their height, but for the middle classes of both England and the United States, formality was already waning by the 1850s.[2] As the nineteenth century progressed and the twentieth century began, formal standards for proper mourning gave way to a pattern of more informal services but sustained notions of proper etiquette and fashion. A lag in the array of available undertakers' services in western New England may have modulated somewhat the formality of their expressions of bereavement and consolation, but it did not deter mourners from engaging in mainstream practices or inhibit their familiarity with the expectations of a wider culture. Stages in the life course were also important dimensions in the experiences of loss and commemoration.

When Lucy Buffum Lovell's daughter Laura died of cholera infantum, Lovell described in detail the moment when the child died. Her breathing quickened for ten or fifteen minutes, "and then without the least struggle . . . her spirit

Laurel Hill Cemetery. Photo © Carol Betsch.

winged its way to another, better world. Her eyes were sweetly closed by the hand of death, there was no distortion of the muscles, no contraction of the limbs. She was peaceful, and we could scarcely believe that she would not breathe again."[3] Lovell recounted a similarly painful but uplifting experience when her older daughter Caroline died of scarlet fever and she saw "the lamp of life go out." George and Susan Sheldon watched Frankie die, and George surely relived the experience as he watched Hattie Willard breathe "two or three short gasps and all was over." A very different scene is conjured up when one visualizes the railroad accident in West Deerfield as survivors try to help engineer Littlejohn and the brakeman Waltham as they lie dying by the riverbank. Even more horrific was the carnage of the battlefield during the Civil War. And how different all these experiences must have felt from that of the Allen sisters as they assisted at the bedside of their mother, Mary, or one of their aunts after a long life.

It is hard to find in any of these examples the metaphor of the body as a wonderful machine. The corpse does not translate well into a "machine broken," for it cannot be repaired or have its parts replaced. The "lamp of life has gone out" and cannot be relit. Mary Bradbury reminds us that the body is metaphorical for many things, that it is both a signifier and signified, but a corpse takes on another set of connotations.[4] The life course has concluded or has been interrupted prematurely, and the body becomes symbolically the empty vessel in which life formerly resided.

Throughout the period I am concerned with, family members and friends continued to treat the bodies of the deceased with love and respect. Until the funeral industry undertook these roles, the family and closest friends prepared the body for burial and kept it in the family home until the funeral service.[5] Lucy Lovell's description of combing and braiding Caroline's hair one last time, and her declaring it a privilege to do so, speaks volumes about the intimate contact between a parent and the corpse of a child. This level of contact diminished as the undertaker assumed an ever larger role.

Lucy Lovell attended the funerals of her children and in her diary mentions hymns sung and consolations offered. Among the middle and upper classes of Victorian England, women were actively discouraged from attending funerals and participating in funeral processions and burials, even when a spouse or child was involved. The ostensible purpose was to spare women the emotional strain, but it was also feared that their alleged inability to contain their emotions might disrupt the solemnity of the occasion. Victorian America was far more tolerant and inclusive of women's participation in funerals and burials, although some manuals cautioned against active involvement.[6]

The corpse, however revered, embodied other associations as well between 1840 and 1916. It could be seen as a potential source of disease, pollution, and danger if not buried quickly. The odor, or miasma, of decomposition was feared throughout the nineteenth century, and after germ theory became widely accepted, undertakers and physicians were mindful of the threat of disease and advised embalming and timely burial.[7]

In England the sanitary reformer Edwin Chadwick claimed as early as 1843, in his *Report on the Practice of Interment in Towns*, that "a corpse generated feelings of respect and awe only among the comfortable classes" but was treated with little ceremony and even disgust among the working and poor classes.[8] This claim was certainly an exaggeration, perhaps stemming from Chadwick's own class biases. For New England, descriptions of wakes and accounts in the *Greenfield Gazette and Courier* speak to both respect and ceremony on the part of working-class Irish and other immigrants. Regardless of how an individual body is regarded after death, even though it is inanimate, it is never entirely neutral or mute to those who engage with it.

Bradbury, citing J. Prior and other social historians, also reminds us of the importance of the actual presence of a body to the social processes of death.[9] A physician or coroner declares the individual dead, the family or undertaker prepares the body, the bereaved mourn, the clergy eulogize, and the state records the body. Soldiers whose bodies are never found disrupt this social process and make closure more difficult. In the "good death" even the corpse had a role to play by attending the service and looking its best.

When the famous Deerfield artist George Fuller died in 1884, at the age of sixty-two, his son Robert Higginson Fuller began a series of entries in his mother's diary to chronicle the events. George Fuller was born in Deerfield and after leaving for some years, he returned in 1859 to live on and work the family farm. As he became more successful as a painter, he maintained a studio at his Deerfield home as well as a residence in Brookline and another studio in Boston. He was failing rapidly in the spring of 1884 while in Brookline. Over five days' time Robert H. Fuller described in the diary his father's weakening condition, his partaking of brandy, gruel, and beef tea, the doctors' visits, and the diagnosis of Bright's disease, or kidney failure. On the afternoon of March 20 Fuller was briefly animated, talking and seeming "like his old self," but he died in the early hours of March 21.

The body of George Fuller was called upon by his family to perform at two funeral services. The first, on March 23 in Brookline, came under the direction of the Unitarian minister, Mr. Brown. "All the leading artists of Boston came out to have a last look. . . . Father looked so calm and peaceful with such a noble look on his brow that it was hard to believe that he was anything more than asleep." The next day the family entourage took the train to Deerfield. "Reverend Buckingham preached the service and mother liked his remarks

George Fuller (1822–1884),
photographed by Allen and
Rowell, 1883. Courtesy of
PVMA.

very much indeed." They proceeded to the cemetery, where "Mr. Buckingham made a few further remarks." The family returned to the cemetery on
the morning of the twenty-fifth "and found the grave covered with beautiful
flowers, still fresh, and among them a white lily sent by Mary Field."[10] In 1886,
the writer William Dean Howells, who had been among the distinguished
attendants at Fuller's funeral in Brookline, published a tribute titled *George
Fuller: His Life and Works*.[11] George Fuller, renowned native of Deerfield, had
fulfilled admirably all the tasks required of the dying and deceased in late
nineteenth-century America.

By the 1880s, hospitals in Boston had advanced a long way toward their modern
role in caring for the sick and dying, but there was little question that George
Fuller would die at home. For the middle and upper classes in the United
States, home was still the proper place for care of the dying in their final days
or hours. City hospitals during the nineteenth century were more focused on
the acute illnesses of the poor and working classes and on the medical needs
of those without families or who were travelers or recent immigrants to the

city. Ironically, these same potential patients feared a trip to the hospital and the possibility of being experimented on with some new surgical method or vile treatment and then autopsied in the event of death.[12] Someone who lived at home in the presence of family, whether affluent or of modest means, would die at home. For residents of Franklin County, unless death was unexpected, perhaps happening in a workplace accident, there was no other choice until near the close of the nineteenth century.[13]

As we have seen, even without hospitals, death became increasingly medicalized between 1840 and 1916. By the 1850s, in middle- and upper-class households, a physician was usually present in the final hours before death, whether of a child, like Laura and Caroline Lovell, or an adult. Doctors treated consumptive young women and the mothers who died in childbirth. In the early years of the tuberculosis sanitarium movement, many patients might have convalesced for a long time in an institution, but, like Esther Grout, they came home to die.[14] In the years after the Civil War, a doctor's attendance was no less common and, emboldened by improvements in surgery and the discoveries of pathogens after 1870, the attending physician became ever more confident and proactive in trying to save the dying patient.[15] George Fuller's doctor consulted with other physicians before giving his final diagnosis of Bright's disease. He administered "a powder" on the afternoon before Fuller's death but warned the family that the patient would not fully recover.[16] Before the mid-nineteenth century, artistic images of the bedside in the hour of death were likely to include a minister; after that time it was more likely to be a physician at the bedside.

Sociologists and psychologists of death, such as Bradbury, suggest that as death became more medicalized, it also came to be regarded as less sacred and less "natural." Bradbury and others have gone so far as to observe that in contemporary Western society, we have a notion of "the good medical death."[17] In the good medical death, all the "deathwork professionals," from doctors and coroners to embalmers and funeral directors, use their skills to make death a controlled and managed sequence that is as comfortable as possible for the dying person and his or her family and friends. Death today is often regarded less as a natural process and more as the failure of medical science and technology to cure. The good medical death finds its origins in the nineteenth-century doctor's attempts to treat the dying person, to make him or her comfortable with laudanum or another sedative, and to assist the family in obtaining the services of a competent undertaker.

As George Sheldon observed in his comments on the trappings of funerals in the 1890s, the commercialization of death was also advancing as the years progressed. Small-town funerals never affected the accessories of the more elegant city funerals. Victorian-era funerals in Protestant America were generally less formal but derivative versions of English customs. Funerals in the United States, Canada, and Australia were less expensive and more subdued than those in England, though the farther one traveled into the countryside from London, the less formality one found in English funerals as well.[18] Still, funeral expenses could be prohibitive for middle-class families who felt obligated to make such expenditures.

Even after the height of Victorian mourning had passed in England, services could be elaborate. Pat Jalland consulted the 1869–71 edition of *Cassell's Household Guide*, published in London, and found that whereas an inexpensive funeral in England could cost as little as three pounds, five shillings, an expensive one might cost fifty-three pounds. That sum "secured a hearse and four horses, two mourning-coaches with four horses, twenty-three plumes of rich ostrich feathers, a strong elm shell with stout outer lead coffin, two mutes, and fourteen men as pages, feathermen, and coachmen, complete with truncheons and wands."[19] Such an extravagant display would have attracted considerable attention in Boston on its way to Mount Auburn, never mind Greenfield. One American etiquette book cautioned that "the hired mutes and heavy trappings of woe which are still in use at funerals in England are entirely abandoned in this country."[20]

Colonel George Duncan Wells's military funeral in 1864 was the most ornate service I discovered in the records for Franklin County. A highly respected native of Greenfield, Wells served in the First and Thirty-fourth Massachusetts Regiments of the Union Army and saw action at Harper's Ferry, Bull Run, Harrisonburg, Newmarket, and other battle sites. He was killed in action at Cedar Creek in the Shenandoah Valley of Virginia on October 12, 1864. His body was one of the few from Franklin County that was recovered and made it home from the war. It may have arrived "in a pine box," but its interment was by no means modest.

The remains arrived in Greenfield on October 21 and lay in state in Washington Hall until the funeral.[21] The procession to the Unitarian church included a hearse drawn by a team of horses, followed by a solitary horse with an empty saddle, led by a soldier on foot. The Shelburne Falls band paraded and played, and some fifty uniformed Union soldiers marched with the hearse. Washington Hall and the church were decorated with black and white drapery and flags-in-mourning. Every pew was filled, and many additional mourners stood outside. Stores were closed in town. Citizens lined the streets to pay their respects as an estimated two thousand mourners proceeded to Green River Cemetery. Upon Wells's interment the military escorts fired a volley of shots.[22]

Later funerals, such as George Fuller's in 1884, Edgar Buckingham's in 1894, and George Sheldon's in 1916, continued to exhibit the commercializing forces emergent in the growing funeral industry, but commercialization was

Colonel George Duncan Wells's family plot in Green River Cemetery. Photo ©
Carol Betsch.

not the same thing as extravagance and certainly not the same as Victorian
formality. Prominent men like these three did have well-attended services
with grand eulogies, many floral tributes, and costly undertaker's expenses.
Yet Sheldon's funeral was described as "simple, as he would have wished."
Buckingham's funeral was "simple but impressive." The most noteworthy
feature of Buckingham's funeral procession apparently was the orderly group
of schoolchildren who followed the body to the grave.[23] Even George Fuller's
funeral in Brookline, though attended by many noteworthy members of
Boston's artistic community, was held in his home, and the "exercises . . . were
of the simplest character."[24]

I found no record of what Fuller, the artist, Buckingham, the minister, or
Sheldon, the country gentleman, historian, and statesman, wore in their caskets,
but it is safe to assume that, as was true for the businessmen of the county, it
was probably their best suits and not shrouds. From at least the beginnings
of the Gilded Age (circa 1870–1900) and thereafter, the suit betokened the

more secular and commercializing trends appearing in burial customs. For men, heavenly shrouds were falling out of fashion in favor of a well-tailored suit. The world of commerce had penetrated the sacred domains of family and church. For women, the Victorian guardians of home and faith, evidence suggests that robes and shrouds persisted longer.[25]

Just as the white Anglo-Saxon Protestant man might stand before his doctor, unmarked by any predisposition to disease or deficiency, so too the corpse might be described as possessing a bearing appropriate to a person's ethnicity and class. It was said of George Fuller that "his massive brow was free from trace of sickness or pain. A soft and peaceful expression almost shown [*sic*] on his face. The hand of the destroyer appeared so lightly laid upon him it seemed that we might hope for its withdrawal and that the light of his eyes might at any moment beam upon us."[26] Lengthy obituaries, sermons, and eulogies occasionally were devoted to women of note, such as C. Alice Baker and Catherine Yale, but men garnered the far larger share of such tributes.

As sites of commemoration and remembrance, cemeteries and their assemblages of tombstones were by far the most important material representations of death. If at times neglected in the seventeenth and early eighteenth centuries, during the nineteenth and early twentieth centuries, the gravesite became a primary locus for expressions of love, honor, and grief by the survivors of the deceased. George and Susan Sheldon's selection of Frankie's stone provides a telling example of the thoughtfulness and seriousness of this act, as do many other stones in the cemeteries of the four Franklin County towns. Just as older people sometimes took the initiative in planning their own services, so the dying person and his family might collaborate to select an appropriate stone and epitaph. The stone and its inscription represented an intimate connection between the deceased and his or her surviving loved ones, but these objects conveyed other messages as well.

The choice of an appropriate marker was dictated by many considerations, including dominant social ideologies and conventions regarding size, shape, and style; the availability of materials such as slate, sandstone, granite, and marble; and matters of emotional attachment, personal taste, and economic means.[27] Archaeologists and other students of gravestones have observed a general trend that holds for many cemeteries in New England and upstate New York. Even though social inequalities always existed in New England towns, in the early nineteenth century, class differences were not displayed prominently in cemeteries. The sizes of gravestones varied little. The shapes tended to be similar and the type of stone fairly uniform. The impression one gains when entering an early graveyard or cemetery is that of a shared, communal standard that veiled underlying socioeconomic differences.[28]

Allen Sisters, *The Old Burying Ground*, c. 1900. Courtesy of PVMA.

From the second half of the nineteenth century into the early twentieth, gravestones became much more variable in size and material, and many prominent markers were erected to glorify family names and individual successes. In keeping with other commercializing processes, these trends reached their height during the Gilded Age, and families of means often created plots with a large central stone with the gradual addition of accompanying markers for "Father," "Mother," "Sister," Brother," and so on. Scanning a cemetery of this period, one is struck by the variability and implied status differences reflected in the different sizes and styles of grave markers. Randall McGuire believes these variations reflect the rise of capitalism and Social Darwinism, which emphasized individual success over social equality. The grouping of family gravestones and accompanying monuments perpetuated the "cult of domesticity" in the cemetery and reified the Victorian ideal of family.[29] Although such patterns can easily be overstated, there is a chronological coherence in New England cemeteries that roughly conforms to these changes in cultural preferences.[30]

What the descriptions of larger trends fail to capture is the subtle differences and emotional expressions that individual stones evoke regardless of grandiosity or expense. Yes, Frankie Sheldon's and Hattie Willard's stones are diminutive in comparison with George Fuller's, Edgar Buckingham's, and George Sheldon's, but evidence of a parent's love and loss is visible in them. By embellishment, epitaph, or both, theirs and those of many other children manifest intense feelings of loss. This is true of stones dedicated to spouses as well, although when a husband and wife in the late nineteenth century had individual stones, the wife's would never be the larger of the two. On gravestones of that time, a wife's inscription often included the words "wife of" or "relict of," followed by the husband's name. Such stones might also display an epitaph expressing considerable affection and devotion by the deceased's husband or children.

When we encounter the small, unadorned marker of an infant or the middling gravestone of someone who died of advanced age, bearing only a name and a date of death, we cannot assume any less emotional connection or investment from their loved ones or that these markers are evidence of lower socioeconomic status. Nor should we necessarily assume that a heavily festooned gravestone signifies deep and unqualified affection. As Sarah Tarlow has commented with respect to cemeteries, it must always be understood that people are "subtle, complex, emotional," and motivated by a variety of intentions.[31] The military cemetery, for example, with its identical gravestones in perfect alignment, is mute about the emotional attachments and family connections of the deceased, yet we know they existed, and in variety. The military cemetery's expanse of lawn with its uniform relief sends its own

Gravestone of Hattie Willard, Laurel Hill Cemetery, Deerfield.
Photo © Carol Betsch.

message, but it is a message of numbers rather than of individual testimonies. The gravestone is a metaphor for death but embodies many meanings, and the cemetery is a complex cultural landscape.

Commemoration and consolation, too, take many forms. The Victorian culture of mourning placed considerable emphasis on bereavement and on expressions of condolence, consolation, and commemoration. The dying person could participate directly by giving or bequeathing treasured possessions to valued friends or family members. When Samuel Willard willed books to George Sheldon, perhaps as an expression of gratitude for his assisting at Hattie's death, the bequest was also a tribute to their long-standing friendship. Books, jewelry, and even common household items were often given away at the time of death, not so much as a distribution of wealth as tokens of remembrance.

Portraits or photographs commissioned by parents or other family members were a desired form of remembrance, as demonstrated by the posthumous photograph of Edward Hitchcock's son Harry and the reference in Sheldon's diary to a photograph's being taken of Hattie Willard. These and other "likenesses" became poignant records of lost loved ones for many families in the second half of the nineteenth century.[32]

In a book about death and the bereaved, published in 1865, Thomas Baldwin Thayer writes, "In every home there is an enshrined memory, a sacred relic, a ring, a lock of shining hair, a broken plaything, a book, a picture, something sacredly kept and guarded, which speaks of death, which tells as plainly as words, of some one long since gone." Karen Halttunen suggests that these personal mementos were valued because they permitted the bereaved to weep and mourn over a representation of the deceased in the privacy of the home in a way that would have been unacceptable publicly.[33] These items, especially hair or a photograph taken either before or after death, carried additional symbolic meaning.

Gravestone of Frankie Sheldon, Laurel Hill Cemetery. His epitaph has worn away: "By guardian Angels led / Safe from temptation, safe from sin's pollution / He lives, whom we call dead." Photo © Carol Betsch.

Memorial hair wreath, c. 1860. Courtesy of PVMA.

"How full thou art of memories, severed tress!"[34] Probably no single item exemplified the embodiment of a deceased loved one in late nineteenth- and early twentieth-century America, where the keeping of mementos and visual likenesses was widespread, than hair. Literally a part of the deceased's body, it carried the texture, color, and form of one of the person's most distinguishing features. References even allude to the fragrant, lingering scent of a child or spouse. So popular was the collecting and embellishment of locks of hair from a living or deceased loved one that some women specialized in making hair jewelry and art. Mrs. E. L. Hammond operated a hair shop in Greenfield in the 1870s that did hair jewelry by commission. When Mrs. Hammond closed her shop in Greenfield in March 1876, she published an advertisement in the *Gazette and Recorder* advising all patrons to pick up their uncollected pieces by February 15.[35] Potential patrons of such shops were occasionally warned of unscrupulous establishments that used hair collected or purchased from hairdressers or barbershops rather than the actual hair for which the commission was made.

Mourning jewelry, consisting of rings, bracelets, brooches, and especially lockets, was popular in England and the United States between 1840 and 1916. Like other objects, these could be bequeathed or given away by the deceased before death or by a surviving loved one. A locket containing a likeness of the deceased, a lock of hair, or both, provided an intimate and daily reminder of the person gone. The jewelry might be made of silver or gold, and a stone of black jet or clear stones such as diamonds might be chosen to include in a piece for later stages of mourning, but many items were fashioned from the hair itself. Braided, woven, or knotted hair was incorporated into bracelets and brooches and used in other memorial pieces such as braided bookmarks and crocheted or knotted art framed as wall hangings. The Victorian fascination with hair ran deep and wide, extending well beyond mourning jewelry. For the living, a lock of hair was also an expression of friendship and intimacy and a favored topic of poetry and other forms of literature. The interest was primarily in women's hair, but the lock of a lost child or husband was also highly valued in cases of mourning.[36]

For some twenty-first-century Americans, the notion of collecting and memorializing a lock of hair is unsettling; for others it is no different from collecting a lock of hair or other memento from, for example, a famous living person.[37] More unsettling perhaps is the tradition of posthumous photography and portraiture. Yet as others have pointed out, with today's ubiquity of professional and lay photography, it is easy to forget that for many nineteenth- and early twentieth-century families, a posthumous photograph might have been the only record available of a child or other loved one. Furthermore, people at the time were more familiar with death, because it was a common occurrence and because most people died at home. Still, the surreal quality of some memorial imagery cannot be denied. Surviving family members might be pictured seated around a dead child, for example, or the child might lie in a carriage, suggesting motion and activity that would never again take place.[38]

One particularly jarring and evocative mourning portrait comes from the Franklin County town of Ashfield, adjacent to Shelburne. Edwin Romanzo Elmer (1850–1923) was a local artist and inventor whose much adored child, Effie, died at the age of nine and a half of what was believed to be a heart ailment.[39] Shortly after the child's death, Elmer painted a portrait, titled *Mourning Picture*, of the family in front of the house he had built. Effie is shown playing with her pets and toys while her parents sit in the background, dressed in full mourning attire. Analysts of this work point out the shaded background in which the parents are seated, in contrast to the sunlit space in which Effie

Edward Romanzo Elmer, *Mourning Picture*, 1890, oil on canvas, 27 15/16 x 36 in. Smith College Museum of Art, Northampton, Mass., Purchased SC 1953:129.

plays. It has also been suggested that this painting, more than simply an attempt to freeze a moment in time, is an attempt "to mitigate death's finality through art."[40] Such artifacts of commemoration kept alive the memory of the deceased, if only in a material way.

When Harriet Allen, a young woman in her early twenties, died in the summer of 1855, her parents received a sheaf of letters that were adept and genteel in their expressions of condolence. One began, "My dear friend, I need not say to you that I have sympathized most deeply with you and yours in this recent sad & trying bereavement." Yet another: "My dear friend, I have heard of your great affliction, & the sudden and unexpected death of your daughter Harriet. Permit me to condole with you for this great—this overwhelming loss. You are philosopher enough to know that our destiny is not in our hands, and that there is a Power above us that orders all things for the right."[41] During late July and August, more such letters arrived, addressed to one or both parents or to Harriet's older sister. The craft of the consolation letter had risen to something of an art in New England in the mid-nineteenth century, and it would persist for many decades.

Between about 1830 to 1890, a flurry of women's almanacs, etiquette books, and mourning manuals advised the emerging middle class of the proper conventions, attire, and modes of correspondence to observe in the event of a death in a family with whom one was close. Details were specified right down to the black-bordered stationery one should use when writing letters of condolence—advice that may have prompted a postscript by one friend of the Allens, written on the margin of unbordered paper, saying, "Excuse this expression of my feelings *on this paper* but real sympathy is in thought & not in expression."[42] Karen Halttunen writes that "for the middle classes of mid-nineteenth-century America, mourning the dead was the most powerful sentiment of all and the most resistant to public expression through empty social forms."[43] The meshing of Victorian formality and propriety with New England values honoring frugality and avoidance of vanity and ostentation created a distinctive North American pattern of mourning. Feelings were to be genuine, "natural," and "right." Services had to be construed as "simple," like those attributed to Fuller and the others. At the same time, the expression of sentiment and the performance of mourning allowed the middle class to demonstrate its sincerity and gentility.

The evidence indicates that many middle-class people of Franklin County and a wider swath of New England embraced the cult of mourning and observed its practices. Seldom a week went by when the *Greenfield Gazette and Courier* and other local newspapers failed to include a little poem or vignette about an untimely or honorable death. Whether it was an anonymous poem on the last page by "A mother" or a printing on the front page of Longfellow's "The Sleeping Dead,"[44] each piece expressed a sentimentality that was supposed to be natural to middle-class women and acquired by middle-class men of good breeding and education. Many pieces were clipped and found their way into memorial albums and scrapbooks collected by young homemakers. Some became the basis for penmanship lessons for young girls.[45] This genre appears to have reached its peak at mid-century, although many examples can be found right into the twentieth century.[46] By the end of the nineteenth century, however, local newspapers leave one with the impression that the increasing numbers of advertisements for undertakers and purveyors of monuments were gradually crowding into the space available for poems about death.

Another avenue open to the bereaved or simply to ordinary citizens with an interest in death and the afterlife was the comfort of "consolation literature."[47] Just as "Mother, do not weep" poetry, attributed to dying children, asked parents not to cry because the child was destined for a better place, so consolation literature assured readers that heaven was a knowable place where the bereaved would again meet their loved ones. Written primarily by Protestant clergymen and Christian women, scores, if not hundreds, of books, short stories, and religious tracts conveyed consolation themes. The heyday of this genre was from the 1830s to the 1880s, but the form persisted into the early twentieth century. Ann Douglas cites the story of little Eva in Harriett Beecher Stowe's *Uncle Tom's Cabin* as an example of the consolation theme in mainstream literature and as a popular subject—the dying young girl. On her deathbed Eva bestows locks of her hair to Uncle Tom and others.

Of the many women writing consolation literature, probably none was more widely recognized than Elizabeth Stuart Phelps, who was born in Boston in 1844. Her first major adult book was *Gates Ajar* (1868), followed by *Beyond the Gates* (1883) and *The Gates Between* (1887). *Gates Ajar*, along with *Uncle Tom's Cabin*, one of the most popular novels of the later nineteenth century, tells the story of Mary, a New England girl and sister of a young soldier killed in the Civil War. Mary finds heaven not a distant and elusive place but a warm and accessible one where her brother watches over her and where the earthbound bereaved can communicate with their loved ones. A feature of Phelps's writing and that of many others was what Douglas refers to as the domestication of heaven, a homey, earthlike place where mothers could eventually meet their lost children, and wives, their deceased husbands.[48]

The broad appeal of these novels and short stories bears witness to the unanswered longing of so many parents and loved ones. Novels like *Uncle Tom's Cabin* and *Gates Ajar* were ubiquitous in New England and were quoted in newspapers and other sources. George Sheldon knew *Uncle Tom's Cabin* well enough to quote from it in his diary, and it is safe to assume that a person of Susan Sheldon's background and experience read something published earlier than but like *Gates Ajar*. If there is a transition in the consolation literature of the later part of the nineteenth century, it would appear to be toward a more dramatic, theatrical style.[49]

The post–Civil War years and the emerging Gilded Age stirred up choppy waters for the middle class to navigate with regard to commemoration of the dead. For Protestants, traditional Yankee values of sincerity and simplicity were being challenged by the commercial forces that impinged on virtually all aspects of life. The predominantly Roman Catholic population of immigrants further inspired a desire by Yankees to set themselves apart by demonstrating their economic dominance. One way to do this was to choose more formal and expensive funeral services, attire, and gravestones, but this was a stage on which Irish merchants and skilled workers could perform as well. Halttunen argues that as early as the 1850s, the middle-class residents of North American cities were leaving behind the codes of sincerity and "right feelings" while retaining the social forms of gentility, including mourning, and even taking them to a more formal level.[50]

In Franklin County and perhaps other parts of rural New England, this disjunction seems to have lagged somewhat. The Reverend Mumford certainly wanted people to trust his sincerity and true feelings when, regarding Hattie Willard's service, he claimed to be impressed by the "evident reality in the grief" and the "artlessness in the expressions of sympathy."[51] The grief over a lost child or spouse was genuine, but the "simplicity" of the funeral services of the Sheldon and Fuller families and their acquaintances may have been more perceived than real.

The solemnity of the cult of mourning provided a target for critics and satirists. As early as 1828 the *Greenfield Gazette and Courier* ran an article arguing that mourning apparel was a mockery in the absence of true grief, and where true grief was present, it was an "indifferent" gesture. The writer went on to state that the principal objection to the practice of wearing mourning clothes was that "it is useless, inconvenient, and expensive."[52] In 1841, the *Gazette and Courier* published an announcement saying, "The proprietors have determined to follow the example of the State, and raise a revenue from dead folks." It then warned that the newspaper was going to start charging a fee for lengthy obituaries, "to check the swarm of these notices which come in upon us. They are, generally speaking, interesting to but very few, and they crowd out matter which is interesting to many."[53] The newspaper ran the occasional article on the "peculiarities of French funerals."[54]

Correspondence regarding death and funerals was not always solemn and consoling. In 1850, Edward Russell wrote matter-of-factly to "Brother Hawks" to tell of "Mother's Death." He explained that "she wanted to see you much" and "I should have written you before, but her death has been almost daley [*sic*] expected since I received your letter." He then assured his brother that she was "handsomely buried" and that he will come visit soon if "any business can be had" nearby.[55] Louisa Higginson, in a letter to her brother Waldo, describes a tedious funeral she attended in 1862 in which she found "the overflow of human sympathy" to be "rasping." "It lasted ages," she said, and she feared "going into hysterics."[56] P. Cooley, a South Deerfield resident, recalled hearing as a child that a coffin slid off a sleigh on its way to the cemetery. The drivers had to retrace their route and found that the coffin had slid off on a sharp bend in the road. Following the marks in the snow, they found the occupied coffin down an embankment.[57]

"I didn't attend the funeral, but I sent a nice letter saying I approved of it." Samuel Clemens, or Mark Twain (1835–1910), may be the American writer from this period who is best known for his wit and sarcasm about death and the afterlife. His character Emmeline Grangerford in *The Adventures of Huckleberry Finn*—she is the deceased daughter of Colonel Grangerford—wrote the "Ode to Stephen Dowling Bots, Dec'd." Emmeline also drew morbid pictures and kept a scrapbook of obituaries, accidents, and other "cases of patient suffering." Huck expresses the opinion that considering her morbid disposition when alive, "she was having a better time in the graveyard." Scholars attribute Twain's inspiration for Emmeline's poem to the works of sentimental poets such as Lydia Maria Child and especially Julia A. Moore.[58] Twain's short story "Captain Stormfield's Visit to Heaven" was aimed directly at Elizabeth Stuart Phelps's *The Gates Ajar*, lampooning the homelike scenes and friends united in Phelps's version of heaven. In Captain Stormfield's heaven, people age in both directions, parents meet their now grown children, and Stormfield grows quickly weary of sitting on clouds and playing the harp.[59] Other social critics of the period found this form of consolation literature outlandish and oppressive as well.

Twain, however, had from childhood endured many personal losses. When he was born on November 30, 1835, his mother had already lost three other children. His older sister, Margaret, died in 1839, his brother Benjamin in 1842, and his father in 1847, when Twain was eleven. He then lost his younger brother, Henry, in a steamship accident in 1858. After he and Olivia (Livy) Langdon married in 1870, they lost their son Langdon in 1872, and Twain's reportedly favorite daughter, Olivia Susan (Susy), died in young adulthood in 1896. Livy died in 1904, and Twain's daughter Jean in 1909. By the time Twain himself died in 1910, he had, like George Sheldon, witnessed members of his family passing at all stages of the life course.[60]

Twain thought at an early age that he "carried the seed of death in him." He felt responsible for his brother Henry's death, he thought he had contributed to his son Langdon's death by leaving him uncovered on a winter's carriage ride shortly before the boy died, and he felt extreme guilt about not returning from a European tour before the death of his daughter Susy.[61] Twain saw his dead sister Margaret and brother Benjamin in the house at the times of their passing, observed Livy holding their dead son Langdon, and said that he had seen his own father's autopsy through a keyhole in the door of the doctor's office. He knew well the face of death.

As a son, sibling, and parent, Twain must have known and experienced every possible emotion surrounding death. Harold Bush has pointed out that despite Twain's critiquing of sentimental poetry, he was also strongly attached to it. What he thought were excessive expressions of grief, he himself expressed before and after Susy's death. During a lecture tour in 1888 that took him to Smith College in nearby Northampton, Massachusetts, he recited James Whitcomb Riley's sentimental poem "The Absence of Little Wesley." Perhaps even more surprisingly, he composed two elegiac poems after Susy's death, "In Memoriam" a year after she died and "Broken Idols" a year later. "In Memoriam" ends with these lines:

> They stand, yet, where erst they stood
> Speechless in that dim morning long ago;
> And still they gaze, as then they gazed,
> And murmur, It [the light] will come again;
> It knows our pain—it knows—it knows—
> Ah surely it will come again.

Using Twain as a prime example and consulting current psychoanalytic theories of grieving, Bush argues that the mourning of a deceased child is likely to be profoundly life changing and that long periods of bereavement are normal.[62]

Mark Twain maintained firm connections to the Connecticut River valley and New England in the late nineteenth and early twentieth centuries. He and his family lived downriver from Franklin County in Hartford, Connecticut, for much of that time. He lectured throughout New England often, and he was a frequent visitor to the region. One of his closest friends of more than forty years was William Dean Howells, the novelist and editor of the *Atlantic Monthly* and the man who eulogized George Fuller's "life and works." Asked to the celebrated Ashfield Dinners, where Howells had spoken on more than one occasion, Twain wrote to decline an oft-repeated invitation: "A few years ago I was growing old and rheumatic. But all that is changed now. I *am* old and rheumatic."[63]

Perhaps there is something to be made of the Yankee stoicism said to be characteristic of rural New Englanders and the fatalism attributed to the Irish and other immigrants who arrived in the nineteenth and early twentieth centuries. Aspects of character and custom do have their place. But normative cultural patterns and stereotyped attributions of character fail to capture adequately the tangled web of illness, loss, and grief I found cast over this valley. The one persistent theme I discovered was the genuine, heartfelt grief of a parent at the loss of a child. Mark Twain's anger and cynicism over many forms of loss gave us Captain Stormfield, but with the loss of his own children his profound sadness gave us "In Memoriam."

The inhabitants of the Connecticut Valley of Massachusetts, like those everywhere and anywhere else, found their individualized ways to bury and memorialize their departed. They selected from a wide array of religious liturgies, community expectations, family practices, and personal emotions. And the richer they were, and we are, for it.

At the time of George Sheldon's death, an era had ended, but the dawn of the new era was not auspicious. After 1916 the United States would enter the "war to end all wars." At least twenty-eight hundred Massachusetts soldiers would die in World War I. In September 1918 the influenza pandemic would strike and ultimately kill another estimated eighteen thousand Massachusetts citizens, many of them soldiers.[64] Oh, and the woman who lingered at the graveside on that Memorial Day visit? She was Kathleen Belanger, nurse, emergency medical technician, and the mother of Sergeant Gregory Belanger of Deerfield, a decorated Iraq war veteran killed in action August 27, 2003. She, perhaps more than anyone else who visited the cemetery that day, could empathize with the mothers of Deerfield who came before her.

APPENDIXES:
Data Collection and Evaluation

Frequent reference is made to historical data in several chapters. Over many years before I began writing this book, my students and I collected data available on vital statistics, the censuses, and public health. These data came from a variety of official sources often including original records from the offices of town clerks as well as manuscript and published sources from the towns and the state of Massachusetts. In most cases summaries of these data have been published elsewhere, and citations in the chapter notes point to those publications for the reader interested in further background. However, as a foundation for key chapters in the book and for the reader interested in seeing a glimpse of the results on which observations and generalizations have been made, I include a few examples in the figures below.

The figures are, for the most part, based on data that are not heavily massaged. They are faithful to the counts available or derivable from the original data, but with some control for age and sex composition, disease type, and so forth. Thus, the precise numbers are not subjected to estimation techniques and are reflective of what nineteenth-century statisticians might have observed had they graphed the data in the manner presented here. There is likely some over- or underestimation, but the trends are reliable.

Appendix A. Infant Mortality (Chapter 3)

The slow rise and then long and somewhat steady decline of infant mortality can be observed in figure 1. Note the peak of infant deaths in the 1870s. The impact of the 1918 influenza pandemic can also be observed in 1918. Current infant mortality rates in Massachusetts are among the lowest in the nation and compare favorably with many European countries. According to the National Center for Health Statistics, the U.S. infant mortality rate was 6.86 per 1,000 live births in 2005, but rates varied by ethnicity and access to prenatal care. The rate in Massachusetts was closer to 5.

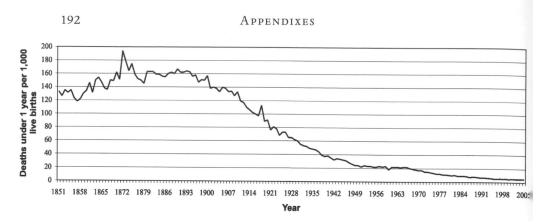

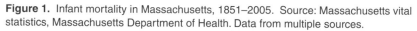

Figure 1. Infant mortality in Massachusetts, 1851–2005. Source: Massachusetts vital statistics, Massachusetts Department of Health. Data from multiple sources.

Infant Mortality in the Study Area

A comparison of infant mortality in the state, Franklin County, and in the four-town study area illustrates the comparability of the subregions in addition to highlighting some specific differences. For example, the rate for the state of Massachusetts includes Boston and the large manufacturing cities such as Lowell, Lawrence, and Fall River. The small cities and towns of western Massachusetts never reached the levels in these major cities, with the exception of the mill city of Holyoke, Massachusetts, located in Hampden County, farther south on the Connecticut River. This suggests that Franklin County was a more favorable environment, at least where infant survivorship is concerned. In figure 2 note that the overall rate for Franklin County is well below the state and four-town averages. This is because the other towns in Franklin County were among the smallest and most rural in the state, with lower rates of infant mortality. The four-town values correspond closely to the state pattern, with the exception that the 1870s mortality peaks were staggered differently.

Primary Causes of Infant Mortality in the Study Area, 1850–1910

Virtually all of the research on the nineteenth- and early twentieth-century United States and Europe demonstrates that gastrointestinal infections were the primary cause of serious illness and death of children under two. This is also true for many parts of the world today, wherever sanitary conditions and hygienic practices are difficult to maintain. Even given the somewhat crude diagnostic capabilities of the late nineteenth century and variety of terms used to assign cause of death, it is possible to ascertain the relative impact in the study area. Figure 3 shows our estimate of the relative impacts of various major causes of death in the Connecticut Valley.

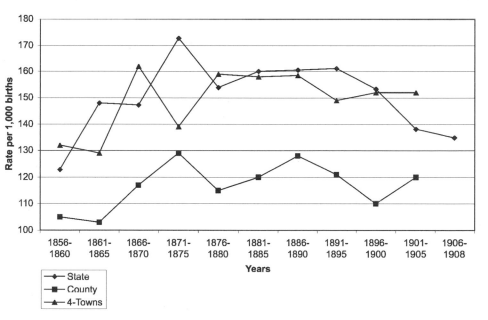

Figure 2. Infant mortality in the state, Franklin County, and four-town study area, 1850–1908. Values based on three- or five-year averages.

Figure 3. Principal causes of death in infants as inferred from the cause-of-death records, Deerfield, Greenfield, Montague, and Shelburne, 1850–1910.

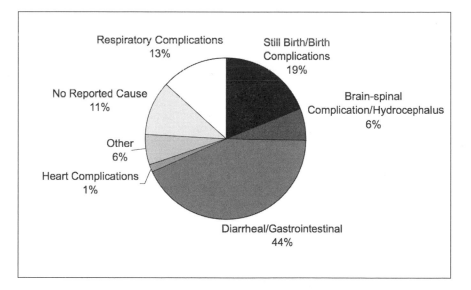

Appendix B. Scarlet Fever (Chapter 4)

The scarlet fever epidemics that plagued New England and much of the United States in the mid- to late 1800s took a significant toll on children in the Connecticut Valley. My research team compiled data on the period between 1850 and 1910 and on two of the most serious epidemics that hit the four-town study area. and their impact could readily be seen.

The graphs for scarlet fever are based on approximately 220 deaths that were reliably diagnosed as scarlet fever or scarletina. This is obviously an undercount of the real numbers but still sufficient to reveal unambiguous trends. As figure 1 shows, the three contiguous towns of Deerfield, Greenfield, and Shelburne suffered the most; the town of Montague, on the other side of the Connecticut River, apparently had several fewer deaths.

The point was made in Chapter 4 that after infants and toddlers survived to age two, it was childhood fevers, and particularly scarlet fever, that were most threatening to survivorship. In figure 2 I plot the incidence of scarlet fever with age. Note how the trajectory rises rapidly commencing at about age two and then decreases as children's immune systems mature and as they reach puberty.

Figure 1. Scarlet fever deaths of children under 16 years in the four-town study area.

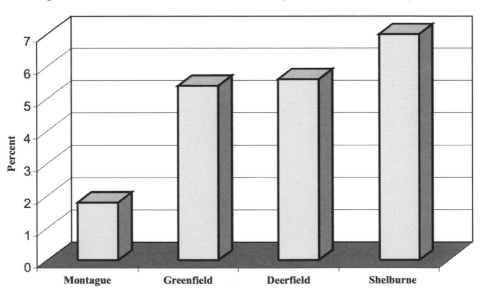

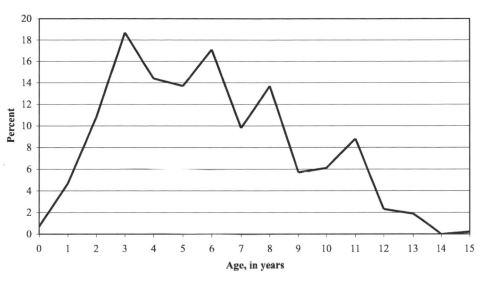

Figure 2. Scarlet fever deaths of children under 16, 1850–1910, as percentage of total deaths.

Scarlet fever deaths could occur in any given year since streptococcal bacteria were ubiquitous and easily transmitted. However, in certain years the cases reached epidemic proportions, as we see in 1858–59, and 1867–68. Such a spike could occur because of the virulence of the strain of bacteria occurring locally; it could also be the result of other infections that weakened children and made them more susceptible. For example, gastrointestinal infections or a measles outbreak could weaken many children, who then succumbed to the subsequent streptococcal infection. Figure 3 illustrates the annual impact of scarlet fever.

As observed with infant mortality, gastrointestinal diseases often show a strong seasonal peak at certain times of the year, and in temperate latitudes that period is often in the late summer and early fall. We were interested in whether or not scarlet fever showed seasonality, and so we graphed the two epidemics across the months of the year to assess whether children were more vulnerable at certain periods. As can be observed in figure 4, there was a strong January peak in the 1859 epidemic, but that pattern was virtually absent in the 1867 epidemic. It is also possible to see a slight trend toward a higher percentage of deaths in the period of May, June, July. This pattern has been observed in other studies for major cities in the northern hemisphere.

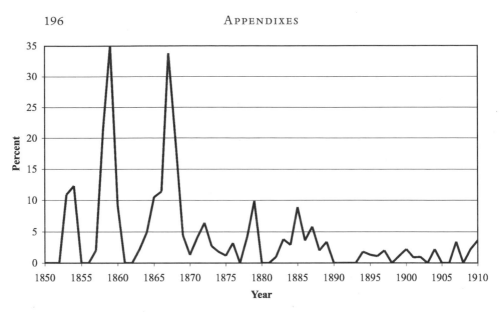

Figure 3. Epidemic mortality from scarlet fever in the four-town study area, 1850–1910. Note the peaks in 1859 and 1867.

Figure 4. Seasonality in the scarlet fever epidemics of 1858–59 and 1867–68. Despite the strong peak in January for the 1859 epidemic, seasonality provides a weak signal for scarlet fever.

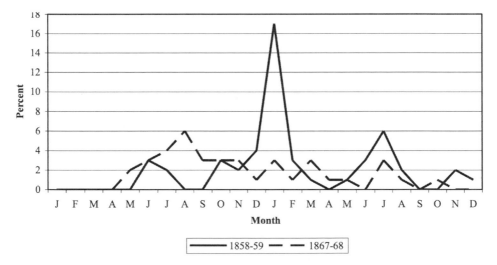

Appendix C. Tuberculosis in Young Women (Chapter 5)

As noted in Chapter 5, the fact that girls and young women showed a higher susceptibility to mortality from tuberculosis was understood to be the case even in the late nineteenth century. In fact, Samuel W. Abbott in his frequently cited report, "The Vital Statistics of Massachusetts, A Forty Years' Summary," published in 1897, created a graph to illustrate a comparison between England and Massachusetts for this phenomenon (pp. 788–89). It is difficult to reproduce an adequate copy, but it is worth presenting here for the sheer power of the information and the influence it had on early thinking about tuberculosis. In figure 1 the darker line represents the rate of mortality for females between 1851 and 1895, and the lighter, or dotted, line represents the rate for males. The long persistent trend of higher female mortality in Massachusetts was of concern, but the fact that the two lines were merging and crossing toward the end of the century was a source for optimism. Abbott noted that the crossover for England occurred much earlier, in 1866 (p. 789).

In the four-town study area and in Franklin Country, the decline in tuberculosis mortality followed a similar trend between 1850 and 1905. Initially,

Figure 1. "Phthisis" mortality in Massachusetts and England, per million population, 1851–1895. Source: *A Forty Years' Summary,* 788.

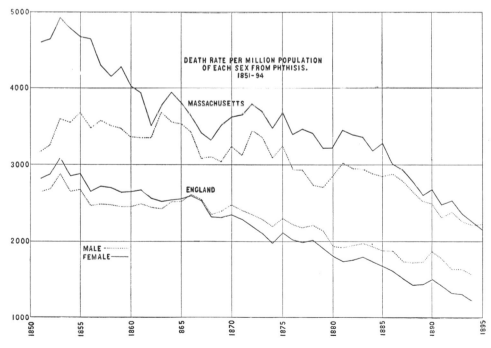

female deaths were significantly higher than male deaths, and the two rates tended to merge over time. In the Connecticut Valley case, the crossover begins approximately 1885 rather than 1895. Rates for the four-town area are expressed per 10,000 population, rather than per million population. The graph comparisons for male and female tuberculosis mortality are based on 1,969 total deaths over the study period, of which 1,888 are of known age, 843 male and 1,045 female.

As described in Chapter 5, much of this difference in rates of death in the earlier decades was the result of increased deaths of girls and young women between their early teen years and their late twenties. This is illustrated in figure 3, which presents tuberculosis mortality by age. Note that there are two crossovers of the male and female data, each of which may be of interest. Male rates become higher than female rates at around the age of 40 years, and then female rates again cross over to become higher than males in the 70-79 age group. This latter occurrence presumably is due to the fact that heart disease is much higher for men at this age than for women. (Again, the graph comparisons for male and female tuberculosis mortality are based on 1,969 total deaths over the study period, of which 1,888 are of known age, 843 male and 1,045 female.)

Figure 2. Tuberculosis mortality by year and by sex in the four-town study area, 1855-1905. Source: Nicole Falk Smith, "The Problem of Excess Female Mortality: Tuberculosis in Western Massachusetts, 1850–1910," M.A. thesis, Department of Anthropology, University of Massachusetts Amherst, 2008.

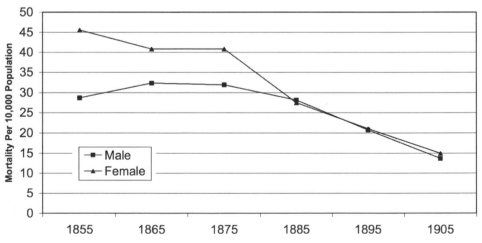

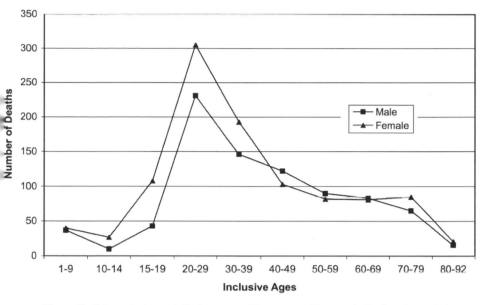

Figure 3. Tuberculosis mortality by age and by sex over life span in the four-town study area, 1850–1910. Source: Smith, "The Problem of Excess Female Mortality."

Appendix D. Old Age (Chapter 7)

In Chapter 7 it was pointed out that in Massachusetts in the nineteenth and early twentieth centuries, as is true today, the chronic diseases appear more frequently as a cause of death in the elderly than they do in individuals in the younger age groups. Infectious diseases, however, still played an important role in elderly deaths. A comparison of the leading causes of death in the elderly in the state records for Massachusetts versus those for Deerfield may reflect some real differences, as well as possibly some differences in diagnostic capabilities and choices. Old age was listed as a cause far more commonly in Deerfield than it was in the state as a whole. Both stroke and apoplexy were used by Deerfield physicians, yet they were probably grouped together by the Massachusetts Office of Vital Statistics. Cancer and nephritis may not have been as easily diagnosed by the doctors of Deerfield as it was by a wide sampling of physicians in the state by 1910.

The relative proportion of deaths by each of the major ten causes for Deerfield are shown in figure 2. If I had grouped apoplexy and stroke together, the two would have overtaken the fourth-ranked cause, tuberculosis. These examples serve as reminders of how complex diagnosis was in the early twentieth century (as it is now), and how categories that were to some extent subjective and sometimes meant different things to different diagnosticians could complicate matters. Yet, there is relative good correspondence among these eight causes, and actual differences plus sampling processes could certainly account for some of the disparity. As noted above, the broad trends are discernible, and it is not an interpretive stretch to group a variety of, for example, gastrointestinal causes of infant death into a meaningful category or two, or to make reasonable assessments about categories like apoplexy and stroke. But caution is warranted in trying to be too precise about many attributed causes of death between 1840 and 1916.

Figure 1. Eight leading causes of death in Massachusetts (1910) and Deerfield (1900–1910).

MASSACHUSETTS STATE	DEERFIELD, MASSACUSETTS
1. Heart Disease	1. Old Age
2. Stroke	2. Pneumonia
3. Pneumonia	3. Heart Disease
4. Cancer	4. Tuberculosis/Consumption
5. Nephritis (Bright's)	5. Stroke
6. Pulmonary Tuberculosis	6. Apoplexy
7. Diarrhea	7. Lungs (other)
8. Old Age	8. Cancer

Figure 2. Ten leading causes of death in population aged 60 years and over, Deerfield, 1900–1910.

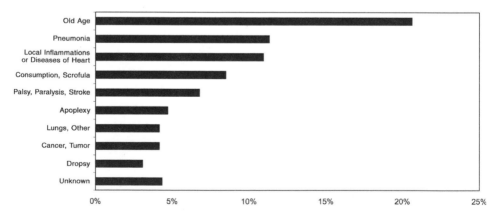

NOTES

Introduction

1. See Gary Laderman, *Rest in Peace: A Cultural History of Death and the Funeral Home in Twentieth-Century America* (New York: Oxford University Press, 2003), 1.

2. Philippe Ariès, *Western Attitudes toward Death: From the Middle Ages to the Present*, trans. P. M. Ranum (Baltimore: Johns Hopkins University Press, 1974).

3. *National Vital Statistics Reports* 56, no. 10 (2008): 7.

4. Despite these extraordinary reductions in infant and childhood mortality, the United States is still not the gold standard. As of 2005, the United States ranked thirty-sixth in the world for lowest infant mortality and thirty-eighth for greatest life expectancy. As good as our prospects are, citizens of most of western Europe, Japan, and other east Asian countries fare better. See, e.g., Population Reference Bureau, "Countries with the Highest and Lowest Life Expectancy," at www.prb.org/pdf07/07WPDS_Eng.pdf, and Geography IQ at www.geographyiq.com/ranking/rankings.htm, for the rankings under "people."

5. Katherine Ott, *Fevered Lives: Tuberculosis in American Culture since 1870* (Cambridge: Harvard University Press, 1996), 1.

6. For useful discussions of the importance of an anthropological perspective on health and how the new medical anthropology views notions of sickness and healing, see Merrill Singer, "The Development of Critical Medical Anthropology: Implications for Biological Anthropology," in *Building a New Biocultural Synthesis: Political-Economic Perspectives on Human Biology*, ed. Alan H. Goodman and Thomas L. Leatherman, 93–123 (Ann Arbor: University of Michigan Press, 1998); Donald Joralemon, *Exploring Medical Anthropology* (Boston: Allyn and Bacon, 1999); James Trostle, *Epidemiology and Culture* (Cambridge: Cambridge University Press, 2005).

7. For examples, see Joralemon, *Exploring Medical Anthropology*; Margaret Lock and Deborah Gordon, *Biomedicine Examined* (Boston: Kluwer, 1988); Byron Good and Mary-Jo DelVecchio Good,"Learning Medicine" in *Knowledge, Power, and Practice: The Anthropology of Medicine and Everyday Life*, ed. Shirley Lindenbaum and Margaret Lock, 81–107 (Berkeley: University of California Press, 1993).

8. Ott, *Fevered Lives*.

9. For examples of medical anthropological analysis of American medicine, see Hans A. Baer, *Biomedicine and Alternative Healing Systems in America: Issues of Class, Race, Ethnicity, and Gender* (Madison: University of Wisconsin Press, 2001), esp. 7–49, and Merrill Singer and Hans A. Baer, *Critical Medical Anthropology* (Amityville, NY: Baywood, 1995), 181–202.

10. Deborah Gordon refers to this delineation in hindsight as the assumption that it is the "cumulative progression toward the unfolding of truth about nature's diseases." Gordon, "Tenacious Assumptions in Western Medicine," in *Biomedicine Examined*, ed. Margaret Lock and Deborah Gordon, 19–56 (Boston: Kluwer, 1988). For examples of a newer medical history that problematizes traditional narratives, see the exceptional collection of essays in *Locating Medical History: The Stories and Their Meanings*, ed. Frank Huisman and John Harley Warner (Baltimore: Johns Hopkins University Press, 2004).

11. Examples of works in which illness and death or death and loss are considered processually include Stephen M. Stowe, *Doctoring the South: Southern Physicians and Everyday Medicine*

in the Mid-Nineteenth Century (Chapel Hill: University of North Carolina Press, 2004), and Julie-Marie Strange, Death, Grief, and Poverty in Britain, 1870–1914 (New York: Cambridge University Press, 2005). For illness and medicine in a midwestern regional context see Lucinda M. Beier, A Matter of Life and Death: Health, Illness and Medicine in McLean County, 1830–1995 (Bloomington: McLean County Historical Society, 1996).

12. Philippe Ariès, Centuries of Childhood: A Social History of Family Life, trans. R. Baldick (New York: Vintage, 1962), 39.

13. Lawrence Stone, The Family, Sex, and Marriage in England, 1500–1800 (New York: Harper & Row, 1979), cited in Pat Jalland, Death in the Victorian Family (New York: Oxford University Press, 1996), 121. Sheila R. Johansson, "Neglect, Abuse, and Avoidable Death: Parental Investment and the Mortality of Infants and Children in the European Tradition," in Child Abuse and Neglect: Biosocial Dimensions, ed. Richard Gelles and Jane Lancaster (New York: Aldine, 1986).

14. Nancy Scheper-Hughes, Death without Weeping: The Violence of Everyday Life in Brazil (Berkeley: University of California Press, 1992). There are those who counter Scheper-Hughes's argument with other interpretations of the mothers of northeastern Brazil. See, for example, Marilyn K. Nations and L. A. Rebhun, "Angels with Wet Wings Won't Fly: Maternal Sentiment in Brazil and the Image of Neglect," Culture, Medicine, and Psychiatry 12, no. 2 (1998): 141–200; Ruthbeth Finerman, "'Parental Incompentence' and 'Selective Neglect': Blaming the Victim in Child Survival," Social Science and Medicine 40, no. 1 (1995): 5–13; Patrice L. Engle, review of Death without Weeping: The Violence of Everyday Life in Brazil, by Nancy Scheper-Hughes, Medical Anthropology Quarterly 8, no. 3 (1994): 346–49.

15. Jalland, Death in the Victorian Family; Linda Pollock, Forgotten Children: Parent-Child Relations from 1500 to 1900 (New York: Cambridge University Press, 1983).

16. For contrasts between working-class and elite practices in England, see Strange, Death, Grief, and Poverty.

17. Ann Douglas, "Heaven Our Home: Consolation Literature in the Northern United States, 1830–1880," in Death in America, ed. D. E. Stannard, 49–68 (Philadelphia: University of Pennsylvania Press, 1975).

18. Jessica Mitford, The American Way of Death (New York: Simon and Schuster, 1963); see also James Farrell, Inventing the American Way of Death, 1830–1920 (Philadelphia: Temple University Press, 1980).

19. My thinking on the problem of recording history is strongly shaped by my collaboration with Elinor Ochs and Andre Gingrich on "Recording Time," Wenner-Gren International Symposium, Mallorca, Spain, March 2000.

20. My thinking here on the difficulties for historians of recapturing past experience is influenced by the writings of Joan Scott (historian) and William Roseberry (anthropologist) and conversations with professional friends and colleagues Marjorie Abel and Elinor Ochs.

21. Michael Sappol, A Traffic of Dead Bodies: Anatomy and Embodied Social Identity in Nineteenth-Century America (Princeton, N.J.: Princeton University Press, 2002), 12.

22. Sarah Tarlow, Bereavement and Commemoration: An Archaeology of Mortality (Malden, Mass.: Blackwell, 1999), 6.

Chapter 1. Histories of Illness and Death

1. Burial Records of the First Church of Deerfield for 1841; Vital Statistics of Deerfield, Massachusetts, to 1850; Stephen West Williams daybook, 1836–43, Williams Family Papers (hereafter WFP), Pocumtuck Valley Memorial Association Library, Deerfield, Mass. (hereafter PVMA Library).

2. Although his training in New York was only for approximately five months, Williams wrote to his friend and Deerfield resident Elihu Hoyt that he was attending "twenty to thirty lectures a week, " that he was devoting considerable time to training in surgery, and that it was the "busiest time in my life." Letter to Elihu Hoyt, February 21, 1813, box 4, folder 5, WFP, PVMA Library.

3. The Massachusetts legislature approved the Vital Registration Act in 1842, which provided standardized forms for collecting and reporting births, deaths, and marriages by every town clerk in the Commonwealth. The governor signed the act in March of that year.

4. J. Ritchie Garrison, *Landscape and Material Life in Franklin County Massachusetts, 1770–1860* (Knoxville: University of Tennessee Press, 1991), 214, 314. In an exchange of letters with Oliver Wendell Holmes, the father of the famous Supreme Court judge, Williams had inquired about positions in Boston. Holmes wrote back that finding such a position might be difficult for a country doctor. Box 11, folders 1, 2, WFP, PVMA Library.

5. An expanded version of the address was published later that year in the society's journal. Stephen West Williams, "A Medical History of the County of Franklin, in the Commonwealth of Massachusetts," *Massachusetts Medical Society Communications, 1842–1848* 7 (1842): 1–76; quot. 1, 19, 21–22.

6. Philadelphia could vie for this title in the 1840s.

7. Though less symmetrical an ending date than 1920, 1916 marks the death of an important historian of Deerfield, George Sheldon, and the end of the "long" nineteenth century. The following year, the United States entered World War I and a new era and regime of mortality.

8. See, e.g., Paul Starr, *The Social Transformation of American Medicine: The Rise of a Sovereign Profession and the Making of a Vast Industry* (New York: Basic Books, 1982).

9. The phrase is drawn from Psalm 90: "'The days of our years are threescore years and ten; and if by reason of strength they be fourscore years, yet is their strength labour and sorrow; for it is soon cut off, and we fly away."

10. For example, see, the introduction to Laurie Garrett, *The Coming Plague: Newly Emerging Diseases in a World out of Balance* (New York: Farrar, Straus and Giroux, 1994), 4–12.

11. Ronald Barrett, Christopher W. Kuzawa, Thomas McDade, and George J. Armelagos, "Emerging and Re-Emerging Infectious Diseases: The Third Epidemiologic Transition," *Annual Review of Anthropology* 27 (1998): 247–71.

12. For the critical approach, see Joseph Carvalho III, "Rural Medical Practice in Early 19th-Century New England," *Historical Journal of Western Massachusetts* 4 (Spring 1975): 1–15. For the apologetic approach, see J. Worth Estes, introduction to *Medicine and Healing*, Proceedings of the Dublin Seminar for New England Folklife, ed. Peter Benes (Boston: Boston University Press, 1992), 8–12.

13. U.S. Bureau of the Census, *The Statistical History of the United States from Colonial Times to the Present*, Bicentennial Ed. (New York: Basic Books, 1976), 11.

14. For an overview on the high rates of urban mortality in the U.S. over this period, see Michael R. Haines, "The Urban Mortality Transition in the United States, 1800–1940," *Annales de Demographie Historique* 2001 (1): 33–64.

15. The local historian Amelia Miller wrote that "Sheldon's concerns with history were always to commemorate, to preserve, to collect, and to record." Amelia Miller, foreword to *A History of Deerfield, Massachusetts*, facsimile of the 1895–96 ed. (Deerfield: PVMA, 1972).

16. James H. Cassedy, *Demography in Early America: Beginnings of the Statistical Mind, 1600–1800* (Cambridge: Harvard University Press, 1969), 29–30.

17. Barbara G. Rosenkrantz, *Public Health and the State: Changing Views in Massachusetts, 1842–1936* (Cambridge: Harvard University Press, 1972), 21–23.

18. Pat Jalland, *Death in the Victorian Family* (New York: Oxford University Press, 1996), 2.

19. Margaret Lock, introduction to Lock and Deborah Gordon, *Biomedicine Examined* (Boston: Kluwer, 1988), 8.

Chapter 2. Life and Death in Massachusetts, Deerfield, and the Connecticut River Valley, 1620–1840

1. Timothy Dwight, *Travels in New-England and New York*, 4 vols. (New Haven, Conn.: T. Dwight, 1821), 1:65. The preface suggests that Dwight visited Deerfield in the fall—the most beautiful

time of year—in 1797. Son of a prominent family (Jonathan Edwards was his grandfather), Dwight was a noted author, scholar, and theologian, who became president of Yale in 1795.

2. Stephen West Williams, for example, provides a litany of the epidemics that struck Deerfield and surrounding towns between 1787 and 1841 in his *Medical History of the County of Franklin, in the Commonwealth of Massachusetts* (Boston: The Society, 1842). Overall, however, mortality was still relatively low during those years.

3. Rodolphus Dickinson, *Geographical, Statistical & Historical View of the Town of Deerfield* (Deerfield: Graves and Wells, 1815), Pocumtuck Valley Memorial Association Papers, PVMA Library.

4. Stephen West Williams, "Medical and Physical Topography of the Town of Deerfield, Franklin Co., Massachusetts," *Boston Medical and Surgical Journal* 15, no. 2 (1836): 197–203.

5. William Cronon, "Telling Tales on Canvas: Landscapes of Frontier Change," in *Discovered Lands, Invented Pasts: Transforming Visions of the American West*, ed. Jules David Prown, 37–87 (New Haven: Yale University Press, 1992). See also Martha Hoppin, "Depicting Mount Holyoke: A Dialogue with the Past," in *Changing Prospects: The View from Mount Holyoke*, ed. Marianne Doezema, 31–61 ([South Hadley, Mass.]: Mount Holyoke College Art Museum; Ithaca, N.Y.: Cornell University Press, 2002).

6. Goist was likely influenced not directly by Cole but rather by one of several landscape artists of lesser note who chose this general location for valley subjects—most notably the Oxbow. Perhaps it was William Henry Bartlett and his *Valley of the Connecticut, from Mount Holyoke* (ca. 1838). See Hoppin, "Depicting Mount Holyoke," 32–37.

7. For more information on Native settlement of the region and the Contact Period, see Peter A. Thomas, "In the Maelstrom of Change: The Indian Trade and Cultural Process in the Middle Connecticut River Valley, 1635–1665" (Ph.D. diss., University of Massachusetts Amherst, 1976); and Margaret Bruchac, "Historical Erasure and Cultural Recovery: Indigenous People in the Connecticut River Valley" (Ph.D. diss., University of Massachusetts Amherst, 2007).

8. Although English-descended Americans continued to experience occasional epidemics of these diseases, the impact on Native populations tended to be proportionally more lethal. There is a substantial literature on the concept of "virgin soil" populations. I use the term here to refer to lack of prior exposure of Native Americans to several Old World pathogens and the diminished resistance they had to those pathogens for a variety of environmental and immunological reasons. By using the term, however, I am not implying, as some have, any genetic deficiencies in resistance among Native populations.

9. Elizabeth A. Fenn, *Pox Americana* (New York: Hill and Wang, 2001), 88–103. See also Ann M. Becker, "Smallpox in Washington's Army: Strategic Implications of the Disease during the American Revolutionary War," *Journal of Military History* 68, no. 2 (2004): 381–430.

10. See, e.g., Alfred W. Crosby, *The Columbian Exchange: Biological and Cultural Consequences of 1492* (Westport, Conn.: Greenwood, 1972); Henry F. Dobyns, *Their Number Become Thinned: Native American Population Dynamics in Eastern North America* (Knoxville: University of Tennessee Press, 1983); David Cook Noble, *Born to Die: Disease and New World Conquest, 1492–1650* (New York: Cambridge University Press, 1998). For a discussion of the Massachusetts experience with reference to archival sources, see Neal Salisbury, *Manitou and Providence: Indians, Europeans, and the Making of New England, 1500–1643* (New York: Oxford University Press, 1982).

11. The Deerfield raid is a complex story, involving French and English competition for this region and other issues. It has been a folkloric tradition since at least the early nineteenth century. For a thorough discussion of the raid and its aftermath, see Evan Haefeli and Kevin Sweeney, *Captors and Captives: The 1704 French and Indian Raid on Deerfield* (Amherst: University of Massachusetts Press, 2003). For details of the numbers killed and taken, see 279–91.

12. Margaret Bruchac makes the point that Williams drew on indigenous knowledge, while at the same time disparaging the knowledge of "old women and Indian doctors." See Bruchac, "Historical Erasure and Cultural Recovery," 227–34.

13. Haefeli and Sweeney, *Captors and Captives*, 15–16.

14. Paul Jenkins, *The Conservative Rebel: A Social History of Greenfield, Massachusetts* (Greenfield: Town of Greenfield, 1982), 58–72.

15. Dwight, *Travels in New-England and New York*, 1:86. See also James H. Cassedy, *American Medicine and Statistical Thinking, 1800–1860* (Cambridge: Harvard University Press, 1984), 5–6.

16. Williams, "Medical and Physical Topography of the Town of Deerfield," 201.

17. David Hackett Fischer, *Albion's Seed: Four British Folkways in America* (New York: Oxford University Press, 1989), 111–12. The age-adjusted rate for the United States was 8 per 1,000 in 2004. *National Vital Statistics Reports* 55, no. 19 (2007): 1. See Ernest Caulfield, "A History of the Terrible Epidemic, Vulgarly Called the Throat Distemper, as It Occurred in His Majesty's New England Colonies Between 1735 and 1740," *Yale Journal of Biology and Medicine* 11, no. 3 (January 1939): 219–72.

18. Rates estimated for the Connecticut Valley appear lower than those estimated by Fischer. See, e.g., Richard S. Meindl and Alan C Swedlund, "Secular Trends in Mortality in the Connecticut Valley: 1700–1850," *Human Biology* 49, no. 3 (1977): 389–414.

19. The first director of the College of Medicine in Philadelphia was Dr. John Morgan, who had received his training in Edinburgh and London. For more on the history of American medical schools and their connections to Europe, see Cassedy, *American Medicine*, and *Medicine and American Growth, 1800–1860* (Madison: University of Wisconsin Press, 1986); W. F. Bynum, *Science and the Practice of Medicine in the Nineteenth Century* (Cambridge: Cambridge University Press, 1994); J. Worth Estes and David M. Goodman, *The Changing Humors of Portsmouth: The Medical Biography of an American Town, 1623–1983* (Boston: F. A. Countway Library of Medicine, 1986). Bynum claims that Americans were much more consumers of medical thinking than producers until the last third of the nineteenth century. Bynum, *Science and the Practice of Medicine*, xiii.

20. Bynum, *Science and the Practice of Medicine*, 3. See also James Trostle, "Early Work in Anthropology and Epidemiology: From Social Medicine to the Germ Theory, 1840 to 1920," in *Anthropology and Epidemiology*, ed. Craig R. Janes, Ron Stall, and Sandra M. Gifford, 35–57 (Boston: D. Reidel, 1986).

21. Hence the term *heroic medicine*. Bynum, *Science and the Practice of Medicine*, 4–17. It is alleged that when President George Washington became ill with severe sore throat, his doctors took approximately eighty ounces of blood from him within twelve hours. He died shortly thereafter.

22. For more on body snatching and anatomy riots, see Michael Sappol, *A Traffic of Dead Bodies: Anatomy and Embodied Social Identity in Nineteenth Century America* (Princeton, NJ: Princeton University Press, 2002). A Franklin County doctor of some prominence, Charles Knowlton of the nearby town of Ashfield, who subsequently became a pioneer in the American birth control movement, admitted to body snatching. See S. J. W. Tabor, "The Late Charles Knowlton, M.D.," *Boston Medical and Surgical Journal* 45 (September 10 and 24, 1851), cited in Robert E. Riegel, "The American Father of Birth Control," *New England Quarterly* 6 (1933): 474–75.

23. Quoted in Wellness Directory of Minnesota, *The History of Medicine: The Revolutionary War*, www.mnwelldir.org/docs/history/history02.htm (accessed November 2008).

24. At the time of the American Revolution, according to Paul Starr, "there appear to have been about 3,500 or 4,000 physicians, 400 of them had formal medical training, perhaps half as many held medical degrees." Starr, *The Social Transformation of American Medicine* (New York: Basic Books), 40. This elite, Starr points out, was almost entirely in the larger cities. Local histories often point to a significant presence of degreed doctors in small towns and cities, and Starr reports that even in rural areas doctors were in plentiful supply (64).

25. Lawrence Dame, M.D., transcripts, Records of the Franklin District Medical Society (FDMS), 1851–1923, PVMA Library.

26. Lawrence Dame, M.D, "Chronological Listing of Practicing Physicians in Deerfield," box 4, FDMS, PVMA Library.

27. George Sheldon, *A History of Deerfield, Massachusetts*, 2 vols. (Deerfield: PVMA, 1895–96), 2:381. Williams was apparently never a judge of probate. Kevin Sweeney, personal communication.

28. Papers of Thomas Williams New York Historical Society, dlib.nyu.edu:8083/nyhsead/ servlet/SaxonServlet?source=/williams.xml&style=/saxon01n2002.xsl&part=body#series7 (accessed May 2006). See also Stephen West Williams, *American Medical Biography, or Memoirs of Eminent Physicians, Embracing Principally Those Who Have Died since the Publication of Dr. Thacher's Initial Work on the Same Subject* (Greenfield, Mass.: L. Merriam, 1845).

29. William Stoddard Williams, receipt, box 10, fol. 3, WFP, PVMA Library.

30. Many sources repeat this observation; for example, Barrett Wendell, *Cotton Mather, The Puritan Priest* (New York: Dodd, Mead, 1902), 298.

31. Meindl and Swedlund, "Secular Trends in Mortality"; David E. Stannard, ed., *Death in America* (Philadelphia: University of Pennsylvania Press, 1975), 18.

32. See David E Stannard, "Death and the Puritan Child," in Stannard, *Death in America*, 9–29.

33. For the Puritan, according to Gordon Geddes, "assurance of salvation lay less in the subjective response of the believer than in the Christ who had accomplished it." Geddes, *Welcome Joy: Death in Puritan New England* (Ann Arbor, MI: UMI Research Press, 1981), 8.

34. Fischer, *Albion's Seed*, 114; Susan McGowan, history educator, PVMA, personal communication. Laws were passed by the Massachusetts General Court restricting "excessive" funeral expenditures. See Robert W. Habenstein and William M. Lamers, *The History of American Funeral Directing*, 5th ed. (Brookfield, WI: National Funeral Directors Association, 2001).

35. There is an extensive literature on mortuary practices and gravestone changes in New England; see Charles O. Jackson, ed., *Passing: The Vision of Death in America*, vol. 2 of *Contributions in Family Studies* (Westport, Conn.: Greenwood Press, 1977); David E. Stannard, *The Puritan Way of Death: A Study in Religion, Culture, and Social Change* (New York: Oxford University Press, 1977), 9–29; Catherine C. Macdonald, "'The Dust They Left Behind': Community and the Persistence of Mortuary Funerary Practices in the Connecticut River Valley, 1650–1850" (BA thesis, Amherst College, 2007). Kevin Sweeney, "Where the Bay Meets the River: Gravestones and Stonecutters in the River Towns of Western Massachusetts, 1690–1910," *Markers: The Journal of the Association for Gravestone Studies* 3 (1985): 1–46; Karen Halttunen, personal communication, 2007.

36. Sheldon, *History of Deerfield*, 2:885.

37. M. R. Haines, "The Use of Model Life Tables to Estimate Mortality for the United States in the Late Nineteenth Century," *Demography* 16, no. 2 (1979): 289–312.

38. Quoted in A. J. Jaffe and W. I. Laurie, "An Abridged Life Table for the White Population of the United States in 1830," *Human Biology* 14 (1942): 352.

39. For more on the history of therapeutics in the nineteenth century see John Harley Warner, *The Therapeutic Perspective: Medical Practice, Knowledge, and Identity in America, 1820–1885* (Cambridge: Harvard University Press, 1986).

40. The origins of smallpox inoculation—or variolation—may have been in China, India, or quite possibly the Middle East, and there is reasonable evidence that the development and use of inoculation in Asia and the Middle East precedes Europe's adoption of the method by many years. Cotton Mather advocated for smallpox variolation in Boston and reportedly learned about the method from his black slave, Onesimus. Sheldon Watts, *Epidemics and History: Disease, Power, and Imperialism* (New Haven, Conn.: Yale University Press, 1997), 112–13. See also Fenn, *Pox Americana*, 32; Harriet A. Washington, *Medical Apartheid: The Dark History of Medical Experimentation on Black Americans from Colonial Times to the Present* (New York: Doubleday, 2007), 71–73.

41. Some cases were reported by local physicians, but many of these may have been misdiagnoses. A significant smallpox epidemic occurred during the American Revolution, affecting all the colonies and not just New England. For details, see Fenn, *Pox Americana*. Williams does report a smallpox epidemic in Deerfield, and presumably the Connecticut Valley, in 1777. Williams, *Medical History of the County of Franklin*, 11. Edward Jenner is alleged to have learned of using cowpox from a Dorset farmer. Watts, *Epidemics and History*, 116.

42. Yellow fever is caused by a virus carried by mosquitoes. It is generally thought of as a tropic disease today, but it affected many temperate port cities in early America.

43. This research was conducted under grants from the National Science Foundation and the National Institutes of Health. For the findings on these four towns, see Meindl and Swedlund, "Secular Trends in Mortality"; Richard S. Meindl, "Environmental and Demographic Correlates of Mortality in Nineteenth Century Franklin County Massachusetts" (Ph.D. diss., University of Massachusetts Amherst, 1979); Alan H. McArdle, "Mortality Change and Industrialization in Western Massachusetts, 1850–1910" (Ph.D. diss., University of Massachusetts, 1986). For the Commonwealth of Massachusetts, see Maris A. Vinovskis, "Mortality Rates and Trends in Massachusetts before 1860," *Journal of Economic History* 32 (1972): 184–213; Haines, "Use of Model Life Tables." The reference to "we" and "our" in this section reflects the many scholars and collaborators involved in this research.

44. According to the most recent available data on infant mortality in the United States, the rate is 6.7 per thousand live births. *National Vital Statistics Reports* 57, no. 14 (2009): 1.

45. In Massachusetts in this period, "dropsy" would most likely refer to swelling and retention of fluids, possibly congestive heart disease; "catarrh" to a bad cold or respiratory infection; and "bilious fever" to an intermittent fever accompanied by diarrhea and vomiting.

46. R. Gutman, "Birth and Death Registration in Massachusetts, III: The System Achieves a Form, 1849–1869," *Millbank Memorial Fund Quarterly* 37, no. 3 (1959): 302–10.

47. James Deane, "Biographical Sketch of the Late Stephen West Williams, M.D.: Communicated for the *Boston Medical and Surgical Journal*," *Boston Medical and Surgical Journal* 2 (1855): 29–32. For a critical view of medical training prior to the mid-nineteenth century, see Kenneth M. Ludmerer, *Learning to Heal: The Development of American Medical Education* (New York: Basic Books, 1985), 11–20.

48. Williams, *Medical History of the County of Franklin*, 25.

49. This summary is based on Deane, "Biographical Sketch of the Late Stephen West Williams," and Jane Winchester, "Introducing Stephen West Williams, M.D: First President of the Franklin District Medical Society" (paper presented at 150th anniversary of FDMS, April 25, 2001, Greenfield, Mass.; spiral-bound copy in the FDMS papers of PVMA and Historic Deerfield Libraries, Deerfield, Mass.).

50. For more on the debate about irregulars, see, e.g., Walter L. Burrage, *A History of the Massachusetts Medical Society: With Brief Biographies of the Founders and Chief Officers, 1781–1922* (Norwood, Mass.: Plimpton Press, 1923), chap. 3.

51. For more on Sylvester Graham, see Stephen Nissenbaum, *Sex, Diet, and Debility in Jacksonian America: Sylvester Graham and Health Reform* (Westport, Conn..: Greenwood, 1980). Deerfield had its own expert on dyspepsia: native son Edward Hitchcock, professor of natural history and eventual president of Amherst College. He published his lectures in Hitchcock, *Dyspepsy Forestalled and Resisted: Lectures on Diet, Regimen, and Employment* (Boston: R. Lord and Holbrook, Peirce and Parker, 1831).

52. For more on Thomsonianism and therapeutic debates between irregulars and regular physicians, see Warner, *Therapeutic Perspective*, 37–80.

53. John C. Gunn, *Gunn's Domestic Medicine: A Facsimile of the First Edition* (1830; Knoxville: University of Tennessee Press, 1986), 2, 4. In the introduction, Charles Rosenberg points out that Gunn was especially popular in the South and West but had wide circulation in the East as well. The book went through fourteen printings before 1820 and sixty-eight printings by 1920 (v).

54. Stephen West Williams, *Notice of Some of the Medical Improvements and Discoveries of the Last Half Century: And More Particularly in the United States of America, Read before the Franklin Medical Society of the State of Massachusetts* (New York: Van Norden & Amerman, 1852), 34–36.

55. Stephen West Williams to Dr. William Bull (1762–1842), Miscellaneous Family Papers, Bull Family Folder, PVMA Library. Stephen West was referring to a bylaw restricting consultations with irregulars and was strongly in favor of Franklin's having its own society.

56. Stephen West Williams says that one epidemic in Deerfield may have been introduced by someone who traveled to Hartford and returned with the fever. Williams, *Medical History of the County of Franklin*, 15.

57. U.S. Bureau of the Census, *Historical Statistics of the United States from Colonial Times to the Present*, Bicentennial Ed. (Washington, DC: U.S. Government Printing Office, 1975). "Urban" and "rural" are somewhat imprecise distinctions. By Massachusetts law any community attaining a population of twenty-five hundred or more is designated as a city, but in the nineteenth century many such towns were, by principal occupations and landscape, decidedly "rural."

58. Dr. Humphrey Gould, Bill of Mortality for Rowe, in Williams, *Medical History of the County of Franklin*, 68.

59. For more on the economic development of these communities and the region, see Jenkins, *Conservative Rebel*; J. Ritchie Garrison, *Landscape and Material Life in Franklin County Massachusetts, 1770–1860* (Knoxville: University of Tennessee Press, 1991); Christopher Clark, *The Roots of Rural Capitalism: Western Massachusetts, 1780–1860* (Ithaca: Cornell University Press, 1990). Also, since the 1820s, agriculture in the region had been moving away from subsistence to an ever-widening array of cash crops.

60. Travel times are discussed in Garrison, *Landscape and Material Life*, 214–16.

Chapter 3. Cholera Infantum

1. The pneumonia-diarrhea complex also includes pneumococci for bronchial infection, Shigellae, Salmonella, *E. coli*, etc., for gastro-intestinal infection. An acute bout of diarrhea will often precipitate pneumonia in infants and young children.

2. Williams said 54, the parish minister said 40. George Sheldon, *History of Deerfield, Massachusetts*, 2 vols. (Deerfield, Mass.: Pocumtuck Valley Memorial Association, 1895–96), 2:781–82.

3. Stephen West Williams, *A Medical History of the County of Franklin, in the Commonwealth of Massachusetts* (Boston: The Society, 1842), 14–15.

4. Mary Willard diary, box 1, folder 3, Willard Family Papers, PVMA Library, p. 93.

5. Stephen West Williams account book, WFP, PVMA Library, #13187, p. 88. As early as 1839, Williams partnered with Dr. A. Sumner Haskell, presumably because of Williams's busy schedule of lecturing at regional medical colleges and other professional activities.

6. Stephen West Williams, "Observations on Dysentery, and on the Use of Astringents, Particularly the Cerussa Acetata and Opium in the Cure of the Complaint," *American Journal of Medical Science* 3, n.s. (1842): 127–31.

7. "Records of the Church of Deerfield," PVMA Library Archives.

8. Williams account book. It is difficult to ascertain exactly who treated whom, but judging from the account books, between 1841 and 1843 Haskell saw the majority of patients, with Williams traveling farther and seeing what appear to be more select patients, and probably following up with friends and family close to home.

9. According to Williams's account book, he treated both John G. Williams's and David Sheldon's children, though not necessarily for these precise conditions and times (pp. 52, 66).

10. Vital Records of Deerfield, Historic Deerfield Library. The original Vital Records of Deerfield are archived in the Town Clerk's Office, South Deerfield, Mass. A compilation of the vital records to the year 1850 can be found in Thomas W. Baldwin, comp., *Vital records of Deerfield, Massachusetts to the year 1850* (Salem, Mass.: Higginson Book Co.), 1920. Copies of the records from 1675 to 1898 are available on microfiche from Jay Mack Holbrook, Holbrook Research Institute, Oxford, Mass. (1987), and the Historic Deerfield Library. An electronic file of the vital records to 1910 was created from the originals by Alan C. Swedlund and collaborators over a period of years; a CD titled *Census and Vital Records of the Town of Deerfield, Massachusetts, through 1910* is archived for restricted use at the Historic Deerfield Library. I use this electronic file when referring to vital statistics in this and subsequent chapters.

11. Reprinted in *Greenfield Gazette and Courier*, September 28, 1863. *Hall's Health at Home, or Hall's Family Doctor*, by W. W. Hall, M.D., was published in Hartford, Conn., and Cincinnati,

Ohio, and, after its initial publication in 1872, went through multiple editions. It was often cited in local newspapers and could be found in the libraries of many New England middle-class homes.

12. John C. Gunn, *Gunn's Domestic Medicine: A Facsimile of the First Edition* (1830; Knoxville: University of Tennessee Press, 1986), 353.

13. *Greenfield Gazette and Courier*, July 27, 1841, 2.

14. Dr. Jacob Bigelow, of Harvard, generalized in 1835 that most medical men thought deaths could be reduced by letting the disease take its natural course. Quoted in Paul Starr, *The Social Transformation of American Medicine* (New York: Basic Books, 1982), 55.

15. Stephen West Williams was elected to the Vermont Medical Society in 1815. He had been a member of the Massachusetts Medical Society since 1817 and in 1839 became an honorary member of the Connecticut Medical Society. In the 1830s and early 1840s he was a member of the Hampshire District Medical Society of Massachusetts and the Franklin District Medical Society. He was actively recruiting for the latter organization in 1851 and became its first president. See Stephen W. Williams, *The Genealogy and History of the Family of Williams in America, more particularly of the descendants of Robert Williams of Roxbury* (Greenfield, Mass.: Merriam & Mirick, 1847). See also Jane Winchester, "Introducing Stephen West Williams, MD," paper presented at the 150th anniversary of the Franklin District Medical Society, Deerfield, Mass., April 25, 2001.

16. Malcolm Read Lovell, ed., *Two Quaker Sisters: From the Original Diaries of Elizabeth Buffum Chace and Lucy Buffum Lovell* (New York: Liveright, 1937), xxiv–xxx. Hereafter page numbers appear in text.

17. See, e.g., Gary Laderman, *The Sacred Remains: American Attitudes toward Death, 1799–1883* (New Haven: Yale University Press, 1996); Karen Sánchez-Eppler, *Dependent States: The Child's Part in Nineteenth-Century American Culture* (Chicago: University of Chicago Press, 2005); Martha Sandweiss, ed., *Photography in Nineteenth-Century America* (New York: Harry N. Abrams, 1991).

18. J. L. Lovell opened a studio in Amherst in 1856, the earliest photographic studio in western Massachusetts. He made several photographs for Amherst College, and for Edward's father, Edward Hitchcock Sr., who had been a professor of natural history and president of Amherst College. John Lyman Lovell Folder, Special Collections, Jones Library, Amherst, Mass.

19. Ann Douglas, *The Feminization of American Culture* (New York: Knopf, 1977). See also Viviana A. Rotman Zelizer, *Pricing the Priceless Child: The Changing Social Value of Children* (New York: Basic Books, 1985), 25–26.

20. See Alan M. Kraut, *Silent Travelers: Germs, Genes, and the "Immigrant Menace"* (Baltimore: Johns Hopkins University Press, 1995). The Irish came in the 1840s, followed closely by Germans, and after the Civil War significant numbers of French Canadians migrated into the valley.

21. Lemuel Shattuck and others, *Report of the Sanitary Commission of Massachusetts* (1850; reprint, Cambridge: Harvard University Press, 1948), 200–201.

22. Edward Jarvis, M.D., "Infant Mortality," in *Fourth Annual Report of the State Board of Health of Massachusetts*, Public Document no. 34 (Boston: Wright & Potter, 1873), 195.

23. Boston Medical Commission to Investigate the Sanitary Condition of the City, *The Sanitary Condition of Boston: The Report of a Medical Commission* (Boston: Rockwell and Churchill Printers, 1875), 180.

24. Irish made up approximately 25 percent of Deerfield's population in the federal census of 1870. This number is estimated by tabulating the households in which parents or household heads were identified as being born in Ireland in the 1870 manuscript census for Deerfield, available on microfilm, Historic Deerfield Library. See also Stacy Pomeroy, "A Fragile Community: The Irish in Deerfield, Massachusetts, 1850–1880" (Smith College student paper, 1976, held in main stacks, Historic Deerfield Library).

25. *Greenfield Gazette and Courier*, January 31, 1859. Brief articles about Irish and German immigrants appear in several issues of the *Gazette and Courier* during this period. Frequently, as in this piece, they pay a qualified compliment to the foreign born, and then indulge in ethnic stereotyping.

26. The epidemic of 1872 is bracketed by economic recessions or depressions that persisted through much of the 1870s.

27. The ages at death could be important here. Between one and two years of age would have been the time mothers weaned and started supplemental feeding. Since teething generally begins at approximately six to seven months, most deaths in the first six months can reflect supplemental feeding prior to teething. This practice, in turn, suggests that mothers were having difficulty nursing, were forced to rely on wet nurses, or were using contaminated milk or water, or both.

28. For an insightful discussion of recovering experiences of the poor in Britain, see Julie-Marie Strange, *Death, Grief, and Poverty in Britain, 1870–1914* (Cambridge: Cambridge University Press, 2005), 10–26.

29. Stephen West Williams and other doctors would occasionally serve the poor and indigent and bill the town for the expenses. See. e.g., Stephen West Williams Memorandum book, 1847–1851 (part of #13185), WFP, PVMA Library.

30. The events described here are based on the 1870 manuscript federal census and the 1872 register of vital statistics for the town of Deerfield, and also various documents on labor opportunities at this time. The deaths and families are real. William and Sarah Corless, the parents of Sarah and Mary, do not appear in the 1870 federal census of Deerfield. No doubt they emigrated from Ireland, and quite possibly they were related to Thomas and Margaret Corless, who do appear in the census, living in Cheapside. The circumstances are based on a knowledge of the likely conditions of Cheapside during this period. According to the 1870 census, the Thomas Corlesses lived in a multifamily dwelling, and I found no evidence for sewer or piped drinking water in this neighborhood until at least the 1880s. On the basis of the information available, I infer that families of Thomas and William were living in the same house.

31. For a discussion of the discourse on unfit mothers, see Alan C. Swedlund and Helen L. Ball, "Nature, Nurture, and the Determinants of Infant Mortality: A Case Study from Massachusetts, 1830–1920," in *Building a New Biocultural Synthesis: Political-Economic Perspectives on Human Biology*, ed. Alan H. Goodman and Thomas L. Leatherman, 191–228 (Ann Arbor: University of Michigan Press, 1998).

32. Williams, *Medical History of the County of Franklin*, 23.

33. Shattuck and others, *Report on the Sanitary Commission*, 84.

34. Lawrence Dame, M.D., transcripts, Franklin District Medical Society Papers, 50, PVMA Library. Carbolic acid is a derivative of benzene, used sometimes as an antiseptic, but poisonous and even potentially fatal if taken internally.

35. Ibid., 58.

36. Ibid., 61, 64.

37. See Harry F. Dowling, *Fighting Infection: Conquests of the Twentieth Century* (Cambridge: Harvard University Press, 1977), chap. 1; John Harley Warner, *The Therapeutic Perspective: Medical Practice, Knowledge, and Identity in America, 1820–1885* (Cambridge: Harvard University Press, 1986), 276–82.

38. The first two of three epidemics of Asiatic cholera in North America that were part of world pandemics during the nineteenth century broke out in 1832 and 1849. Deerfield residents were well aware of the epidemics, but not from personal experience, since they affected primarily the coastal cities. Boston also escaped the high mortality experienced by some other cities in 1832. Charles E. Rosenberg, *The Cholera Years: The United States in 1832, 1849, and 1866* (Chicago: University of Chicago Press, 1962), 49.

39. C. E. A. Winslow, foreword to Shattuck and others, *Report on the Sanitary Commission*.

40. Shattuck and others, *Report on the Sanitary Commission*, 84.

41. The categories were Endemic and Epidemic Diseases, Nervous System, Respiratory Organs, Digestive Organs, Organs of Circulation, Diseases of Uncertain Seat, Urinary and Genital Organs. Massachusetts, Registry and Returns of Births, Marriages, and Deaths, *First Annual Report* (Boston: Dutton and Wentworth, Printers to the State, 1843), 81–116.

42. Barbara G. Rosenkrantz, *Public Health and the State: Changing Views in Massachusetts, 1842–1936* (Cambridge: Harvard University Press, 1972), 23–25, 30–33.

43. Ibid., 27.

44. Samuel Warren Abbott, "The Vital Statistics of Massachusetts: A Forty Years' Summary (1856–1896)," in *Twenty-eighth Annual Report of the State Board of Health of Massachusetts*, Public Document no. 34 (Boston: Wright & Potter, 1897), 713–829.

45. Rosenkrantz, *Public Health and the State*, 24–25.

46. Shattuck and others, *Report on the Sanitary Commission*. Shattuck's report includes reference to Stephen West Williams's work on Franklin County, e.g., 78.

47. Stephen West Williams to Lemuel Shattuck, April 7, 1851, Lemuel Shattuck Papers, Massachusetts Historical Society, Boston. Shattuck's letters to Williams have not been located to my knowledge. The correspondence between Shattuck and Williams reveals the state's early interest in the vital events occurring in the rural counties and Williams's interest in making those events known to the state.

Chapter 4. The Fevers of Childhood

1. In the nineteenth century *statist* could be a title of self-identification or a term ascribed to one who embraced the power of the state to administer to the welfare of its citizens, and who supported the collection of statistical data on citizens.

2. Streptococcal bacteria could also be transmitted in contaminated sources, such as milk, food, or clothing.

3. Susan McGowan and Amelia F. Miller, *Family and Landscape: Deerfield Homelots from 1671* (Deerfield, Mass.: Pocumtuck Valley Memorial Association, 1996), 190. In 1859 Joseph ("Jesse") Stebbins's parents were living in the house marked Cowles on the map.

4. The Franklin District Medical Society was founded in 1851; the Franklin Medical Society, of regular physicians, was founded years earlier.

5. Benjamin Platt Thomas, *Abraham Lincoln: A Biography* (New York: Knopf, 1952), 220. Cited in Harry F. Dowling, *Fighting Infection: Conquests of the Twentieth Century* (Cambridge: Harvard University Press, 1977), 60.

6. Diary excerpts of Lucy Buffum Lovell, in *Two Quaker Sisters: From the Original Diaries of Elizabeth Buffum Chace and Lucy Buffum Lovell*, ed. Malcolm Read Lovell (New York: Liveright, 1937), 96.

7. Ibid., 102–3. Caroline's brother Edward, Lucy Lovell's remaining child, became ill with scarlet fever two days after Caroline and died a few days later.

8. George Sheldon opens his diary with an explanation of why he started it: "A sort of record of Farm operation. Local events and Miscellaneous matters . . . generally—commenced on the day of Father's Death, April 2, 1860." Sheldon diary, George Sheldon Papers, PVMA Library.

9. Samuel Willard, "Will of Samuel Willard," in Sheldon Papers, box 1, Folder 5, PVMA Library.

10. Mumford was substituting for the local minister, the Reverend James K. Hosmer, who was away in the war.

11. Frank Wright was probably an amateur photographer living in the Wapping section of Deerfield. Records show that a man named Frank Wright was living in the family homestead at this time, and there is no record of a professional photographer named Frank Wright in the area.

12. Lovell, *Two Quaker Sisters*, 104–5.

13. The modern history of embalming in the United States begins with efforts during the Civil War primarily to preserve Northern soldiers for their return home. Domestic embalming was not a common practice until the early 1900s. Robert W. Habenstein and William M. Lamers, *The History of American Funeral Directing*, 5th ed. (Brookfield, Wis.: National Funeral Directors Association, 2001).

14. Pat Jalland, *Death in the Victorian Family* (New York: Oxford University Press, 1996), 119–42; Karen Sánchez-Eppler, *Dependent States: The Child's Part in Nineteenth-Century American Culture* (Chicago: University of Chicago Press, 2005), 101–48.

15. *Greenfield Gazette and Courier*, May 26, 1862.

16. Cemeteries of Deerfield, transcriptions by Edith Clark Nyman, Historic Deerfield Library.

17. "Resignation" was first published in 1849 in *The Seaside and the Fireside*. According to Christoph Irmscher, Longfellow wrote the poem after the death of his own daughter. Irmscher, *Longfellow Redux* (Urbana: University of Illinois Press, 2006.), 46.

18. Autographs book of George Sheldon, p. 63, letter dated February 14, 1860. PVMA Library.

19. In gravestone iconography, the handshake often symbolizes eternal friendship. Association for Gravestone Studies, *Symbolism in the Carving on Gravestones*, AGS Field Guide no. 8 (Greenfield, Mass., 2003).

20. Translated by H. Martin Wobst, Department of Anthropology, University of Massachusetts Amherst, February 4, 2004. The condition of the stone makes exact translation difficult.

21. Tracy Chevalier, *Falling Angels* (New York: Dutton, 2001), is a highly readable novel that provides a realistic portrayal of young children strongly influenced by the culture of mourning.

22. Poem from obituary of Luany B. Wilcox, *Greenfield Gazette and Courier*, February 8, 1864, p. 3. For other examples of words from children, see Sánchez-Eppler, *Dependent States*, 140–48.

23. Dowling, *Fighting Infection*, 56–57. It should be noted that while scarlet fever was "relatively easy" to diagnose by doctors who had seen a lot of it, the poor training and inexperience that characterized many physicians during this period could easily lead to a misdiagnosis of something like measles, as in the case with the Lovell child.

24. See W. F. Bynum, *Science and the Practice of Medicine in the Nineteenth Century* (Cambridge: Cambridge University Press, 1994), 225–26; Anne Hardy, *The Epidemic Streets: Infectious Disease and the Rise of Preventive Medicine, 1856–1900* (Oxford: Clarendon, 1993), chap. 3; T. McKeown and R. G. Record, "Reasons for the Decline of Mortality in England and Wales during the 19th Century," *Population Studies* 16 (1967): 94–122.

25. Lawrence Dame, M.D. List of Practicing Physicians of the Franklin District Medical Society. Typescript, FDMS Papers, PVMA Library.

26. Lawrence Dame, M.D., transcribed minutes, meetings of the Franklin District Medical Society, Franklin District Medical Society Papers, PVMA Library, pp. 20, 24.

27. John C. Gunn, *Gunn's Domestic Medicine: A Facsimile of the First Edition; or, Poor Man's Friend* (1830; Knoxville: University of Tennessee Press, 1986), 352.

28. W. W. Hall, M.D., *Health at Home; or, Hall's Family Doctor* (Hartford, Conn.: S. M. Betts, 1872), 431. Hall's *Health at Home*, originally published in 1845, went through many editions. Typical of health advice manuals of the day, it was readily available to literate citizens of western Massachusetts and was sometimes quoted in the local newspapers.

29. See, e.g., Nancy Tomes, *The Gospel of Germs: Men, Women, and the Microbe in American Life* (Cambridge: Harvard University Press, 1998).

30. Data from the 1867–68 epidemic show, however, that more of the children who died were from working-class families than from more affluent families. See, e.g., Hardy, *Epidemic Streets*, 64–79; Dowling, *Fighting Infection*, 230–31; Alan Swedlund and Alison Donta, "Scarlet Fever Epidemics of the Nineteenth Century: A Case of Evolved Pathogenic Virulence?" in *Human Biologists in the Archives: Demography, Health, Nutrition, and Genetics in Historical Populations*, ed. D. A. Herring and A. C. Swedlund, 159–77 (2003).

31. Annual Report, Town of Deerfield, 1883. PVMA Library. The state legislature passed a law in 1884 requiring physicians and parents to report a number of serious infectious diseases, including scarlet fever, to the selectman or local board of health, see Rosenkrantz, 110.

32. Walter L. Burrage, *A History of the Massachusetts Medical Society: With Brief Biographies of the Founders and Chief Officers, 1781–1922* (Norwood, Mass.: Plimpton Press, 1923), 136–37.

33. Massachusetts, Registry and Return of Births, Marriages, and Deaths in the Common-wealth, *Seventeenth Annual Report* (Boston: William White, Printer to the State, 1859), 62; also see table X.

34. Massachusetts, Registry and Return of Births, Marriages, and Deaths in the Common-wealth, *Eighteenth Annual Report* (Boston: William White, Printer to the State, 1861), 68.

35. Cited in ibid., 72.

36. See, e.g., Barbara G. Rosenkrantz, *Public Health and the State: Changing Views in Massachusetts, 1842–1936* (Cambridge: Harvard University Press, 1972), 27.

37. Sánchez-Eppler, *Dependent States*, 143. Sanchez-Eppler also sees in the writings of parents, friends, and relatives of the deceased during this period a desire for more reliable information from the medical experts, evidence that even the institutional medical authority has a personal relation to grief (personal communication).

Chapter 5. Dutiful Daughters, Pallid Young Women

1. Lemuel Shattuck and others, *Report of the Sanitary Commission of Massachusetts* (1850; reprint, Cambridge: Harvard University Press, 1948).

2. Samuel Warren Abbott, "The Vital Statistics of Massachusetts: A Forty Years' Summary (1856–1895)," in *Twenty-eighth Annual Report of the State Board of Health of Massachusetts*, Public Document no. 34 (Boston: Wright & Potter, 1897), 786–89; Caren A. Ginsberg and Alan C. Swedlund, "Sex-Specific Mortality and Economic Opportunities: Massachusetts, 1860–1899," *Continuity and Change* 1, no. 3 (1986): 415–45.

3. Consumption deaths, however, do show fluctuations. There was a peak in some Connecticut Valley towns in the 1870s, while the region and the state as a whole were experiencing an ongoing decline in numbers of consumption deaths per population. For example, see Alan H. McArdle, "Mortality Change and Industrialization in Western Massachusetts, 1850–1910" (PhD diss., University of Massachusetts Amherst, 1986), 154–58 and fig. 31; Abbott, "Vital Statistics of Massachusetts," 762.

4. Shattuck and others, *Report of the Sanitary Commission*, 94–95. The pattern of excess female mortality held true for Britain as well, as reported in the *Lancet* (1881), ii. 1, 108, cited in Anne Hardy, *The Epidemic Streets: Infectious Disease and the Rise of Preventive Medicine, 1856–1900* (Oxford: Clarendon, 1993), 257.

5. Germ theory, however, was not the overarching and integrated concept it is sometimes made out to be. See, e.g., Nancy J. Tomes and John Harley Warner, eds., introduction to "Re-thinking the Reception of the Germ Theory of Disease: Comparative Perspectives," special issue, *Journal of the History of Medicine and Allied Sciences* 52, no. 1 (1997).

6. See, e.g., Linda Bryder, "'Not always one and the same thing': The Registration of Tuber-culosis Deaths in Britain, 1900–1950," *Social History of Medicine* 9, no. 2 (August 1996): 253–65. The contrasts were strongly class-based and often racialized as well. See, e.g., Katherine Ott, *Fevered Lives: Tuberculosis in American Culture since 1870* (Cambridge: Harvard University Press, 1996), 1–52, 142. See also Hardy, *Epidemic Streets*, 217. Causes of death listed in the vital records of Deerfield reveal that the term *tuberculosis* was used very seldom before 1900. As tuberculosis became the more definitive diagnosis when the bacillus was present, some doctors continued to use *consumption* for what they thought was a hereditary form and even noted that consumptives were more susceptible to tuberculosis. See, e.g., Joseph G. Richardson, *Health and Longevity* (New York: Home Health Society, 1914), 2:1248–50.

7. See, e.g., Ott, *Fevered Lives*, esp. 9–52; for narratives about consumptive patients, see also Susan Sontag, *Illness as Metaphor* (New York: Farrar, Straus and Giroux, 1978); Sheila Rothman, *Living in the Shadow of Death* (New York: Basic Books, 1994).

8. For a comprehensive look at images of the consumptive, see Thomas Dormandy, *The White Death: A History of Tuberculosis* (New York: New York University Press, 2000).

9. Dr. George Derby, secretary of the Massachusetts Board of Health, suggested in *Second Annual Report*, in 1871, that the fate of individuals with a "consumptive tendency" was poor

for one "choosing to make shoes in an ill-ventilated shop" as opposed to living "the life of a lumberman in the open air." Quoted in Charles Harrington, "The Work of the State Board of Health," in *Tuberculosis in Massachusetts*, ed. Edwin A Locke (Boston: Wright & Potter, 1908), 11. People of different ethnicities, however, were believed to respond differently to the disease. Jews, for example, were thought to have a "relative immunity." H. Linenthal, "Sanitation of Clothing Factories and Tenement-House Workrooms," in ibid., 28.

10. Boston Medical Commission to Investigate the Sanitary Condition of the City, *The Sanitary Condition of Boston: The Report of a Medical Commission* (Boston: Rockwell and Churchill Printers, 1875), 65–67. Shattuck, however, in an 1845 report on the conditions of Boston, identified the circumstances of the Irish, rather than their race, as the principal issue and observed that other classes in similar circumstances would probably show the same results. Cited in Barbara Gutmann Rosenkrantz, *Public Health and the State: Changing Views in Massachusetts, 1842–1936* (Cambridge: Harvard University Press, 1972), 20.

11. W. W. Hall, M.D., *Health at Home; or, Hall's Family Doctor* (Hartford, Conn.: S. M. Betts, 1872), 647.

12. For example, Ott, *Fevered Lives*, 39–45; Rothman, *Living in the Shadow of Death*, 3, 131–75. Elijah Spencer Fuller, for example, traveled to California, New Mexico, and even Chihuahua, Mexico, while he was suffering from tuberculosis in the mid-1850s. Journal of Elijah Spencer Fuller, box 125, Fuller-Higginson Family Papers, PVMA Library.

13. Esther Grout diary, PVMA Library.

14. The exception in treatments for most middle-class patients would be the gradually increasing emphasis on diet, more fresh air, and exposure to sunlight.

15. Derby, *Second Annual Report*, quoted in Harrington, "Work of the State Board of Health," 11–12.

16. Ott, *Fevered Lives*, 9.

17. See, e.g., Abbott, "Vital Statistics," 788; Hardy, *Epidemic Streets*, chap. 8.

18. Dr. George Derby noted the decline in *Fourth Annual Report of the State Board of Health of Massachusetts*, Public Document no. 34 (Boston: Wright & Potter, 1873).

19. Advocacy for a state board of health linked to consumption and sanitary reform can be found in Henry I. Bowditch, *Consumption in New England* (Boston: Ticknor & Fields, 1862).

20. For a discussion of the creation of the State Board of Health, see Rosenkrantz, *Public Health and the State*, esp. chap. 2.

21. Henry I. Bowditch, *Public Hygiene in America* (1877; reprint, New York: Arno Press, 1972), 451–62.

22. Lyman Bartlett to Alfred Bartlett, July 23, 1861, Bartlett Family Papers, box 2, folder 3, PVMA Library. From Dickinson Hill, Lyman pointed out that Bowditch would see the Deerfield and Connecticut Valleys and beyond, and could take note of the various climates and topographies.

23. *Greenfield Gazette and Courier*, November 21, 1867, 2; reprinted from the *New York Tribune*.

24. Nancy J. Tomes, "American Attitudes toward the Germ Theory of Disease: Phyllis Allen Richmond Revisited," *Journal of the History of Medicine and Allied Sciences* 52, no. 1 (1997): 17–50, clearly illustrates the timing of an emerging "germ theory of disease" in Europe and the United States and notes that already in the early to mid-1870s articles about germ theory were appearing in places such as the *Boston Medical and Surgical Journal* and the *New York Medical Record* (24–25).

25. Ott, *Fevered Lives*, 16–19, 100–110.

26. My conclusions about housing location and structure, like the family data, are drawn from the 1870 manuscript census. I inferred or, at times, pinpointed locations by following the census taker's (George Sheldon's) route through the town using the 1871 Beers Atlas of Franklin County. Since deaths occurred throughout the decade, I cannot confirm that these women died in the locations where I originally plot them, though the evidence supports my assumption that they were in the same town and likely in the same locations. 1870 Manuscript Census of Deerfield, microfilm, Historic Deerfield Library.

27. In the 1870 census all three of these children are listed as cutlery workers.

28. Richard D. Brown and Jack Tager, *Massachusetts: A Concise History* (Amherst: University of Massachusetts Press, 2000), 210–12.

29. Cheapside matched well Bowditch's high risk factors. Bowditch, *Consumption in New England*, e.g., 76, 85. Bowditch argued in several examples of his writings that low-lying and damp housing was a major factor in the spread of consumption, and several contemporary observers commented that many of the Commonwealth's more recent immigrants, and particularly the Irish, seemed more susceptible to the disease. See also Boston Medical Commission, *Sanitary Condition of Boston*, e.g., 122–33.

30. These comments about the "wallet shop" were common nineteenth-century assertions for why women should not work outside the home.

31. "At home" appears often as the occupation of young women in nineteenth-century censuses. Occasionally they might be listed, like Margaret Herron, as "farm laborer," but we know these young women worked actively in many roles on the farmstead, including doing piecework and home manufacturing. Marjorie R. Abel, "Women's Work in the Western Massachusetts Rural Economy," in *Labor in Massachusetts: Selected Essays*, ed. Kenneth Fones-Wolf and Martin Kaufman, 30–52 (Westfield: Institute for Massachusetts Studies, Westfield State College, 1990); Marjorie R. Abel and Nancy Folbre, "A Methodology for Revising Estimates: Female Market Participation in the U.S. before 1940," *Historical Methods* 23, no. 4 (1990): 167–76.

32. According to the 1870 census for Deerfield, there were thirty-nine "black" citizens living in Deerfield, twenty-one adults and eighteen children. The Smiths had six children. Of the male adults, two are listed as "farm laborer," five as "laborer," one as a butcher, and one as a servant. Among female adults, one is listed as "housekeeper," one as "servant," one as a "hotel cook," and one as a "kitchen girl," in the same hotel. Six women are listed as "keeps house." Five families live in black, male-headed households; the remaining live in the households or hotel of their white employers. All appear to have lived in the Mill River and South Deerfield areas.

33. Details about these families are drawn from the 1870 manuscript census and Deerfield vital records.

34. *Greenfield Gazette and Courier*, September 29, 1875.

35. Ibid., May 15, 1876. The stigma associated with consumption arose because it was considered a "filth" disease and because of the heritable connotations. The avoidance of naming it as a cause of death among more prominent families probably also contributed to an underestimation of the total numbers of deaths.

36. Ibid., November 27, 1849. Her epitaph reads, "Peaceful in life, happy in Death."

37. Young men typically might well have received more and more elaborate eulogies and obituaries than young women. See Chapter 9 for more on mourning practices for young men and young women.

38. A search through the Franklin County Publication Archive Index (www.publicationarchive. com/) of the *Gazette and Courier*, published weekly between January 1870 and January 1875, revealed at least 215 entries with some reference to the Irish or the immigrant population.

39. Laurel Hill is also the name of a well-known example of the rural cemetery movement located in Philadelphia.

40. George Sheldon and others thought that Deerfield's old burying ground was a place "beautiful for situation" (*History of Deerfield*, 2:879), and it certainly is today. On the rural cemetery movement, see Blanche M. G. Linden, *Silent City on a Hill: Picturesque Landscapes of Memory and Boston's Mount Auburn Cemetery*, rev. ed. (Amherst: University of Massachusetts Press/Library of American Landscape History, 2007). See also Stanley French, "The Cemetery as Cultural Institution: The Establishment of Mount Auburn and the Rural Cemetery Movement," in *Death in America*, ed. David E. Stannard, 69–91 (Philadelphia: University of Pennsylvania Press, 1975).

41. Sheldon, History of Deerfield, 2:879–84; Shirley Majewski, PVMA librarian, and William H. Leno, South Deerfield Cemetery Association, personal communication.

42. Mesmerism and clairvoyance were even topics for discussion by the Franklin District Medical Society at their October 1876 meeting. Minutes of the Franklin District Medical Society, box 4, PVMA Library.

43. Bartlett Family Papers, box 3, folder 1, PVMA Library.

44. Pat Jalland, *Death in the Victorian Family* (New York: Oxford University Press, 1996), 17–38.

45. See, e.g., Ott, *Fevered Lives*, 72–86. Many of these improvements, by isolating patients, were probably as instrumental in preventing the spread of consumption as in curing it.

46. It should be noted that physicians treated many middle-class young women who did not want to be revealed as tubercular. They would have treated their consumptive patients discreetly with the conventional prescriptions of sedatives or syrups or put them on the rest cure, but they would not have talked about it at FDMS meetings.

47. J. F. A. Adams, "The Health of the Farmers in Massachusetts," in *Fifth Annual Report of the State Board of Health of Massachusetts*, Public Document no. 34 (Boston: Wright & Potter, 1874), 183–262.

48. Ginsberg and Swedlund, "Sex-Specific Mortality," 436.

49. It has been observed that the exposure rate in late nineteenth-century America was extremely high, and the majority of Americans were infected but remained asymptomatic. Medical anthropologist D. Ann Herring, personal communication; see also E. R. N. Grigg, "The Arcana of Tuberculosis: III. Epidemiological History of Tuberculosis in the United States," *American Review of Tuberculosis* 78, no. 4 (October 1958): 426–53.

Chapter 6. Reproductive Women, Productive Men

1. Records of the First Church of Deerfield, 1810–1930, box 5, PVMA Library.

2. Lawrence Dame, M.D., transcripts, Records of the Franklin District Medical Society, 1851–1923, PVMA Library, 53.

3. The definitive works on death in childbirth are Irvine Loudon, *Death in Childbirth* (New York: Oxford University Press, 1992); idem, *The Tragedy of Childbed Fever* (New York: Oxford University Press, 2000). For the United States, see also Francis E. Kobrin, "The American Midwife Controversy: A Crisis of Professionalization," *Bulletin of the History of Medicine* 40 (1966): 350–63; Richard W. Wertz and Dorothy C. Wertz, *Lying In: A History of Childbirth in America* (New York: Schocken, 1979); Paul Starr, *The Social Transformation of American Medicine* (New York: Basic Books, 1982), 49–50, 223–25; J. W. Leavitt, "Science Enters the Birthing Room: Obstetrics in America since the 18th Century," in *Sickness and Health in America: Readings in the History of Medicine and Public Health*, ed. Judith Walzer Leavitt and Ronald L. Numbers, 3rd ed., 281–304 (Madison: University of Wisconsin Press, 1997).

4. Starr, *Social Transformation of American Medicine*, 49–50; James H. Cassedy, *American Medicine and Statistical Thinking, 1800–1860* (Cambridge: Harvard University Press, 1984), 80–83.

5. John C. Gunn, *Gunn's Domestic Medicine: A Facsimile of the First Edition, or, Poor Man's Friend* (1830; Knoxville: University of Tennessee Press, 1986), 334.

6. *E. coli, Staphylococcus*, and other bacteria could potentially be involved.

7. There are many summaries of Semmelweis's work. See, e.g., Harry F. Dowling, *Fighting Infection: Conquests of the Twentieth Century* (Cambridge: Harvard University Press, 1977), 56–57; Irvine Loudon, *The Tragedy of Childbed Fever* (New York: Oxford University Press, 2000), 88–110.

8. Lemuel Shattuck and others, *Report of the Sanitary Commission of Massachusetts* (1850; reprint, Cambridge: Harvard University Press, 1948), 91, 101. Another disease of the generative organs that caused a high risk for mothers and newborns was syphilis. But because it was a "hidden disease" that was underreported, and seldom spoken of, its role in obstetrical cases is very difficult to measure or find in case studies.

9. Samuel Warren Abbott, "The Vital Statistics of Massachusetts: A Forty Years' Summary (1856–1895)," in *Twenty-eighth Annual Report of the State Board of Health of Massachusetts*, Public

Document no. 34 (Boston: Wright & Potter, 1897), 764, table 46, 805, table 64. Note that for Shattuck, the denominator was all deaths, for Abbott the number of births.

10. A. McArdle, "Occupational Mortality in Nineteenth-Century Franklin County, Massachusetts" (PhD diss., University of Massachusetts, Amherst, 1985), 216. Death resulting from complications of stillbirth, miscarriage, or abortion contributed to this percentage, no doubt. Abortions were officially criminalized in the 1860s. See Leslie Reagan, *When Abortion Was a Crime: Women, Men, and Law in the United States, 1867–1973* (Berkeley: University of California Press, 1997). The American Gynecological Society estimates that the rate of maternal mortality in the United States was approximately 5.5% in 1915. Taylor E. Stewart, *History of the American Gynecological Society* (St. Louis: C. V. Mosby, 1985), 20.

11. R. S. Meindl and A. C. Swedlund, "Secular Trends in Mortality in the Connecticut Valley: 1700–1850," *Human Biology* 49, no. 3 (1977): 389–414.

12. I am indebted to Shelia Rothman and her book for these details of Deborah Vinal Fiske. Rothman, *Living in the Shadow of Death: Tuberculosis and the Social Experience of Illness in American History* (New York: Basic Books, 1994). The Fiske papers are located among the Helen Hunt Jackson Papers, Tutt Library, Colorado College, Colorado Springs.

13. Ibid., 101.

14. Agnes Gordon Tack diary, 1908–1912, Fuller-Higginson Family Papers, box 49, PVMA Library, p. 1.

15. Ibid., p. 2.

16. Abbott, "Vital Statistics," 819.

17. See Mark Aldrich, *Safety First: Technology, Labor, and Business in the Building of Work Safety, 1870–1939* (Baltimore: Johns Hopkins University Press, 1997).

18. See Paul Jenkins, *The Conservative Rebel: A Social History of Greenfield, Massachusetts* (Greenfield: Town of Greenfield, 1982), 92–116; J. Ritchie Garrison, *Landscape and Material Life in Franklin County Massachusetts, 1770–1860* (Knoxville: University of Tennessee Press, 1991), 218–19.

19. The first passage of a train through the Hoosac Tunnel occurred in February 1875. Carl R. Byron, *A Pinprick of Light: The Troy and Greenfield Railroad and Its Hoosac Tunnel* (1978; Shelburne, Vt.: New England Press, 1996.).

20. George Sheldon diary, George Sheldon Papers, PVMA Library.

21. These figures are drawn from William Fox, *Regimental Losses in the American Civil War, 1861–1865* (Albany, N.Y.: Albany Publishing, 1889), available at www.civilwarhome.com/foxspref.htm. Estimates of numbers vary; the balance of deaths would have occurred in accidents, prisons, and other contexts not specifically related to combat.

22. As with most nineteenth-century nosology, accurate diagnosis of infectious disease as the cause of death in the Civil War is difficult to translate into modern causalities. What is known is that many encampments, field hospitals, and prisoner of war camps of the North and the South suffered from bouts of typhus, typhoid, yellow fever, common dysenteries, and exceedingly high rates of sepsis infection of wounds.

23. Sources vary on the exact numbers. See, e.g., Louis Everts, *History of the Connecticut River Valley in Massachusetts*, 2 vols. (Philadelphia: J. B Lippincott, 1879). Emily J. Harris, "Sons and Soldiers: Deerfield, Massachusetts, and the Civil War," *Civil War History* 30, no. 2 (1984): 157–71.

24. Coincidental with the 1863 draft was the return of Company D of the 52nd Regiment. Company D was largely made up from Deerfield men. Fifteen soldiers did not return; others returned sick and wounded. Harris, "Sons and Soldiers," 164.

25. These numbers and much of the context provided here are drawn from ibid.

26. Jenkins, *Conservative Rebel*, 122–23. Michael H. Frisch, *Town into City: Springfield, Massachusetts, and the Meaning of Community, 1840–1880* (Cambridge: Harvard University Press, 1972), chap. 3.

27. See, e.g., Harris, "Sons and Soldiers," 170. Emily J. Harris, "A Northern Town Responds to the Civil War: Deerfield, Massachusetts, 1861–1865" (paper prepared for Historic Deerfield Summer Fellowship Program, 1978, Historic Deerfield Library), 52, is even more circumspect about the patriotic meaning of hiring substitutes.

28. Estimates vary. See J. David Hacker, "The Human Cost of War: White Population in the United States, 1850–1880," *Journal of Economic History* 61, no. 2 (2001): 486–89.

29. Jenkins, *Conservative Rebel*, 125.

30. One innovation arising from the Civil War was the practice of embalming, and one can literally call it "practice" because it was far from perfected. Bodily fluids were drained and concoctions were formulated which contained some or all of the ingredients arsenic, creosote, mercury, turpentine, and various forms of alcohol. Thomas Holmes, a Civil War physician and embalmer, marketed his formula for three dollars a gallon. Formaldehyde was not discovered until 1867. James C. Lee, "The Undertaker's Role during the American Civil War," *America's Civil War*, November 1996, www.historynet.com/magazines/american_civil_war/3034086.html; Robert W. Habenstein and William M. Lamers, *The History of American Funeral Directing*, 5th ed. (Brookfield, Wis.: National Funeral Directors Association, 2001). Drew Gilpin Faust, *This Republic of Suffering: Death and the American Civil War* (New York: Alfred A. Knopf, 2008), chap. 3.

31. Harris, "Northern Town Responds to the Civil War," 36.

32. "Purpose of Monuments," in *Civil War Monuments of Connecticut*, available at www.chs.org/ransom/overview1.htm. The website is based on David Ransom's study "Civil War Monuments" published in Connecticut Historical Society *Bulletin* 58 and 59 (1993–94).

33. For an enlightening essay on war memorials, see David Glassberg, "Remembering a War," in *Sense of History: The Place of the Past in American Life*, ed. David Glassberg, 23–57 (Amherst: University of Massachusetts Press, 2001). See also Kirk Savage, *Standing Soldiers, Kneeling Slaves: Race, War, and Monument in Nineteenth-Century America* (Princeton, N.J.: Princeton University Press, 1997). On Civil War and memory, see David W. Blight, *Beyond the Battlefield: Race, Memory, and the American Civil War* (Amherst: University of Massachusetts Press, 2002).

34. George Sheldon, *A History of Deerfield, Massachusetts*, 2 vols. (Deerfield, Mass.: PVMA, 1895–96), 2:862. He attributes this idea to "one of the audience" in attendance at the funeral of Colonel George Duncan Wells; possibly he was referring to himself.

35. *Civil War Monuments of Connecticut*, www.chs.org/ransom/036.htm. Also see David F. Ransom, "Notes to Soldier's Monument, Village Common, Main Street, Deerfield, Franklin County, Massachusetts," 7 pages, n.d., PVMA Library. For the cultural significance of community war memorials, see Jay Winter, *Sites of Memory, Sites of Mourning: The Great War in European Cultural History* (New York: Cambridge University Press, 1995), 78–116; Sarah Tarlow, *Bereavement and Commemoration: An Archaeology of Mortality* (Malden, Mass.: Blackwell, 1999), 159–165; and Patrick Hagopian, *The Vietnam War in American Memory: Veterans, Memorials, and the Politics of Healing* (Amherst: University of Massachusetts Press, 2009).

36. Harris, "Sons and Soldiers," 170–71.

37. For the impact of having so few of the deceased returned home during the Civil War, see Gary Laderman, *The Sacred Remains: American Attitudes towards Death, 1799–1883* (New Haven: Yale University Press, 1996), chap. 10; Faust, *This Republic of Suffering*, chap. 3. For England during WWI, see Pat Jalland, *Death in the Victorian Family* (New York: Oxford University Press, 1996), 373–79.

38. Frank Wright Pratt, *Boyhood Memories of Old Deerfield* (Portland, Me.: Southworth-Anthoensen Press, 1936) 248. Pratt says James Hitchcock died in Libby Prison, Richmond, Va., but family papers say he died after being removed from Libby to Andersonville. Hitchcock Family Papers, box 1, folder 14, PVMA Library.

39. The Old Deerfield Grammar School was consolidated with the South Deerfield Grammar School in 1992, and the new school was no longer near the Memorial and the Old Burying Ground. Students still recite the Gettysburg Address in South Deerfield on Memorial Day.

40. Harris, "Sons and Soldiers," 162.

41. *Greenfield Gazette and Courier*, October 28, 1867, 2.

42. Ibid., cited in Byron, *Pinprick of Light*. See also www.hoosactunnel.net/history.php.

43. *Greenfield Gazette and Courier*, December 9, 1867, 2.

44. Agnes Higginson to Stephen Higginson, letter dated August 21, 1862, Fuller-Higginson Family Papers, box 63, folder 3, PVMA Library.

45. Findings of the Massachusetts Board of Railroad Commissioners, May 22, 1886, published in miscellaneous *Greenfield Gazette and Courier* articles for May and June 1886 collected by George Sheldon, O-d 312, C6 1886, PVMA Library. Some accounts give the total of passengers and crew as 46, others as 48.

46. Rev. P. V. Finch, sermon text, *Greenfield Gazette and Courier*, April 17, 1886.

47. Deane attended the May meeting of the Franklin District Medical Society, but matters discussed there were routine, and the minutes report no mention of the accident. FDMS Papers, box 2, 1886, PVMA Library.

48. See Martha Taber, "A History of the Cutlery Industry in the Connecticut Valley," *Smith College Studies in History* 41 (1955): 13–25. Jenkins, *Conservative Rebel*, chap. 9.

49. Antony Disseltile, for example, "shattered" his leg in a belt and was drawn into the grindstone on which he was working. *Turners Falls Reporter*, July 23, 1873, reprinted in Robert L. Merriam et al., *The History of the John Russell Cutlery Company, 1833–1936* (Greenfield, Mass.: Bete Press, 1976), 74.

50. *Greenfield Gazette and Courier*, February 18, 1869.

51. Merriam et al., *History of the John Russell Cutlery Company*, 23.

52. *Greenfield Recorder*, March 17, 1920.

53. See Marjorie R. Abel, "Women's Work in the Western Massachusetts Rural Economy," in *Labor in Massachusetts: Selected Essays*, ed. Kenneth Fones-Wolf and Martin Kaufman, 30–52 (Westfield: Institute for Massachusetts Studies, Westfield State College, 1990). For a broader discussion of family work strategies in New England, see Tamara K. Haraven, *Family Time and Industrial Time: The Relationship between the Family and Work in a New England Industrial Community* (Cambridge: Cambridge University Press, 1982); Louise Lamphere, *From Working Daughters to Working Mothers: Immigrant Women in a New England Industrial Community* (Ithaca, N.Y.: Cornell University Press, 1987), chap. 3.

54. Susan McGowan and Amelia F. Miller, *Family and Landscape: Deerfield Homelots from 1671* (Deerfield: PVMA, 1996), 12, 13.

55. Deerfield Vital Records, PVMA Library; Baptism, Marriage, and Funeral Records of the First Church of Deerfield, 1810–1930, Historic Deerfield Library.

56. Sheldon, *History of Deerfield*, 2:327; McGowan and Miller, *Family and Landscape*, 13.

57. See Viviana A. Rotman Zelizer, *Morals and Markets: The Development of Life Insurance in the United States* (New York: Columbia University Press, 1979), esp. chap. 4.

58. *Greenfield Gazette and Courier*, October 28, 1867.

59. Taber, "History of the Cutlery Industry," 98.

60. J. C. Herbert Emery, "Risky Business? Nonactuarial Pricing Practices and the Financial Viability of Fraternal Sickness Insurers," *Explorations in Economic History* 33 (1996): 195–226.

61. Sharon Ann Murphy, *Life Insurance in the United States through World War I*, available from eh.net/encyclopedia/article/murphy.life.insurance.us. On the relationship of health insurance to life insurance, see John E. Murray, *Origins of American Health Insurance: A History of Industrial Sickness Funds* (New Haven: Yale University Press, 2007, chap 4.

62. William T. Standen, "The Ideal Protection (U.S. Life Insurance Co, 1897)," in Zelizer, *Morals and Markets*, 56–57.

63. Judson MacLaury, *The Job Safety Law of 1970: Its Passage Was Perilous*, www.dol.gov/oasam/programs/history/osha.htm; Raymond L. Bridgman, *Ten Years of Massachusetts* (Boston: D. C. Heath, 1888), 72–87.

64. *Greenfield Recorder*, February 7, 1917.

Chapter 7. Surviving the Odds

1. Samuel Warren Abbott, "The Vital Statistics of Massachusetts: A Forty Years' Summary (1856–1895)," in *Twenty-eighth Annual Report of the State Board of Health of Massachusetts*, Public Document no. 34 (Boston: Wright & Potter, 1897), 718, table 2, 719, 744, table 32.

2. These figures are based on historical life tables in U.S. Bureau of the Census, *Historical Statistics of the United States from Colonial Times to the Present*, Bicentennial Ed. (New York: Basic Books, 1976), 54–56. See also Louis I. Dublin and Alfred J. Lotka, *Length of Life: A Study of the Life Table* (New York: Ronald Press, 1936), 65.

3. David Hackett Fischer, *Growing Old in America* (New York: Oxford University Press, 1978), 228. According to an article in the *Orange Enterprise*, September 11, 1894, Lauriston Durkee made provision in his will for a home for "aged males and females in indigent circumstances." If the home had been created, it would have been the first in Franklin County.

4. The *Merck Manual of Diagnosis and Therapy* includes an expansive section for pediatric disorders, but, in its 18th edition (2006–8) still has only a small subcategory numbering a few pages specifically designated for old age or geriatric disorders. See www.merck.com/mmpe/index.html.

5. This campaign to lower infant and childhood mortality was active throughout the United States, as well as Britain and most of Western Europe.

6. See, for example, Abbott, "Vital Statistics," 801, table 62.

7. See Douglas L. Anderton and Susan Hautaniemi Leonard, "Grammars of Death: An Analysis of Nineteenth-Century Literal Causes of Death from the Age of Miasmas to Germ Theory," *Social Science History* 28, no. 1 (2004): 111–43.

8. There was no category for diabetes yet. Secretary of the Commonwealth, *Sixty-ninth Annual Report of Births, Marriages, and Deaths in Massachusetts*, Public Document no. 1, for the Year Ending December 31st, 1910 (Boston: Wright & Potter, 1911).

9. *Deerfield Vital Statistics* (1900–1910).

10. "797—Senility without mention of psychosis," icd9cm.chrisendres.com/index.php?action=search&srchtext=797. Doctors today would be more likely to determine that an elderly person died of "natural causes," a term very like what the physicians in 1900 were using.

11. Throughout the last quarter of the nineteenth century, the *Greenfield Gazette and Courier* devoted many articles to the long-lived in the various towns served by the paper.

12. When I lecture on death and loss and ask members of the audience who among them reads the obituaries, there is always a stronger showing of hands among the older persons present.

13. For the story of Sheldon's efforts to preserve the past, see Michael Batinski, *Pastkeepers in a Small Place: Five Centuries in Deerfield, Massachusetts* (Amherst: University of Massachusetts Press, 2004), 121–53.

14. Sheldon's friend Edward Hitchcock was a preceptor at Deerfield Academy, then a professor at Amherst College, and finally president of the college from 1845 to 1854. His son Edward was a doctor and a professor at Amherst College and the father of Henry Judson Hitchcock, who is mentioned in Chapter 3.

15. Sheldon is quoting from Harriet Beecher Stowe, *Uncle Tom's Cabin*, chap. 10.

16. Jennie Arms Sheldon, "George Sheldon," typescript, George Sheldon Papers, box 1, folder 2, PVMA Library; Louis H. Everts, *History of the Connecticut River Valley in Massachusetts*, vol. 2 (Philadelphia, J. B. Lippincott, 1879), 692.

17. Joseph G. Richardson, *Health and Longevity*, vol. 1 (New York: Home Health Society, 1914), 543n. Among several ailments, Sheldon complains in his diary of stomach trouble and dyspepsia, referring to it as his "old stomach ake." George Sheldon diary, George Sheldon Papers, PVMA Library. In truth, dyspepsia no doubt affected all classes, but much was made of its being a disease of the middle class and their hectic, overindulgent lifestyles.

18. Robert Grant Irving, "George Sheldon, Historian," Heritage Foundation Summer Fellowship Program, 1961, Historic Deerfield Library, p. 21.

19. This following sequence is pieced together from both computerized linkage of vital statistics records of Deerfield and the genealogical section of Sheldon's *History of Deerfield*, vol. 2, and the manual linkage of extensive family papers found in the Memorial Libraries of PVMA and Historic Deerfield, Inc.

20. As mentioned in Chapter 3, David and Julia's first daughter, Julia Lucretia, died of dysentery in 1842. Their second daughter, born after the death of the first, was named Julia Althea.

Giving a second child the same name as that of a previously deceased child was a common practice in New England families, but more common in the eighteenth and early nineteenth centuries than in the late nineteenth. David Hackett Fischer, *Albion's Seed: Four British Folkways in America* (New York: Oxford University Press, 1989), 96. See also, Daniel Scott Smith, "Life Course Norms and the Family System of Older Americans in 1900," *Journal of Family History* 4 (1979): 285–98.

21. According to a brief death notice, Susan Sheldon "had been about as usual during the day" preceding. *Greenfield Gazette and Courier*, October 10, 1881. This entry was likely provided by George himself, a frequent Deerfield correspondent; it appears near the end of a column of news of the town.

22. Both entries are from page 50 of the transcribed Franklin H. Williams diary, 1852–1891, Diary Collection of the PVMA Library, alphabetical box W.

23. Ibid., 67, 72, 74, 75. Mike was a brother, Arthur a son, Amelia a sister.

24. Agnes Higginson Fuller diary, box 20, Fuller-Higginson Family Papers, PVMA Library. In this period Fuller was living in both Cambridge and Deerfield.

25. Sheldon notes that Henry Augustus Wells, born November 24, 1839, was "simple." Sheldon, *A History of Deerfield, Massachusetts*, vol. 2 (Deerfield: PVMA, 1895–96), 368.

26. Elisha Wells letterbook, 1863–67, box 3, Wells Family Papers, PVMA Library.

27. C. Alice Baker to Winthrop Arms, January 4,1906, box 5, folder 11, Arms Family Papers, PVMA Library. Baker was referring to the Beaux-Arts styled Hall constructed by the Boston Horticultural Society in 1901.

28. "Last Will and Testament of Esther Dickinson, Wife of Consider," box 3, folder 11, Dickinson Family Papers, PVMA Library.

29. Quite possibly lamenting the loss of a beautiful yacht as well as their late friend.

30. Obituary of William Stoddard Williams, *Greenfield Recorder*, July 23, 1911; funeral plan, box 17, file 4, William Stoddard Williams Papers, PVMA Library. W. S. Williams was an insurance agent living in Greenfield. Sheldon, *History of Deerfield*, 385.

31. Edward Clarke, *Sex in Education; or, A Fair Chance for the Girls* (Boston: James R. Osgood, 1873) In a somewhat baffling contradiction, many physicians regarded working-class women and those of nonwhite races as hardy and capable of strenuous labor. The medical anthropologist Ann Herring notes that with their rise in influence and authority, doctors were increasingly commenting on moral and political affairs beyond their training, and in effect medicalizing them (personal communication, 2008).

32. The scholarship on this topic is long and consistent in point of view. See, e.g., G. J. Barker-Benfield, *The Horrors of the Half-Known Life: Male Attitudes toward Women and Sexuality in Nineteenth-Century America* (New York: Harper and Row, 1976), Barbara Ehrenreich and Deirdre English, *For Her Own Good: 150 Years of the Experts' Advice to Women* (Garden City, N.Y.: Anchor, 1978); Carroll Smith-Rosenberg, *Disorderly Conduct: Visions of Gender in Victorian America* (New York: Oxford University Press, 1985); Cynthia Eagle Russett, *Sexual Science: The Victorian Construction of Womanhood* (Cambridge: Harvard University Press, 1989); Emily Martin, *The Woman in the Body: A Cultural Analysis of Reproduction* (Boston: Beacon Press, 1992); Diane Price Herndl, *Invalid Women: Figuring Feminine Illness in American Fiction and Culture, 1840–1940* (Chapel Hill: University of North Carolina Press, 1993); Londa Schiebinger, *Nature's Body: Gender in the Making of Modern Science* (Boston: Beacon Press, 1993); Patricia A. Vertinsky, *The Eternally Wounded Woman: Women, Doctors, and Exercise in the Late Nineteenth Century* (Urbana: University of Illinois Press, 1994).

33. Cited in Ehrenreich and English, *For Her Own Good*, 110. It is worth noting that by the early 1900s the number of topics related to uterine problems declines noticeably in the Franklin District Medical Society minutes, and that by 1902 two female doctors, Mary Dole and Jane Goodnough, were elected members to the society. Minutes of the FDMS, box 2, PVMA Library. Mary Dole would go on to become a prominent physician in Greenfield and Northampton. Dole, *A Doctor in Homespun: Autobiography of Mary Phylinda Dole* (Greenfield, Mass.: Private printing, 1941).

34. G. Stanley Hall, *Adolescence; Its Psychology and Its Relations to Physiology, Anthropology, Sociology, Sex, Crime, Religion and Education* (New York: D. Appleton, 1904). Granville Stanley Hall was born in the neighboring town of Ashfield in 1844 and educated at Williams College.

35. Wearing corsets could lead to compressed ribs and in some cases, prolapsed uteruses. As an intervention some doctors would recommend pessaries (devices used to keep the womb in position), which might in turn lead to serious infection and toxic shock syndrome. See Lynnette Leidy, "The Possible Role of the Pessary in the Etiology of Toxic Shock," *Medical Anthropology Quarterly* 8, no. 2 (1994): 198–208.

36. Bureau of the Census, *Statistical History of the United States*; Kevin G. Kinsella, "Changes in Life Expectancy 1900–1990," *American Journal of Clinical Nutrition* 55 (1992): 1196S–1202S. For rural areas, the difference may have been somewhat less. See Michael R. Haines, "The Urban Mortality Transition in the United States, 1800–1940," *Annales de demographie historique* 1 (2001): 33–64.

37. Susan McGowan and Amelia F. Miller, *Family and Landscape: Deerfield Homelots from 1671* (Deerfield: PVMA, 1996), 86–87, 101; Suzanne L. Flynt, *The Allen Sisters: Pictorial Photographers, 1885–1920* (Deerfield: PVMA, 2002), 28–30; Suzanne L. Flynt, curator, PVMA Museum, personal communication, 2008.

38. Maria Stebbins Brown moved to Springfield, Mass.

39. Flynt, *Allen Sisters*, 25–28.

40. Mary Allen to Frances B. Johnston, e.g., January 9, 1897, April 9, 1897, June 4, 1900, excerpts courtesy Suzanne L. Flynt, PVMA Museum. (The Frances Benjamin Johnston papers are housed in the Library of Congress.)

41. My information on the women occupants of the main street during this period is largely drawn from Batinski, *Pastkeepers in a Small Place*, esp. 169–93, with additional insight provided by Suzanne L. Flynt, Susan McGowan, and Shirley Majewski of the PVMA.

42. Ibid., 170; McGowan and Miller, *Family and Landscape*, 69, 145. Records are not definitive regarding details of ownership and occupancy of the Yale house, though they do indicate that its primary occupants were Madeline Yale Wynne and her companion, Annie C. Putnam, and that Catherine Yale lived there on and off between 1884 and 1900 and paid property taxes in Deerfield. Her obituary describes the house, which she and her daughter called "The Manse," as "her real home" for her last twelve years. *Greenfield Gazette and Courier*, March 22, 1900. Regarding the Yale-Wynne house, see also Deborah L. Rotman, "Newlyweds, Young Families, and Spinsters: A Consideration of Developmental Cycle in Historical Archaeologies of Gender," *Journal of Historical Archaeology* 9, no. 1 (2005): 24–26.

43. Sandra F. Mackenzie, "Taxing the Widows and Spinsters: Female Property Ownership and the Deerfield Street, 1864–1910" (paper prepared for Historic Deerfield Summer Fellowship Program, 1974, StS 350.724 M 157t, Historic Deerfield Library), 59–65, fig. 2 (unnumbered page), app. A.

44. "Essay Read before the Woman Suffrage Society in Shelburne Falls, Massachusetts," 1873, box 1, folder 2, Yale Family Papers, PVMA. Also cited in Mackenzie, "Taxing the Widows," 36. (In 1873, Catherine Yale was living in Shelburne Falls, after buying the Willard house in Deerfield for her daughter.)

45. Baker joined several others, including noted author Elizabeth Stuart Phelps, to publish a reply to Clarke's *Sex in Education*. The editor of the volume, and author of the lead essay, was Julia Ward Howe, an abolitionist, social activist, and author of "The Battle Hymn of the Republic." *Sex and Education: A Reply to Dr. E. H. Clarke's "Sex in Education"* (Boston: Roberts Brothers, 1874). Baker's contribution was authored by "C." A copy appears in the PVMA collection, CC-Vol H856s, 1874.

46. See, e.g., Abbott, "Vital Statistics," 760. For a discussion of issues in naming diseases, see Stephen J. Pietzman, "From Bright's Disease to End-Stage Renal Disease," in *Framing Disease: Studies in Cultural History*, ed. Charles E. Rosenberg and Janet Golden, 3–19 (New Brunswick, N.J.: Rutgers University Press, 1992); Anderton and Hautaniemi Leonard, "Grammars of Death," 111–39.

47. *Deerfield Vital Statistics*. Maria Stebbins Brown died in Springfield, Mass., at the residence of her son-in-law. "Death Notice," *Greenfield Gazette and Courier*, November 22, 1890. Her death is not registered in the vital statistics for Deerfield. Pneumonia, we know today, is often a complication of congestive heart failure.

48. Frederick Rossiter, *The Practical Guide to Health* (Mountain View, Calif.: Pacific Publishing, 1913), 64, 357.

49. W. W. Hall, M.D., *Health at Home, or Hall's Family Doctor* (Hartford, Conn.: S. M. Betts, 1872), 494; Richardson, *Health and Longevity*, 469–70.

50. Roy Porter, ed., *The Cambridge Illustrated History of Medicine* (New York: Cambridge University Press, 1996), 218–19.

51. *Greenfield Gazette and Courier*, March 25, 1893.

52. W. F. Bynum, *Science and the Practice of Medicine in the Nineteenth Century* (New York: Cambridge University Press, 1994), 224–26; John Harley Warner, *The Therapeutic Perspective: Medical Practice, Knowledge, and Identity in America, 1820–1885* (Cambridge: Harvard University Press, 1986), 266–83.

53. See Jane A. Winchester, "Footprints along the Connecticut: James Deane, M.D.," typescript, 2003, Main stacks, 926.1 D283w, Historic Deerfield Library, pp. 2–3.

54. The literal and metaphorical comparison of the body to a machine continues to this day in science and medicine.

55. For a medical description of the body as a machine, see, e.g., Richardson, *Health and Longevity*, bk. 5, 283–96. The medical narrative of the machine and bodily perfection was not satisfactorily reconciled with the female body's proneness to illness and imperfection. Discussions of the more delicate constitutions and the "peculiar" diseases of women could reside in the same texts that extolled the male body as a finely tuned machine.

56. Dora Costa, "Why Were Older Men in the Past in Such Poor Health?" National Bureau of Economic Research Working Paper, 2004, web.mit.edu/costa/www/draft4chicago.pdf. Using health survey data coupled with data on Union Army veterans, Costa found that among men ages 60 to 74, functional limitations declined by 0.6 percent per year between 1910 and the 1990s. The decline in chronic respiratory problems, valvular heart disease, arteriosclerosis, and joint and back problems was about 66 percent from the 1900s to the 1970s and 1980s, or 0.7 percent per year.

57. Greenfield's cane was announced in the *Gazette and Courier*, July 7, 1909. There is both truth and folklore surrounding these canes, and it is alleged that a resident of another town died when the selectmen were on their way to deliver it. In 2008, Blanche Hukowicz, age 101 and still living in her own home, was the holder of the Deerfield cane. Deerfield's oldest resident receives a lapel pin; the cane is kept at Town Hall. Many towns lost their canes over the years. See Barbara Staples, *The Bay State's Boston Post Canes* (Lynn, Mass.: Flemming Press, 1997), and web.maynard.ma.us/bostonpostcane/.

58. A list of the earliest recipients has not been found, nor has a search of the newspapers revealed who first received Deerfield's cane.

59. Alice C. Baker, "The Tablinum," *History and Proceedings of the Pocumtuck Valley Memorial Association* 5, no. 2 (1883): 101–4. Also cited in Batinski, *Pastkeepers,* 179–80. See also Alice C. Baker letters to Winthrop Arms, Winthrop Tylor Arms Papers in box 5, folder 11, Arms Family Papers, PVMA Library. In letters dated January 30 and November 25, 1902, Baker disparages the local Irish.

60. Donald R. Friary and Amelia Miller, foreword to *A History of Deerfield, Massachusetts: A Facsimile of the 1895–96 Edition*, by George Sheldon (Somersworth: New Hampshire Publishing, 1972); Sheldon, *History of Deerfield;* Batinski, *Pastkeepers,* 140–53; Robert Grant Irving, "George Sheldon, Historian," paper prepared for Heritage Foundation Summer Fellowship Program, 1961, Historic Deerfield Library, www.americancenturies.mass.edu/collection/itempage.jsp?itemid=5746.

61. *Greenfield Gazette and Courier*, September 3 1910.

62. Irving, "George Sheldon, Historian," 20.

63. Sheldon, *History of Deerfield*, 883, 885; Irving, "George Sheldon, Historian," 21.

64. See Robert W. Habenstein and William M. Lamers, *The History of American Funeral Directing*, 5th ed. (Brookfield, Wis.: National Funeral Directors Association, 2001), 391.

65. Elsie Putnam and the deceased were young women at the time, but this passage illustrates funeral preparations that would extend to older individuals as well. Elsie M. Putnam diary, March 28–31, 1888, Diary Collection, LO2.001, PVMA Library.

66. Names of undertakers gleaned from business directories in PVMA collections.

67. Richard A. Wells, *Manners, Culture, and Dress of the Best American Society* (Springfield, Mass.: King, Richardson, 1890), in PVMA Library, #13876.

68. Rice Family Papers, folder 7, PVMA Library. This appears to be a bill to Mrs. O. W. Rice for her husband, Oscar W. Rice. The wheat was included presumably so that a sheaf might be placed on the coffin during the service or thrown onto the coffin at burial. A handful of dirt, pine branches, or wheat straw were all customary offerings made before the grave was filled in. The average cost of a funeral in the United States today is about six thousand to eight thousand dollars but it can be considerably more, www.funeralplanning101.com/. See also Mark Harris, *Grave Matters: A Journey through the Modern Funeral Industry to a Natural Way of Burial* (New York: Scribner, 2007), 7–14.

69. The eulogy ran on the first page of the *Greenfield Gazette and Courier*, December 30, 1916, and proceeded for four and one-half columns.

70. Ibid., December 27, 1916. For the description of the room and wandering dog, see Irving, "George Sheldon, Historian."

Chapter 8. Managing Disease in the Long Nineteenth Century

1. Lemuel Shattuck and others, *Report on the Sanitary Commission of Massachusetts* (1850; reprint, Cambridge: Harvard University Press, 1948).

2. U.S. Bureau of the Census, *Historical Statistics of the United States from Colonial Times to the Present*, Bicentennial Ed. (New York, Basic Books, 1976), 16, 22, 116. The estimated foreign-born population for 1840 is not as well known as for 1850, but the percentage was considerably less. The major waves of Irish immigration occurred during and following the potato famine, 1845–49, but significant migration began in the 1820s. In Massachusetts the foreign-born population achieved 25 percent by the 1870s.

3. See esp. David Harvey, *The Condition of Postmodernity: An Enquiry into the Origins of Cultural Change* (Cambridge: Blackwell, 1990), 27–31; on Enlightenment assumptions, also see Eric Wolf, *Envisioning Power: Ideologies of Dominance and Crisis* (Berkeley: University of California Press, 1999), 23–30. Harvey dates the rapid acceleration from about 1890; I would put it at least a decade earlier.

4. Ian Hacking, *The Taming of Chance* (New York: Cambridge University Press, 1990).

5. Paul Starr, *The Social Transformation of American Medicine* (New York: Basic Books, 1982).

6. As I discuss in the Introduction, although historians and social scientists have a tendency to carve history into discrete periods, I believe that reality is usually more complex than "eras" and "epochs" imply. Changes in one set of cultural practices might not synchronize well with changes in another set. In New England in the late nineteenth and early twentieth centuries, for example, the culture of medicine stagnated while other social practices changed rapidly. And, to repeat, "disease time" is altogether disrespectful of calendar time. For these reasons, strict chronologies and cutoff points can seem arbitrary and constrain cultural insights. Nevertheless, a general chronology is useful for reviewing the three processes I explore here. I want to avoid the trap of narrowly defined periods or epochs while using some of the key events highlighted by Starr in ibid. and by Henry Bowditch in his *Public Hygiene in America* (1877; reprint, New York: Arno Press, 1972).

7. The apparent anachronism of a progressive in the Victorian era exemplifies the fact that historical eras are prone to slippage and that some individuals are always ahead or behind their times.

8. Bridging the first—the epoch of confidence—and the second—the epoch of statistics—were doctors like Stephen West Williams, who believed strongly in purgatives and emetics but also in the value of collecting accurate "facts."

9. Bowditch, *Public Hygiene*, 5,6.

10. See esp. Hacking, *Taming of Chance*, 47–54. See also Libby Schweber, *Disciplining Statistics: Demography and Vital Statistics in France and England, 1830–1885* (Durham, N.C.: Duke University Press, 2006); James H. Cassedy, *American Medicine and Statistical Thinking, 1800–1860* (Cambridge: Harvard University Press, 1984), 52–67.

11. Its onset precisely matches Bowditch's date for the beginning of his second epoch.

12. Although the ground was already well laid for the state collection of mortality statistics, Paul Rabinow suggests that, more than any other single event, the experience of the epidemic in Paris prompted efforts to measure and account for disease episodes. Rabinow, *French Modern: Norms and Forms of the Social Environment* (Cambridge: MIT Press, 1989), 30–32.

13. See, e.g., John M. Eyler, *Victorian Social Medicine: The Ideas and Methods of William Farr* (Baltimore: Johns Hopkins University Press, 1979), 13–28; David Lilienfeld and Abraham M. Lilienfeld, "The French Influence on the Development of Epidemiology," in *Times, Places, and Persons: Aspects of the History of Epidemiology*, ed. Abraham M. Lilienfeld, 28–37 (Baltimore: Johns Hopkins University Press, 1980). So important was Louis's influence on Bowditch that he dedicated his centennial lecture to him and devoted several pages of discussion of his second epoch to Louis's work.

14. Eyler believes that Louis's training was a significant factor in Farr's developing theories and methods relating to public health, but an even greater influence was the life table techniques developed by the British actuary Thomas Rowe Edmonds. Edmonds had apparently independently rediscovered the relational probabilities of death at different ages that had first been proposed by Benjamin Gompertz and presented in 1825. Eyler, *Victorian Social Medicine*, 71–78.

15. Ibid., 109. In the British system, England was subdivided into vital registration districts.

16. Stephen West Williams, *A Medical History of the County of Franklin, in the Commonwealth of Massachusetts* (Boston: The Society, 1842).

17. Farr, letter of introduction to readers of the Supplement to *Thirty-Fifth Annual Report*, 1875, iii, quoted in Eyler, *Victorian Social Medicine*, 123.

18. Shattuck, letter to readers of the *Fourth Annual Report to the Legislature Relating to the Registry and Returns of Births, Marriages and Deaths in Massachusetts*, 1845, 99, quoted in Barbara G. Rosenkrantz, *Public Health and the State: Changing Views in Massachusetts, 1842–1936* (Cambridge: Harvard University Press, 1972), 21.

19. The long history of numeracy in America is well documented in Patricia Cline Cohen's *A Calculating People: The Spread of Numeracy in Early America* (Chicago, University of Chicago Press, 2nd edition, 1999).

20. On the constitutive nature of statistics, see Jacqueline Urla, "Cultural Politics in an Age of Statistics: Numbers, Nations, and the Making of Basque Identity," *American Ethnologist* 20, no. 4 (1993): 818–43; Susan Greenhalgh, "The Social Construction of Population Science: An Intellectual, Institutional, and Political History of Twentieth Century Demography," *Comparative Studies of Society and History* 38, no. 1 (1996): 26–66; Susan Greenhalgh, "Making up China's 'Black Population,'" in *Categories and Contexts: Anthropological and Historical Studies in Critical Demography*, ed. Simon Szreter, Hania Sholkamy, and A. Dharmalingam, 148–72 (Oxford: Oxford University Press, 2004); Silvana Patriarca, *Numbers and Nationhood: Writing Statistics in Nineteenth-Century Italy* (New York: Cambridge University Press, 1996), 7–12. See also David I. Kertzer and Dominique Arel, eds., *Census and Identity: The Politics of Race, Ethnicity, and Language in National Censuses* (New York: Cambridge University Press, 2002).

21. Farr responded to a letter from Florence Nightingale and cautioned her about "intermingling causation with statistics." He adds, "You complain that your report would be dry. The dryer the better. Statistics should be the driest of all reading." Cited in Theodore M. Porter, *The Rise of Statistical Thinking, 1820–1900* (Princeton, N.J.: Princeton University Press, 1986),

36. Some resistance to the census taker and statist is evident in the occasional political cartoon, or, for example, in Dickens's portrayal of Mr. Gradgrind in *Hard Times*. See, e.g., Hacking, *Taming of Chance*, 117–18.

22. William Farr, "Influence of Elevation on the Fatality of Cholera," *Journal of the Statistical Society of London* 15, no. 2 (1852): 155–83. Farr thought miasmas at the lower elevations might account for the higher rates of cholera near the Thames, but it was actually the proximity to waterborne disease sources.

23. In this example, the consumptive was likely to present more serious symptoms in part because of the dampness and poor quality of the housing but another contributing factor was the association of class and ethnicity with substandard housing and diet.

24. This constitutive process has been addressed in recent medical anthropological research as a kind of shared "citizenship." Adriana Petryna coined the term *biological citizenship* to refer to the Ukrainian citizens and workers affected by the Chernobyl nuclear accident to acknowledge how the state, the medical community, and those affected created a new social and medical class of citizens. Petryna, *Life Exposed: Biological Citizens after Chernobyl* (Princeton, N.J.: Princeton University Press, 2002). Charles L. Briggs and Clara Mantini-Briggs describe the 1992 cholera epidemic in Venezuela as involving sanitary citizenship and unsanitary subjects. Sanitary citizens are those whom politicians, health officials, physicians, and the press deem knowledgeable of modern medicine and whose behaviors are acceptable to these communities. Unsanitary subjects are those who are judged incapable of these understandings or who are unable to access or resistant to the modern health knowledge and facilities sponsored by these institutions. Briggs and Mantini-Briggs, *Stories in the Time of Cholera: Racial Profiling during a Medical Nightmare* (Berkeley: University of California Press, 2003), 10.

25. In England the people who became statists also included the emerging middle class of business and commerce. William Farr came from a family of farm laborers but gained a wealthy patron through his apprenticeship. Eyler, *Victorian Social Medicine*, 1.

26. Bowditch cited in Rosenkrantz, *Public Health and the State*, 55.

27. Theodore M. Porter, *Trust in Numbers: The Pursuit of Objectivity in Science and Public Life* (Princeton, N.J.: Princeton University Press, 1995), 77. In this instance Porter is referring to bureaucrats in Europe, and though he singles out social workers and philanthropists in the United States, I think it would hold for the nineteenth-century bureaucrats as well.

28. Hacking, *The Taming of Chance*, 119. See also ibid., 115–22; Porter, *Trust in Numbers*, 74–78; Alan M. Kraut, *Silent Travelers: Germs, Genes and the 'Immigrant Menace'* (Baltimore: Johns Hopkins University Press, 1994), 32–49, 138.

29. See, Michel Foucault, *The Order of Things; an Archaeology of the Human Sciences* (New York: Vintage Books, 1973); idem, *The History of Sexuality*, trans. Robert Hurley (New York: Vintage Books, 1980).

30. The greatest reductions achieved were in rates of infant mortality, as outlined in Chapter 3. This issue is explored in greater detail in Alan C. Swedlund, "Infant Mortality in Massachusetts and the United States in the Nineteenth Century," in *Disease in Populations in Transition: Anthropological and Epidemiological Perspectives*, ed. A. C. Swedlund and G. J. Armelagos, 161–82 (Westport, Conn.: Bergin and Garvey, 1990); and Alan C. Swedlund and Helen L. Ball, "Nature, Nurture, and the Determinants of Infant Mortality: A Case Study from Massachusetts, 1830–1920," in *Building a New Biocultural Synthesis: Political-Economic Perspectives on Human Biology*, ed. Alan H. Goodman and Thomas L. Leatherman, 191–228 (Ann Arbor: University of Michigan Press, 1998). See also Susan I. Hautaniemi, "Demography and Death in Emergent Industrial Cities in New England" (Ph.D. diss., University of Massachusetts, 2002).

31. See, e.g., Rosenkrantz, *Public Health and the State*, esp. chap. 4. For information on implementation of local water and sewer systems, see Paul Jenkins, *The Conservative Rebel: A Social History of Greenfield, Massachusetts* (Greenfield: Town of Greenfield, 1982), 147, 205; *Deerfield Annual Report*, 1880–81, PVMA Library; Alan H. McArdle, "Mortality Change and Industrialization in Western Massachusetts, 1850–1910" (Ph.D. diss., University of Massachusetts, 1986).

32. Minutes of the FDMS, boxes 1 and 2, PVMA Library. For similar concerns from the Massachusetts Medical Society, see Walter L. Burrage, *A History of the Massachusetts Medical Society: With Brief Biographies of the Founders and Chief Officers, 1781–1922* (Norwood, Mass.: Plimpton Press, 1923).

33. Debby Applegate, introduction to *The Most Famous Man in America: The Biography of Henry Ward Beecher* (New York: Doubleday, 2006).

34. Sheldon clipped the stories from the *Springfield Republican* when Beecher died and filed them in a special envelope. Biography case, L-pqm, 4160, PVMA Library.

35. George Sheldon obituary, *Greenfield Gazette and Courier*, December 27, 1916. It would probably be more accurate to describe Beecher, Sheldon, and others of the American Party as antislavery Free-Soilers. They opposed the expansion of slavery but did not necessarily call for its abolition where it existed. Kevin Sweeney, personal communication. Bowditch was also deeply involved in the antislavery movement, even taking time off from his medical work. Rosenkrantz, *Public Health and the State*, 57–59.

36. George Sheldon obituary. For a political history of Massachusetts during the period of the American Party, see John R. Mulkern, *The Know-Nothing Party in Massachusetts: The Rise and Fall of a People's Movement* (Boston: Northeastern University Press, 1990).

37. These arguments and list of political alliances come primarily from Richard Hofstadter, *Social Darwinism in American Thought* (1944; reprint, Boston: Beacon Press, 1992), 34–36.

38. Charles Sumner was a political ally and acquaintance, if not friend, of George Sheldon's, according to his obituary.

39. Frank Wright Pratt, "The Old Home Spirit," in *History and Proceedings of the Pocumtuck Valley Memorial Association*, vol. 4 (1901), 217.

40. Donald Friary, foreword to *A History of Deerfield: A Facsimile of the 1895–96 Edition*, by George Sheldon (Somersworth: New Hampshire Publishing, 1972), vol. 1.

41. Morgan followed the thinking of the British anthropologist E. B. Tylor in proposing stages in a unilinear form of evolution from simple to complex. Lewis Henry Morgan, *Ancient Society* (New York: H. Holt, 1877).

42. James Kendall Hosmer, *A Short History of Anglo-Saxon Freedom. The Polity of the English-Speaking Race; Outlined in Its Inception, Development, Diffusion, and Present Condition* (New York: C. Scribner's Sons, 1890). See esp. 12, 14–17, 306–8.

43. Rosenkrantz, *Public Health and the State*, 1.

44. Of the seven hundred deaths occurring in the 1849 cholera epidemic in Boston, more than five hundred were attributed to the Irish. See Oscar Handlin, *Boston's Immigrants: A Study in Acculturation*, Revised Ed. (Cambridge: Harvard University Press, 1972), 178; Charles E. Rosenberg, *The Cholera Years: The United States in 1832, 1849, and 1866* (Chicago: University of Chicago Press, 1962), 137–40. Rosenkrantz does point out, however, that Boston was not as hard hit as New York by the 1832 and 1849 epidemics (*Public Health*, 4). Kraut says that the Irish were also blamed in the 1832 epidemic in New York (*Silent Travelers*, 32).

45. Boston Medical Commission to Investigate the Sanitary Condition of the City, *The Sanitary Condition of Boston: The Report of a Medical Commission*, ed. Thomas B. Curtis, M.D. (Boston: Rockwell and Churchill Printers, 1875), 180.

46. For research on how this played out with regard to infant mortality, see Richard A. Meckel, *Save the Babies: American Public Health Reform and the Prevention of Infant Mortality, 1850–1929* (Baltimore: Johns Hopkins University Press, 1991); Swedlund and Ball, "Nature, Nurture, and the Determinants of Infant Mortality."

47. Quoted in Eyler, *Victorian Social Medicine*, 100; this discussion of the germ theory of disease is based on chap. 5.

48. Kraut, *Silent Travelers*.

49. Nancy J. Tomes, "American Attitudes toward the Germ Theory of Disease: Phyllis Allen Richmond Revisited," *Journal of the History of Medicine and Allied Sciences* 52, no. 1 (1997): 17–50; idem, *The Gospel of Germs: Men, Women, and the Microbe in American Life* (Cambridge: Harvard University Press, 1998).

50. Eyler, *Victorian Social Medicine*, 103–7. Bowditch regarded the poor living conditions of the immigrants as one of the major health problems in the state. The issue of urban slums was well recognized, but despite the efforts of Bowditch and his successors, political considerations and limited authorization hampered the effectiveness of the state Board of Health from its founding through the late 1880s. Rosenkrantz, *Public Health*, chap. 2.

51. Tomes, *Gospel of Germs*, 44.

52. Rosenkrantz, *Public Health and the State*, 99.

53. Ibid., 37–42, 99–103.

54. Even Henry Bowditch, as early as the 1870s, was concerned that parents with a "consumptive heredity" not reproduce consumptive progeny and that the state might feel obligated to restrain the marriage of such persons. Bowditch, "Analysis of a Correspondence on Some of the Causes or Antecedents of Consumption," in *Fourth Annual Report of the State Board of Health of Massachusetts*, Public Document no. 34 (Boston: Wright & Potter, 1873).

55. See, e.g., Anna Steese Richardson, "A Year of Better Babies," *Women's Home Companion*, March 1914, 19–20, cited in Alisa C. Klaus, *Every Child a Lion: The Origins of Maternal and Infant Health Policy in the United States and France, 1890–1920* (Ithaca, N.Y.: Cornell University Press, 1993), 145; Laura L. Lovett, *Conceiving the Future: Pronatalism, Reproduction, and the Family in the United States, 1890–1939* (Chapel Hill: University of North Carolina Press, 2007), 132–36, 143–48.

56. See Daniel J. Kevles, *In the Name of Eugenics: Genetics and the Uses of Human Heredity* (Cambridge: Harvard University Press, 1985) chap. 7; Nancy L. Gallagher, *Breeding Better Vermonters: The Eugenics Project in the Green Mountain State.* (Hanover, N.H.: University Press of New England, 1999), 122–26, 174.

57. *Proceedings of the First National Conferences on Race Betterment* (Battle Creek, Mich., 1914), table of contents.

58. Rosenkrantz, *Public Health and the State*, 141–42.

59. *Greenfield Gazette and Courier*, December 12, 1903. The article under the headline explains that in many of the small towns in Franklin County the birth rates are dropping, and that many of the children born are of foreign parentage.

60. *Greenfield Gazette and Courier*, July 2, 1911.

61. Ibid., August 6, 1910.

62. Jenkins, *Conservative Rebel*, 147.

63. Swedlund, "Infant Mortality in Massachusetts," 163–68.

64. Massachusetts conducted its censuses five years after each U.S. census; thus, 1915 is selected rather than 1916. By combining the U.S. census with the Massachusetts census, it is possible to construct a continuous series at five-year intervals.

65. Secretary of the Commonwealth of Massachusetts, *Report of Births, Marriages, and Deaths in Massachusetts* (Boston: Wright & Potter, 1915), vol. 74. The rates for infant mortality are per 1,000 live births (table 51, p. 150). The rates for childhood fevers and tuberculosis are per 100,000 population, averaged over five years and centered on the census year (table 64, p. 211). The report shows the distribution of deaths by age groupings and provides extensive analysis of infant mortality but no extensive analysis of deaths by other age groups. All of these rates are subject to errors because of underenumeration, misclassification of diseases, and changing age structure of the population at risk, but general trends are valid.

66. Ibid. 106–7; Rosenkrantz, *Public Health and the State*, chap. 3; John T. Cumbler, *Reasonable Use: The People, the Environment, and the State, New England, 1790–1930* (New York: Oxford University Press, 2001); Swedlund, "Infant Mortality in Massachusetts," 169–79.

67. *Massachusetts Acts and Resolves* (1884), chaps. 64 and 98, cited in Rosenkrantz, *Public Health and the State*, 110.

68. Rosenkrantz, *Public Health and the State*, 113–15.

69. See, e.g., Harry F. Dowling, *Fighting Infection: Conquests of the Twentieth Century* (Cambridge: Harvard University Press, 1977). For England, Anne Hardy, *The Epidemic Streets: Infectious Disease and the Rise of Preventive Medicine, 1856–1900* (Oxford: Clarendon, 1993), chap. 8.

70. Others have argued, however, that the United States was simply in a late phase of the epidemic wave of tuberculosis and the interventions were not so important. See, e.g., E. R. N. Grigg, "The Arcana of Tuberculosis with a Brief Epidemiologic History of the Disease in the U.S.A.," *American Review of Tuberculosis and Pulmonary Disease* 78 (1958): 151.

71. A focus on how these efforts occurred in Massachusetts is not meant to imply that "the state" was in any way acting alone. It was only one of many bureaucratic entities involved in these same initiatives. Massachusetts turned to England and France from the outset to learn about the measurement and prevention of mortality and continued to do so between 1870 and 1916. Boston, New York, Philadelphia, and Providence watched one another closely. Likewise, New York, Rhode Island, Pennsylvania, and other northeastern states were part of a pioneering consortium of bureaucracies that followed attentively each other's innovations and initiatives. See Gretchen A. Condran and Rose A. Cheney, "Mortality Trends in Philadelphia: Age- and Cause-Specific Death Rates, 1870–1930," *Demography* 19, no. 1 (1982): 97; Gretchen A. Condran and Samuel H. Preston, "Child Mortality Differences, Personal Health Care Practices, and Medical Technology: The United States, 1900–1930," in *Health and Social Change in International Perspective*, ed. Lincoln C. Chen, Arthur Kleinman, and Norma C. Ware, 171–224 (Boston: Department of Population and International Health, Harvard School of Public Health; distributed by Harvard University Press, 1994); John Duffy, *The Sanitarians: A History of American Public Health* (Urbana: University of Illinois Press, 1990).

72. I find virtually no reference in the local or state record which says or implies that the white, male body is inherently flawed, yet I find countless references to the bodies of immigrants and women as flawed. For a discussion of the place of women and immigrants in relation to health, see Martha H. Verbrugge, *Able-Bodied Womanhood: Personal Health and Social Change in Nineteenth-Century Boston* (New York: Oxford University Press, 1988).

73. When white "natives" were deemed unfit or feeble or sick, it was the exception and not a result of their ethnic background. For examples of the white male ideal in discourses of health of the period, and the belief that New England's colonial settlers were thought to be of superior European stock, see the writings of Dudley Sargent, e.g., "The Physical State of the American People," in *Physical Education* (Boston: Ginn, 1906), esp. 20–32.

9. Bodies of Evidence

1. Stanley French, "The Cemetery as Cultural Institution: The Establishment of Mount Auburn and the Rural Cemetery Movement," in *Death in America*, ed. David E. Stannard, 69–91 (Philadelphia: University of Pennsylvania Press, 1975), mentions picnicking, along with walking and moral contemplation, as motivations of the planners involved in the rural cemetery movement. Sarah Tarlow, *Bereavement and Commemoration: An Archaeology of Mortality* (Malden, Mass.: Blackwell, 1999), cites having an emotional epiphany of her own in visiting cemeteries in the Orkney Islands (20–22).

2. For England, see, e.g., Pat Jalland, *Death in the Victorian Family* (New York: Oxford University Press, 1996), 199, and Tarlow, *Bereavement and Commemoration*. For the United States, see Gary Laderman, *The Sacred Remains: American Attitudes toward Death, 1799–1883* (New Haven, Conn.: Yale University Press, 1996); Karen Halttunen, *Confidence Men and Painted Women: A Study of Middle-Class Culture in America, 1830–1870* (New Haven, Conn.: Yale University Press, 1982), 124–52.

3. Quoted in Malcolm Read Lovell, ed., *Two Quaker Sisters: From the Original Diaries of Elizabeth Buffum Chace and Lucy Buffum Lovell* (New York: Liveright, 1937), 66–67, 102.

4. Mary Bradbury, *Representations of Death: A Social Psychological Perspective* (New York: Routledge, 1999), 116–22.

5. For a discussion of the transition to funeral home care and embalming, see Gary Laderman, *Rest in Peace: A Cultural History of Death and the Funeral Home in Twentieth-Century America* (New York: Oxford University Press, 2003), esp. 1–44. Laderman argues that the funeral industry does assume many roles formerly held by friends and family members.

6. See Jalland, *Death in the Victorian Family*, 221. Richard A. Wells, *Manners, Culture, and Dress of the Best American Society* (Springfield, Mass.: King, Richardson, 1890), states that when receiving guests at a funeral "the ladies of the family do not show themselves at all" (315).

7. For concerns about corpses and sanitation in England, see Julie-Marie Strange, *Death, Grief, and Poverty in Britain, 1870–1914* (Cambridge: Cambridge University Press, 2005), 66–73.

8. Jalland, *Death in the Victorian Family*, 213.

9. Bradbury, *Representations of Death*, 118–22; Lindsay Prior, *The Social Organization of Death: Medical Discourse and Social Practices in Belfast* (New York: St. Martin's Press, 1989); Laderman, *Rest in Peace.*

10. Robert Higginson Fuller entries in Agnes Higginson Fuller diary, box 19, Fuller-Higginson Family Papers, PVMA Library. In his account of the Deerfield service, Sheldon reported that as the viewers passed Fuller's casket "strong men bowed and women's tears fell fast." George Sheldon obituary, *Greenfield Gazette and Courier*, December 27, 1916, in ibid., box 121, file 4.

11. William Dean Howells, *George Fuller: His Life and Works* (Boston: Houghton Mifflin, 1886).

12. Paul Starr, *The Social Transformation of American Medicine* (New York: Basic Books, 1982), 150–62; Morris J. Vogel, *The Invention of the Modern Hospital, Boston, 1870–1930* (Chicago: University of Chicago Press, 1980).

13. A hospital run by a physician in a home in Greenfield is reported in approximately 1894. Between 1894 and 1909, at least two properties in Greenfield were rented for use as hospitals serving county residents and staffed by local physicians. The Franklin County Hospital opened in 1910. *Greenfield Gazette and Courier*, June 9, 1953. The Farren Memorial Hospital also opened around 1910 in Turners Falls.

14. Among the exceptions was "Miss Taussig," cited in Chapter 7, who did not return home to die; she was reported to have died in Saranac.

15. It is worth noting, however, that if the treatments recommended in the minutes of the Franklin District Medical Society during the early 1900s were the ones prescribed, the patient and family had little reason for hope, except for a few important breakthroughs, such as the diphtheria antitoxin.

16. George Fuller diary, March 18 and 20, 1884, Fuller-Higginson Family Papers, box 19.

17. Bradbury, *Representations of Death*, 147–49.

18. For a discussion of Australian funerals, see Pat Jalland, *Australian Ways of Death: A Social and Cultural History, 1840–1918* (New York: Oxford University Press, 2002); idem, *Death in the Victorian Family*, 199.

19. Cassell's *Household Guide*, also published in New York and Paris, was a popular reference book on etiquette and domestic science.

20. Wells, *Manners*, 312.

21. We can safely assume that Colonel Wells's body was also embalmed.

22. Duncan Wells obituary, *Greenfield Gazette and Courier*, October 24 1864; Agnes Higginson to Stephen Higginson (her husband) describing the ceremony, October 22, 1864, Fuller-Higginson Papers, box 64, folder 3; Laderman, *Sacred Remains*, notes that the flags, military escort, and other symbols would be common at funerals of military heroes to evoke patriotism and social solidarity (43).

23. The Reverend Edgar Buckingham (of Deerfield) obituary, *Greenfield Gazette and Courier*, May 5, 1894. Buckingham was the son of Joseph T. Buckingham, editor of the *Boston Courier* and active in Boston's "literary life." Edgar attended Harvard and was graduated from the Harvard Divinity School. He served in the First Church of Deerfield from 1868 to 1891; the First Church was a valued pulpit, ranking high among rural churches in the late nineteenth century.

24. George Fuller obituary, *Boston Advertiser*, May 25, 1862, Fuller-Higginson Papers, box 121. The description of these services as "simple" must be held up against the fact that these were elderly, prominent men of high standing in their community. The material culture, the food and beverages served to those attending, and the general decorum of the services would be quite

substantial compared with the "simple" service in a working-class family. But the Protestant elite wanted them at least to appear and to be described as simple.

25. See Lawrence Taylor, "Symbolic Death: An Anthropological View of Mourning Ritual in the Nineteenth Century," in *A Time to Mourn: Expressions of Grief in Nineteenth Century America,* ed. Martha V. Pike and Janice Gray Armstrong (Stony Brook, N.Y.: Museums at Stony Brook, 1982), 39–48. When Susan Crawford died in Topsfield in 1884 she was buried in a shroud. Crawford was the daughter-in-law of the Reverend Robert Crawford, pastor emeritus of Deerfield's Orthodox Congregational Church. Robert Crawford diaries, microfilm, Historic Deerfield Library. When Deerfield's First Congregational Church began hiring Unitarian ministers, a group split off and founded the Orthodox Congregational Church. They were more conservative in doctrine and no doubt in the retention of traditional mortuary practices.

26. The obituary describes his features as "remarkably natural and composed." Fuller obituary, *Boston Advertiser.* A massive brow was considered by this time a definite sign of intellect and of Anglo-Saxon ancestry.

27. Historical archaeologists and others engaged in gravestone studies have devoted a great deal of attention to the landscape and material culture of cemeteries as expressions of ideology and social change. See, e.g., Edward L. Bell, *Vestiges of Mortality and Remembrance: A Bibliography on the Historical Archaeology of Cemeteries* (Metuchen, N.J.: Scarecrow Press, 1994), 259–346; Aubrey Cannon, "The Historical Dimension in Mortuary Expressions of Status and Sentiment," *Current Anthropology* 30, no. 4 (1989): 437–58; Randall H. McGuire, "Dialogues with the Dead: Ideology and the Cemetery," in *The Recovery of Meaning: Historical Archaeology in the Eastern United States,* ed. Mark P. Leone and Parker B. Potter Jr. (Washington, D.C.: Smithsonian Institution Press, 1988), 435–80; Tarlow, *Bereavement and Commemoration,* esp. 108–70.

28. Edwin J. Dethlefsen, "The Cemetery and Culture Change: Archaeological Focus and Ethnographic Perspective," in *Modern Material Culture: The Archaeology of Us,* ed. R. A. Gould and M. B. Schiffer (New York: Academic Press, 1981), 137–59; McGuire, "Dialogues with the Dead," 457–59.

29. McGuire, "Dialogues with the Dead," 459–61.

30. Temporal complexity and regional variation, however, is well demonstrated in Kevin Sweeney, "Where the Bay Meets the River: Gravestones and Stonecutters in the River Towns of Western Massachusetts, 1690–1910," *Markers: The Journal of the Association for Gravestone Studies* 3 (1985): 1–46. Status differentiation may not have been the rule, but it was certainly present in many eighteenth-century cemeteries.

31. Tarlow, *Bereavement and Commemoration,* 24. Tarlow presents an excellent discussion of monuments, metaphor, and emotion in chap. 2. See also Bell, *Vestiges of Mortality and Remembrance,* 259–96.

32. George Sheldon diary, entry for March 17, 1863, PVMA Library. See also Jalland, *Death in the Victorian Family,* chap. 14. Mortuary photography is well represented in Stanley B. Burns, *Sleeping Beauty: Memorial Photography in America* (Altadena, Calif.: Twelvetrees Press, 1990), and Jay Ruby, *Secure the Shadow: Death and Photography in America* (Cambridge, Mass.: MIT Press, 1995). Also see the discussion in Karen Sánchez-Eppler, *Dependent States: The Child's Part in Nineteenth-Century American Culture* (Chicago: University of Chicago Press, 2005), chap. 3. In a letter to Dear Abby published in newspapers in 2005, "Still shocked in Vancouver" says she was offended that her relative took photographs of the deceased.

33. Thomas Baldwin Thayer, *Over the River; or, Pleasant Walks into the Valley of Shadows and Beyond: A Book for the Sick, the Dying, and the Bereaved* (Boston: Tompkins, 1865), 249, quoted in Halttunen, *Confidence Men,* 133.

34. From a poem by Mrs. Lydia H. Sigourney, "The Lock of Hair," in *The Lady's Almanac* (Boston: Shepard, Clark, and Brown, 1860), 85.

35. Mrs. Hammond advertised periodically in the *Greenfield Gazette and Courier* and announced her closing in the February 7, 1876, issue.

36. See, e.g., Elisabeth G. Gitter, "The Power of Women's Hair in the Victorian Imagination," *PMLA* 99, no. 5 (1984): 936–54; Charlotte Gere, *American and European Jewelry, 1830–1914*

(New York: Crown, 1975); Jalland, *Death in the Victorian Family*, 295–99. For an exceptional set of images, see the Hair Mourning Jewelry Virtual Exhibit at www.historic-northampton. org/virtual_exhibits/mourning_jewelry.html (accessed December 2008).

37. This observation is based on an unscientific survey of a small number of undergraduate students.

38. See, e.g., Sánchez-Eppler, *Dependent States,* 120, 134.

39. Effie's age suggests that the cause of death might have been rheumatic fever.

40. Martha V. Pike and Janice Gray Armstrong, eds., *A Time to Mourn: Expressions of Grief in Nineteenth Century America* (Stony Brook, N.Y.: Museums at Stony Brook, 1982), 85.

41. Dickinson Family Papers, box 1, folders 14 and 16, PVMA Library. Letters of sympathy arrived from New York and Boston, as well as from Stockbridge, Mass., and Bangor, Me.

42. J. K. Tyler to F. H. Allen, July 21, 1855, Dickinson Family Papers, box 1, folder 14; emphasis in original.

43. Halttunen, *Confidence Men*, 151. This section is strongly influenced by Halttunen's findings and observations.

44. *Greenfield Gazette and Courier*, December 22, 1856. Memorial poetry is still found in the current local paper, the *Greenfield Recorder* in the form of paid announcements placed by family members, usually on the anniversary of the death of a parent, spouse, or child.

45. Examples of these memory albums and scrapbooks, and children's writing, are available in the collections of the PVMA Library. One scrapbook, titled "Mrs. Emma Brown from Clara," includes obituaries and memorial poetry from approximately 1879 to 1918.

46. While the peak of this genre is probably in the 1850s and 1860s for New England, the *Greenfield Gazette and Courier* continued to have poems on the first and last page of many issues throughout the century. Shirley Majewski, PVMA, personal communication.

47. The single most important source for analysis of consolation literature is arguably Ann Douglas, "Heaven Our Home: Consolation Literature in the Northern United States, 1830–1880," in *Death in America*, ed. David E. Stannard, 49–68 (Philadelphia: University of Pennsylvania Press, 1975). This brief section follows her argument.

48. Ibid., 66.

49. I refer the reader again to Tracy Chevalier, *Falling Angels* (New York: Dutton, 2001), for a very compelling fictional account of the vestiges of Victorian mourning in the early Edwardian period.

50. Halttunen, *Confidence Men*, 96–97, 151–52.

51. *Greenfield Gazette and Courier*, June 8, 1863. As noted earlier, Rev. Mumford replaced Rev. Hosmer for many services in Deerfield while Hosmer was away in the Civil War.

52. Ibid., December 9, 1828, reprinted from *Brook's Daily Monitor*. Another version of this article was published in 1831.

53. Ibid., September 7, 1841, 3.

54. Ibid., October 27, 1883, 2.

55. Edward Russell to Brother Paul Hawks, March 10, 1850, Russell Family Papers, box 1, folder 10, PVMA Library.

56. Louisa Higginson to Waldo Higginson, May 25, 1862, box 55, folder 4, Fuller-Higginson Family Papers. PVMA Library.

57. P. J. Cooley, South Deerfield–Deerfield House Lots, South Deerfield, box 4, PVMA Library.

58. D. B. Wyndham Lewis and Charles Lee, eds., *The Stuffed Owl: An Anthology of Bad Verse* (1979; reprint, New York: New York Review Books Classics, 2003); Mark Twain, *The Annotated Huckleberry Finn*, ed. Michael Patrick Hearn (New York: W. W. Norton, 2001).

59. Douglas, "Heaven Our Home," 65–66; Mark Twain's "Captain Stormfield's Visit to Heaven" was published in 1909.

60. This material and additional discussion of Mark Twain comes from Albert Bigelow Paine, *Mark Twain, a Biography: The Personal and Literary Life of Samuel Langhorne Clemens* (New York: Harper & Brothers, 1912); Justin Kaplan, *Mr. Clemens and Mark Twain: A Biography* (New

York: Simon and Schuster, 1966); Pamela A. Boker, *The Grief Taboo in American Literature: Loss and Prolonged Adolescence in Twain, Melville, and Hemingway* (New York: New York University Press, 1996); Harold K. Bush Jr., "Broken Idols: Mark Twain's Elegies for Susy and a Critique of Freudian Grief Theory," *Nineteenth Century Literature* 57, no. 2 (2002): 237–68; Julio C. Avalos Jr., "An Agony of Pleasurable Suffering: Masochism and Maternal Deprivation in Mark Twain," *American Imago* 62, no. 1 (2005): 35–38; Randall Knoper, personal communication.

61. Langdon died of diphtheria, and this ride probably had no influence on his death.

62. Bush, "Broken Idols," 239–43.

63. Charles Eliot Norton and the Ashfield Dinners, 1879–1903, Betty and Edward Gulick, Ashfield Historical Society, Historic Deerfield Library.

64. W. M. Hauslee, F. G. Howe, and A. C. Doyle, *Soldiers of the Great War*, vol. 2 (Washington, D.C.: Soldiers Record Publication Association, 1920). For influenza, see Secretary of the Commonwealth, *Fourth Annual Report of the State Department of Health of Massachusetts*, Public Document no. 34 (Boston: Wright & Potter, 1919). This is a conservative estimate, the number who died in Massachusetts as a result of the flu epidemic and its complications was probably closer to forty-five thousand. See A. Swedlund, "Everyday Mortality in the Time of Plague: Ordinary People in Extraordinary Circumstances in Massachusetts before and during the 1918 Flu Epidemic," in *Plagues and Epidemics: Infected Spaces Past and Present*, ed. D. A. Herring and A. C. Swedlund (Oxford: Berg, 2010).

INDEX

Page numbers in italics refer to illustrations.

ALAN C. SWEDLUND is professor emeritus of anthropology at the University of Massachusetts Amherst and external professor at the Santa Fe Institute, Santa Fe, New Mexico. He has written and edited numerous articles, chapters, and books on the history of population and health in New England and the American Southwest. Swedlund and his wife, M.A., reside in the town of Deerfield, Massachusetts.